IMAGES
of America

AROUND CARROLLTON

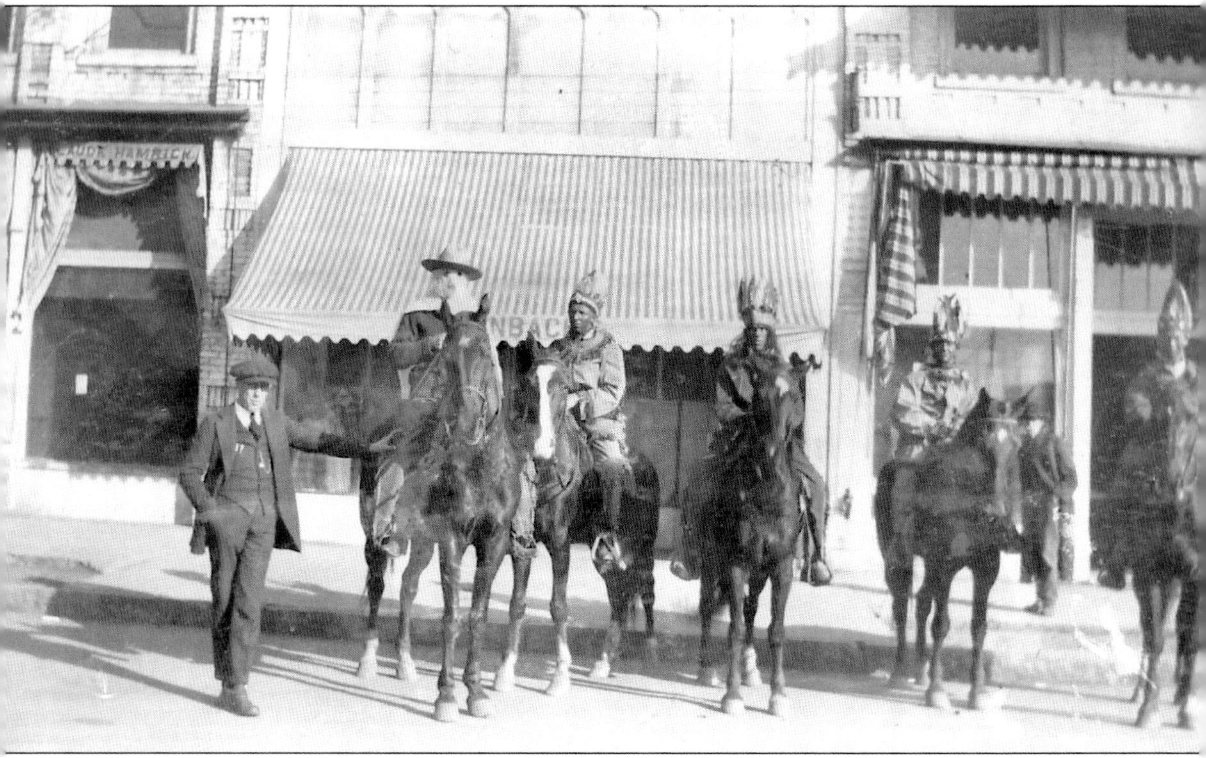

CENTENNIAL PAGEANT, 1927. A pageant that was acted out by a cast of 1,000 people took place in a pasture on Alabama Street about four blocks off Carrollton Square as part of the festivities to mark the county's centennial. F.L. Griffin is the man on foot in this photograph of actors. (Courtesy of Marion McNamara Dobbs.)

ON THE COVER: By the time of Carroll County's centennial in 1927, its frontier and agricultural traditions were declining and being replaced by an urban focus, as reflected in this photograph of the square. Social clubs, new church denominations, higher education, mill industries, and media such as radio and motion pictures brought citizens to town centers like Carrollton. (Courtesy of Marion McNamara Dobbs.)

IMAGES
of America

AROUND CARROLLTON

Suzanne K. Durham

ARCADIA
PUBLISHING

ISBN 978-0-7385-9142-1

Published by Arcadia Publishing
Charleston, South Carolina

Printed in the United States of America

Library of Congress Control Number: 2011939389

For all general information, please contact Arcadia Publishing:
Telephone 843-853-2070
Fax 843-853-0044
E-mail sales@arcadiapublishing.com
For customer service and orders:
Toll-Free 1-888-313-2665

Visit us on the Internet at www.arcadiapublishing.com

For my son, Clay, who gets history

Contents

ACKNOWLEDGMENTS

My sources for much of the caption information in this book have been the various county, city, and school histories written by Joe Cobb, J.C. Bonner, Myron House, and Ben Griffith. I also relied heavily on the early records of the Carroll Service Council, the memoirs of James Mitchell, the bulletins in the university archive's Fourth District A&M School Collection, and the Irvine S. Ingram papers. I found John Bell's history of Carrollton baseball very helpful. Once again, I find it takes a village of encouraging and helpful associates to create a picture book like this. I would like to thank Marion McNamara Dobbs and Jack Dorsey for generously loaning their collections, Lorene Flanders for loaning me to this project, and Dean Sullivan for his technical expertise. I am especially grateful in memoriam to Hall Carmical and Mann Long for having the perseverance to keep a photographic record of their lives "around Carrollton." Saving the best for last: thank you, Luke.

INTRODUCTION

Carroll County is in the west central region of Georgia on the Alabama state line, about 45 miles west of Atlanta. The county was established in 1827 and named for Charles Carroll, of Maryland, who was at the time the last living signer of the Declaration of Independence. Two years later, in 1829, the City of Carrollton was chartered. The county also includes the smaller cities of Bowdon, Mount Zion, Roopville, Temple, Villa Rica, and Whitesburg.

Carroll County has been and continues to be an agricultural region. For many years prior to the Depression, the county was a leading cotton producer within the state. Textile mills operated in Carroll County from the mid-19th century well into the mid-20th century, including the Mandeville, Banning, Lawler, and Carroll mills. When the railroads were built through Carrollton in the 1870s, this became a major transportation hub for raw cotton as well as milled products.

Besides agriculture, Carroll County has the distinction of having been home to several notable educational institutions that have shaped its citizens and whose effects are still felt today. The postbellum Mount Zion Seminary, the Fourth District A&M School in the first decade of the 20th century, and the post-Depression Rural Life and teacher training program at West Georgia College (WGC), now the University of West Georgia, are unique entities that helped define the region as more than a farming community.

There is no better place to scout for vintage photographs that reveal this agricultural and educational history than the archives at the local college library. At the University of West Georgia (UWG), these photographs tell the story of Carrollton and Carroll County for the better part of a century. Thanks to two scrapbooks donated by Woodfin Hall Carmical (1891–1981), we have a refreshing view of life at the Fourth District A&M School from 1910 through 1920. Carmical's *Memory Book* and *My Vacation Days* offer photographs—along with greeting cards, locks of hair, and poems—that give very human faces to the students, teachers, and townspeople from 100 years ago. Carmical was a student, an athlete, and a teacher—not to mention a terrible flirt who seemed to have a crush on no less than a dozen girls during his decade in Carrollton.

As college president Irvine S. Ingram revealed in his papers, the establishment of West Georgia College in 1933 brought a mandate from the Georgia Board of Regents to explore a new direction in education. This was in the midst of the Depression, which devastated an agricultural economy too dependent on a single crop. That new direction focused on filling the need for qualified teachers in rural Georgia. Not only was WGC producing public schoolteachers, it was placing them around Carroll County to help staff the marginal schoolhouses that were the basis of many crossroads communities. The Rural Life program at WGC filled a niche and improved a region in many more ways than just education. The college became a model for other states and even countries trying to uplift their rural populations. Thankfully, the work at WGC in Carroll County was well documented with photographs from the decade-long experiment.

The story of the Mount Zion Seminary cannot be told through pictures alone. Its founder, Dr. James Mitchell (1818–1903), was a cabinet member of President Lincoln and served as his commissioner of emigration in Lincoln's short-lived effort to relocate former slaves away from American soil. For such a highly placed public servant to spend the last quarter century of his life in western Carroll County promoting a higher education standard is worth a graduate thesis. For now, one must be content with the photographic record as collected by former Mount Zion mayor and unofficial historian Jack Dorsey.

In years to come, the name Benjamin M. Long (1881–1973) will become synonymous with Carrollton's photographic history during a large part of the 20th century. He was an insurance agent, amateur photographer, baseball fan, and descendant of one of Carroll County's pioneer families. The Long Collection in the library already has been the basis for two master's theses and a book on buildings in Carrollton. On a visit to the Digital Library of Georgia, it is possible to peruse 88 of Long's photographs, only a small percentage of his total work.

Many of his photographs were donated to the library, and his granddaughter Marion McNamara Dobbs owns many more. In photographing his family and friends, Long captured the sights around Carrollton and Carroll County that citizens of the day would have seen. The picnic havens of Simonton's and Hay's mills, the Bremen train station, and life on the square in Carrollton are just a few of the milieus he captured so well. He was well connected and could take photographs of the city's leading Baptist preachers out of pulpit and on the golf course. Carroll County's centennial in 1927 is well represented in Long's collection. He photographed float after float as they made their way around the square, creating a time capsule of what made Carrollton proud. Long's passion for baseball is reflected in the many team and on-field-play photographs he made. He was also the owner of Carrollton's first team. Carrollton had its own baseball history between 1914 and the 1960s, which Long documented in a way that newspapers did not in the early years.

The Carroll Service Council was organized in 1943 by volunteer citizens to integrate the various charitable and community improvement programs run by churches, civic clubs, and educational institutions at the time. It oversaw public welfare, agriculture, economic growth, youth recreation, religion, and education, functions that in later years would become the responsibility of government agencies. A number of photographs documenting the activities of the service council have been placed in UWG's special collections and are shared in this book.

The earliest photograph published in this book probably dates to the 1880s, and the most recent was taken in 1961. It is hoped that not only the span of years covered in this book, but also the variety of scenes and topics, will satisfy every reader of history around Carrollton.

One

CARROLLTON

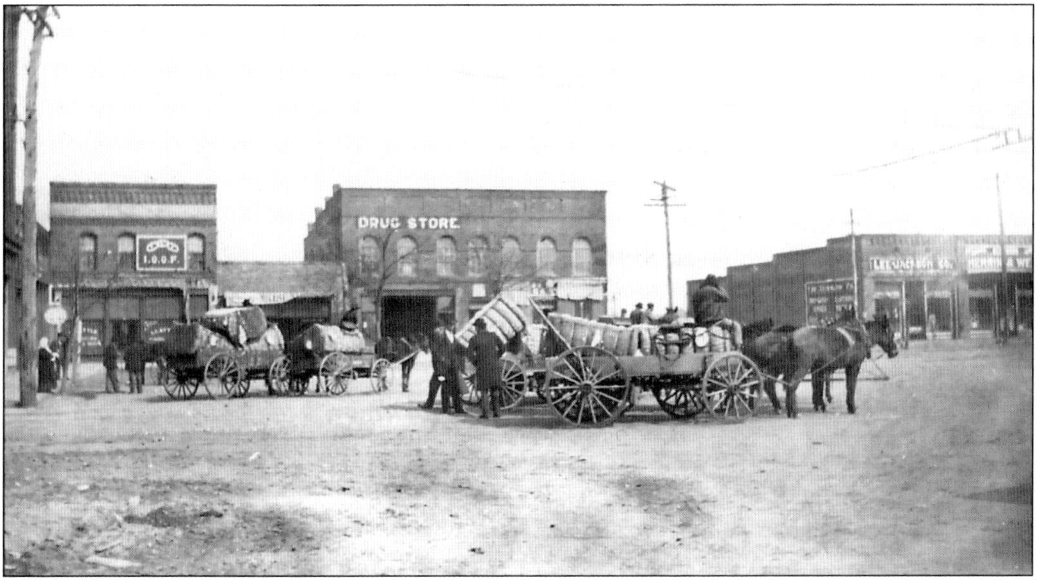

PUBLIC SQUARE, C. 1905. Cotton bales were a common sight on the square in Carrollton as cotton warehouses lined the streets and alleys between the square and the train depot. At this time, it was referred to as Public Square. Later, it would be named for US congressman and native son W.C. Adamson. This view captured the northwest quadrant. (Courtesy of UWG Special Collections.)

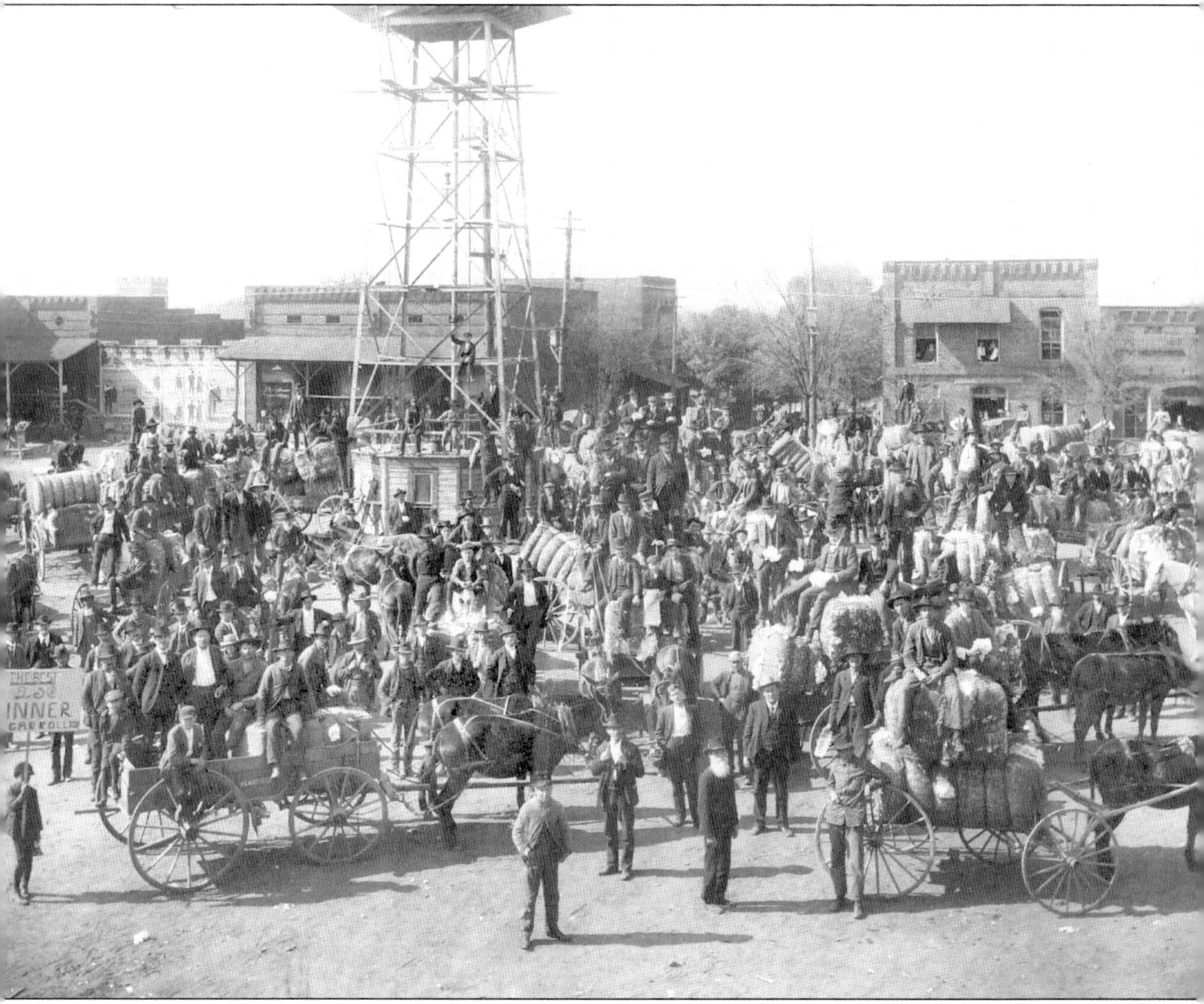

PUBLIC SQUARE, C. 1900. A boy carries a signboard proclaiming a delicious 20¢ dinner while local citizens crowded the square with wagons hauling cotton bales. This view is looking south toward what is now Bradley Street. At the time, it was called Depot Street because of the train station. When this photograph was taken, a water tower stood in the center of the square. The first courthouse was a simple structure on the south side of Newnan Street, and the second one was erected in the square in 1837. A masonry courthouse eventually replaced it around the beginning of the Civil War. In 1893, a fourth courthouse was built where today's courthouse stands at Newnan and Dixie streets. It burned in 1927, and the current building was constructed in 1929. (Courtesy of UWG Special Collections.)

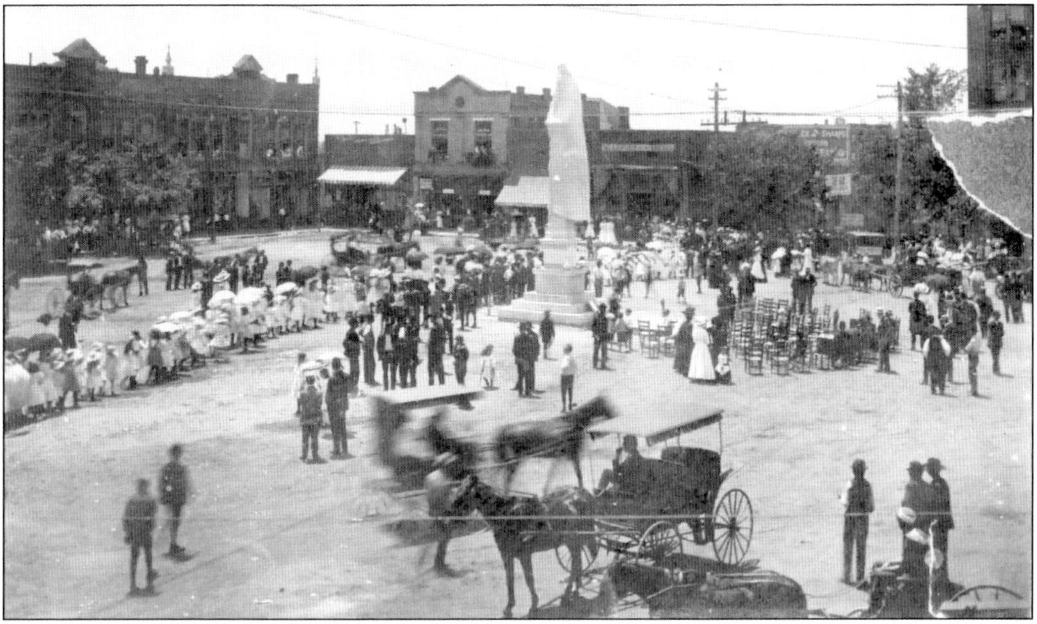

Confederate Monument, 1910. As in many towns and cities across the South, the United Daughters of the Confederacy and Confederate veterans raised money to erect a Confederate Monument in Public Square. In this photograph, an unveiling ceremony is about to take place. The statue now stands at the county courthouse on Newnan Street. (Courtesy of Marion McNamara Dobbs.)

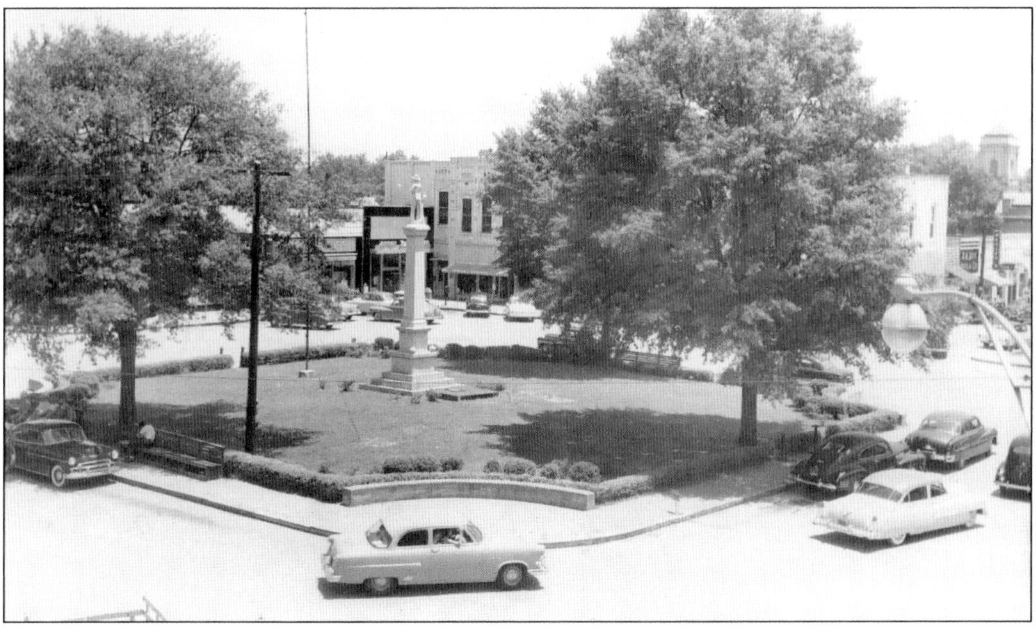

Confederate Monument, 1954. This photograph, with a northeastward view, was taken from the southwest quadrant of the square and shows the Confederate Monument, which faces north down Rome Street. In 1958, the statue and park were removed and replaced with a traffic signal. This allowed traffic to flow through the square, and was part of the modernization of Carrollton. (Courtesy of Marion McNamara Dobbs.)

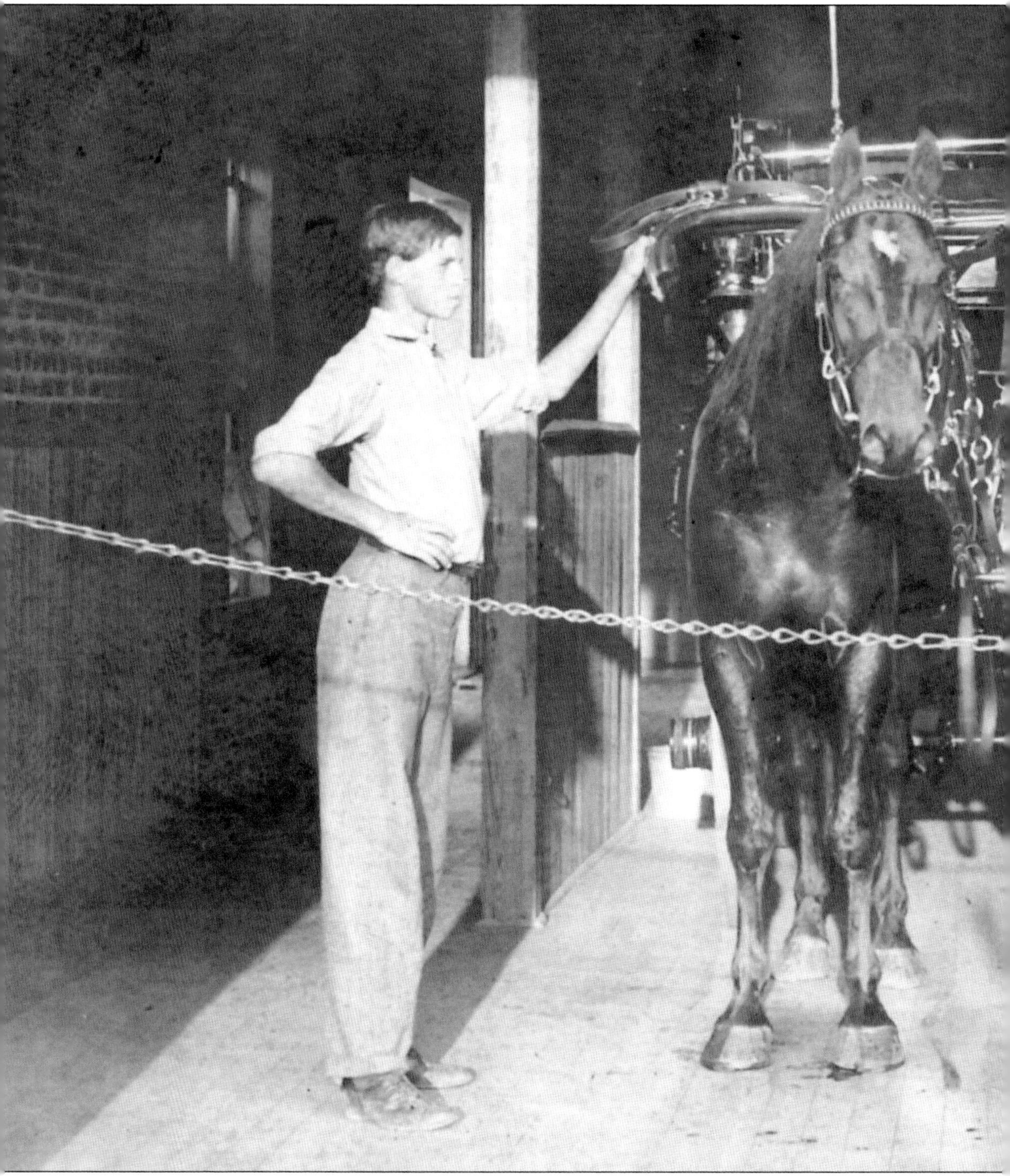

CARROLLTON FIRE STATION, C. 1905. Fear of fire prompted Carrollton City Council to pass an ordinance in 1889 to require all buildings from the square to the first alleys off Newnan, Rome, Alabama, and Depot Streets to be built out of brick. Fires were common and often devastating to the old wooden structures. In 1892, five buildings burned on the square, and in 1893, fire destroyed 15 structures on Newnan Street. In 1905, the fire station was located at the corner of Rome

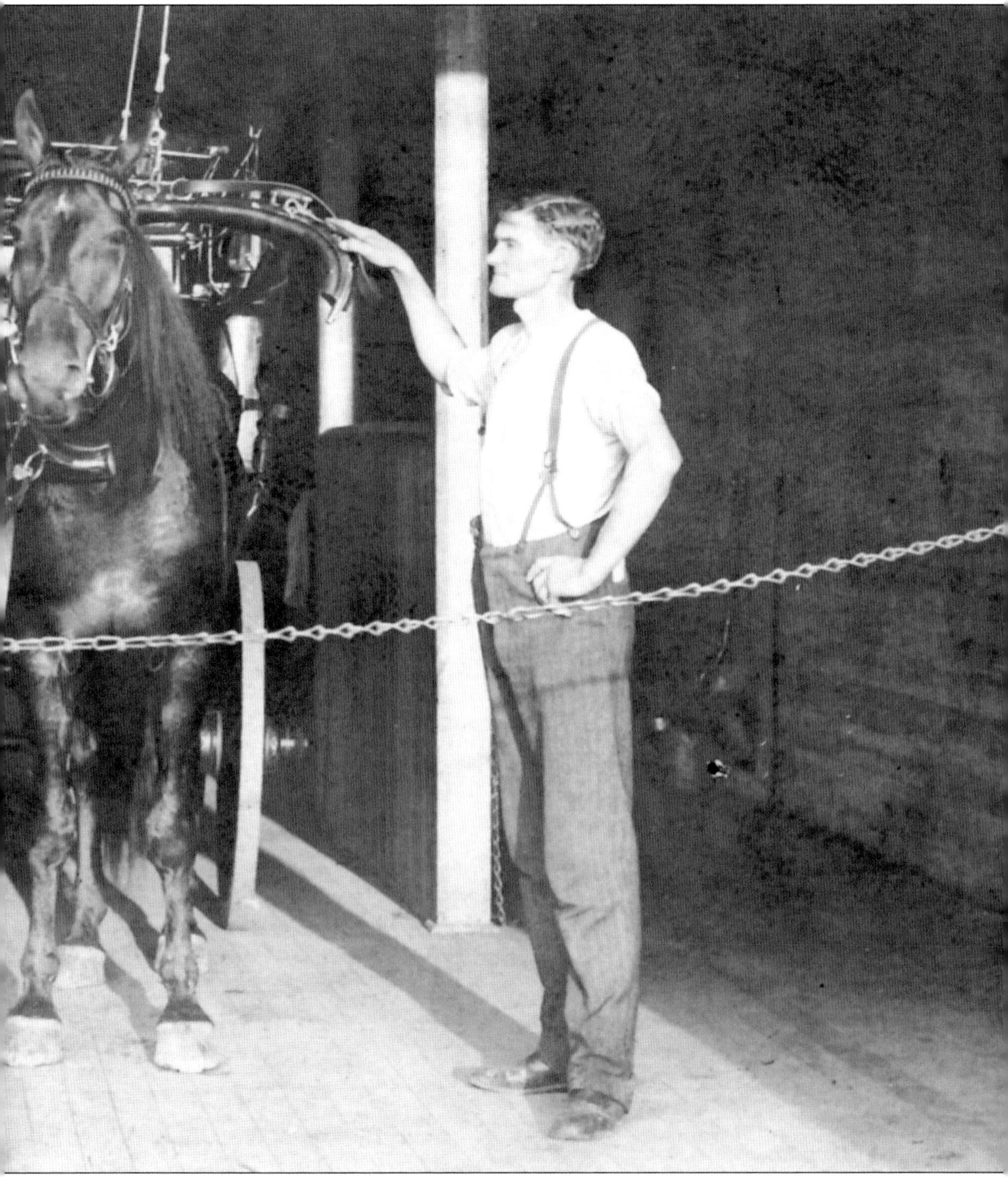

Street and North Alley, which later became City Hall Avenue when City Hall was constructed in 1914. The fire department got its first motorized equipment in 1916. This photograph was in postcard format and found in the Georgia Archives, whose staff gave it to UWG. (Courtesy of UWG Special Collections.)

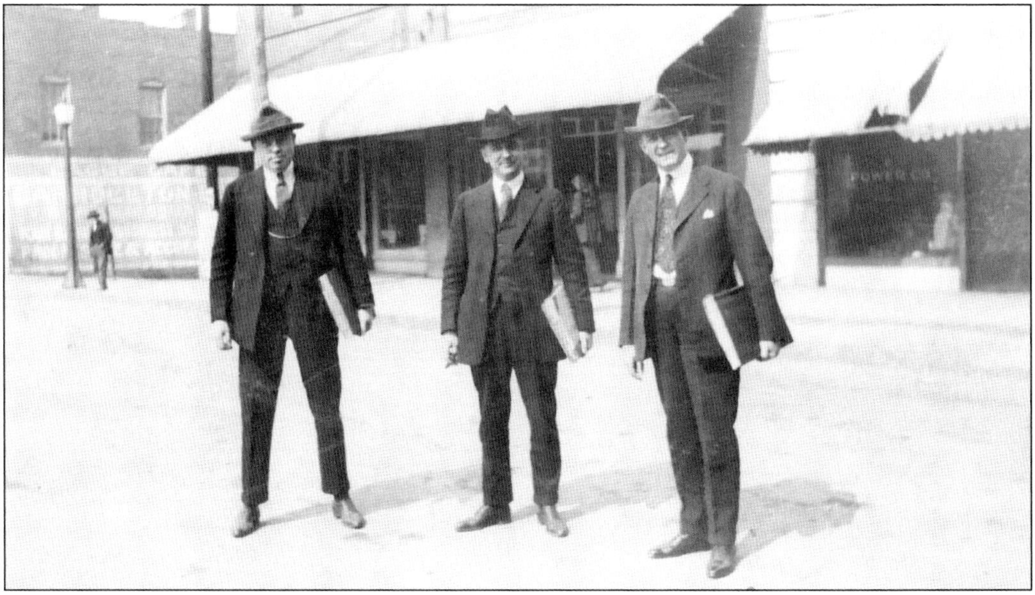

INSURANCE MEN, 1921. These insurance men were associates of the photographer Benjamin "Mann" Long, whose office was in the northeast quadrant of the square. The lamp post in this photograph is at the corner of Rome Street. The men are, from left to right, George Campbell, Alvin Wildwood, and George Gantt. (Courtesy of Marion McNamara Dobbs.)

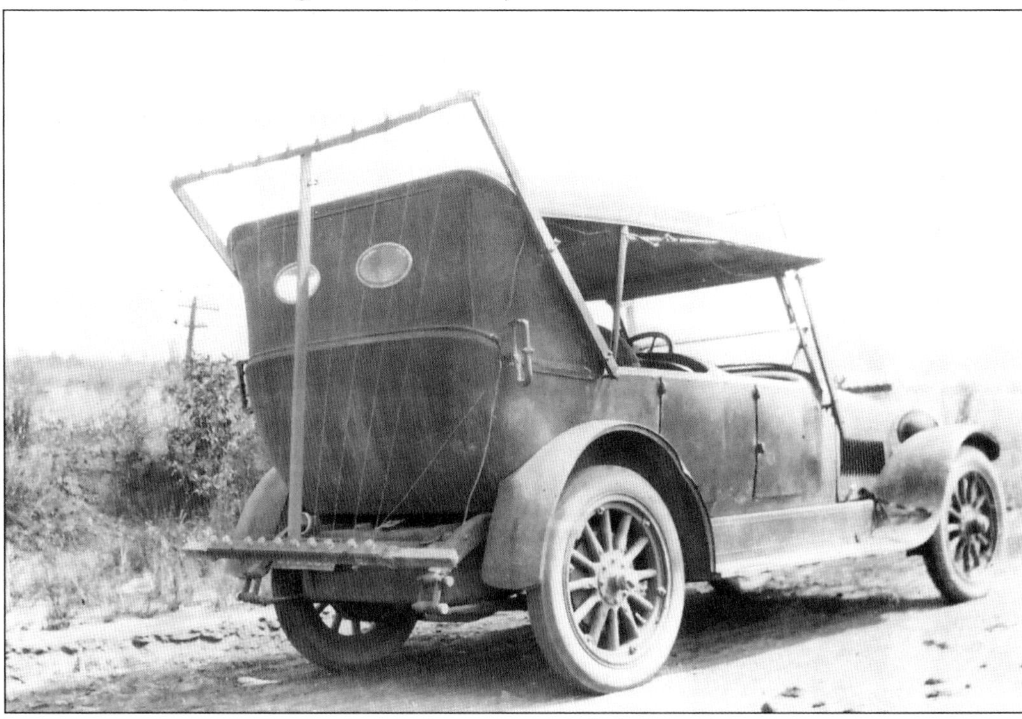

FIRST CAR RADIO, C. 1920. This Hudson automobile belonged to Benjamin "Mann" Long of Carrollton and was said to feature the first car radio in Carroll County. The antenna was strung along the back, over the top, and across the windshield of the car. (Courtesy of Marion McNamara Dobbs.)

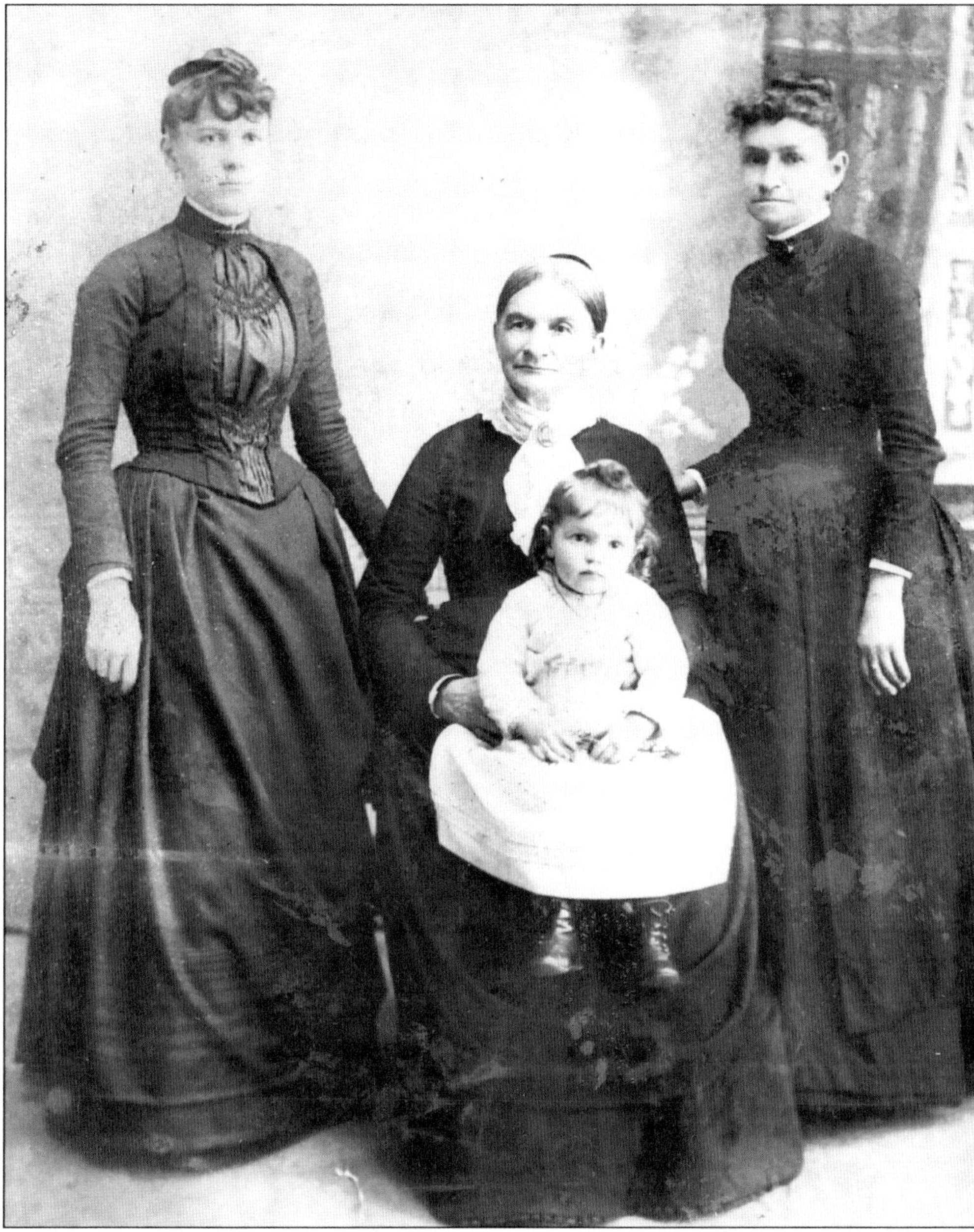

MANDEVILLE DESCENDANTS, C. 1885. Four generations of the Appleton Mandeville family are captured in this studio portrait. His wife, Mary Stewart, is seated, and at right is her daughter, Salina Mandeville Colclough. At left is Salina's daughter, Mary Lou Colclough West. Mary Lou's daughter, Marion Frances, is seated on Mary Stewart's lap. Appleton Mandeville came to Carrollton in 1833 from New York. He and his wife raised 10 children and celebrated their golden wedding anniversary in 1885 in Carrollton. Appleton was responsible for the planting of maple trees on what was known as the Bowdon Road, today called Maple Street. Mandeville's son L.C. Mandeville was an organizer of Mandeville Mills, which dominated the city's industry for decades. Many of the mill's buildings still stand and have been converted to living spaces. (Courtesy of Marion McNamara Dobbs.)

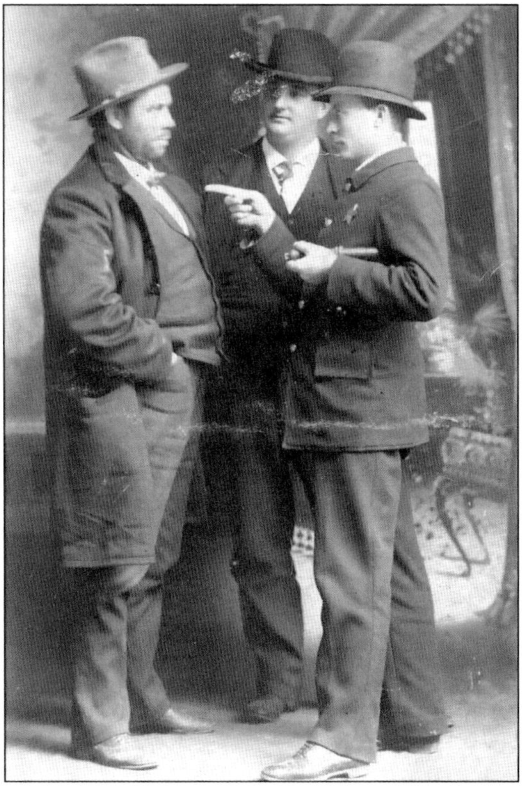

Carrollton Police, c. 1895. This carte de visite image from the late 19th century was taken at a Carrollton photography studio and is part of the Crider family collection. Benjamin H. Crider was chief of Carrollton police at the turn of the century. Perhaps he is pictured here pointing at an unsavory looking character. Tragically, Crider was killed in a shoot-out in 1900 when he was 30 years old. (Courtesy of UWG Special Collections.)

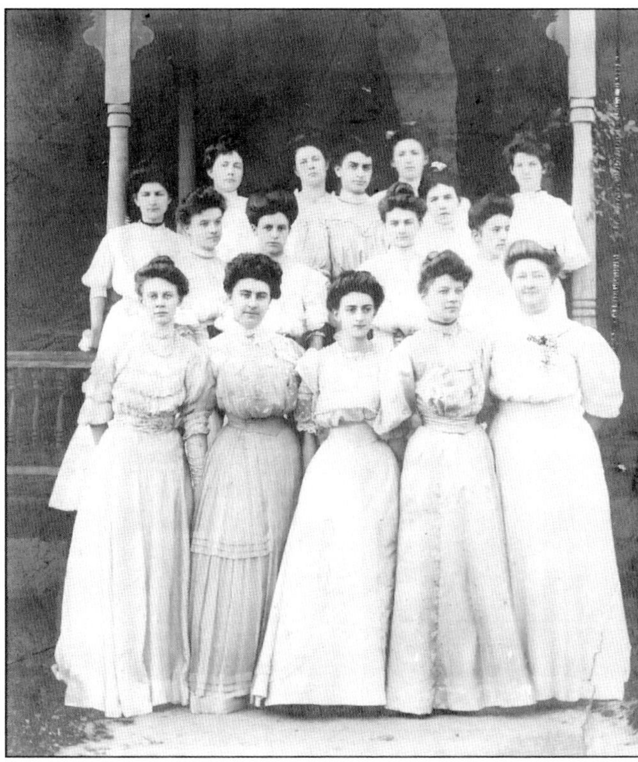

Bridal Shower, 1907. Cora Mae Simonton, second from right in the first row, was given a bridal party at the home of a Mrs. Wiley, who lived at 74 Maple Street. The party was given by Cora Mae's sister, Susie Bess, who is pictured at far left in the first row. Cora Mae was married on April 2, 1907. (Courtesy of Marion McNamara Dobbs.)

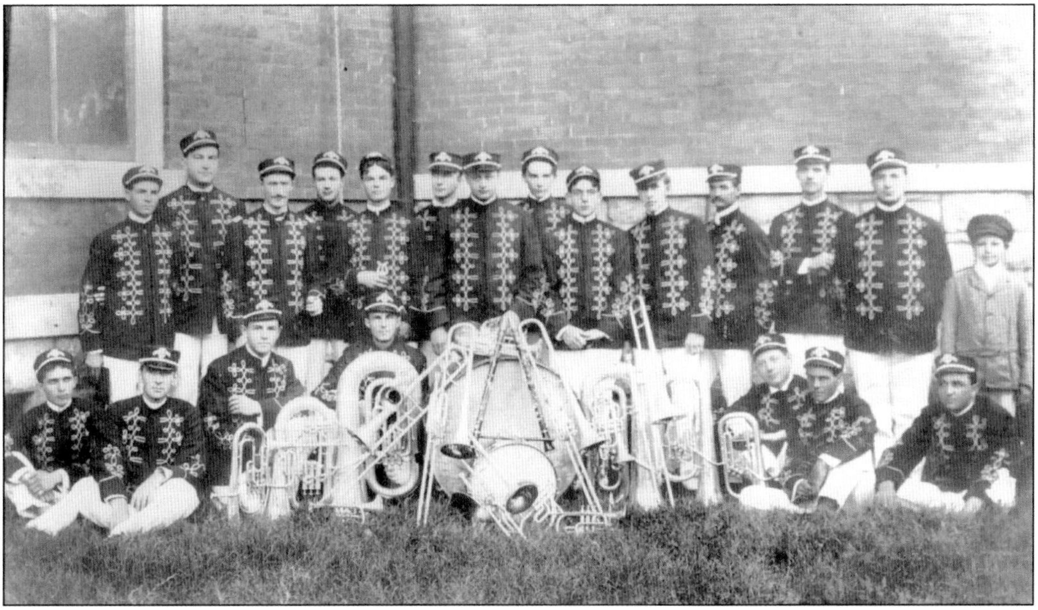

Carrollton Band, c. 1910. Band members are, from left to right, (first row) John Butler, W.A. Upshaw, George Hamrick, Will Perry, Bob Adams, Howard Smith, and Daniel Hearn; (second row) Jasper Holloway, V.B. Toney, George Gray, J.E. Thornton, Joe Holloway, R.E. Foster, B.C. Bass, A.B. Pace, Ben New, Hugh Lee Griffin, William Campbell, Slipper Jones, Albert Jones, and Boyd Holloway. (Courtesy of Marion McNamara Dobbs.)

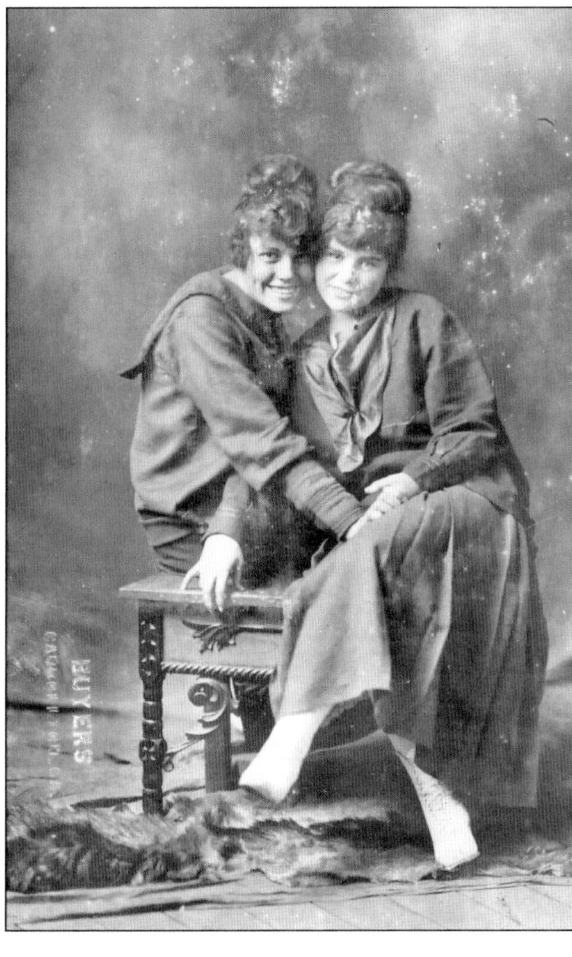

"From Dupy and Kitty Oct. 23, 1916." These young women had their photograph taken at a Carrollton studio for a friend who taught at the Fourth District A&M School. The Buyers Photograph Company advertised its services with the saying, "Our Lens is like Love—blind to every defect." (Courtesy of UWG Special Collections.)

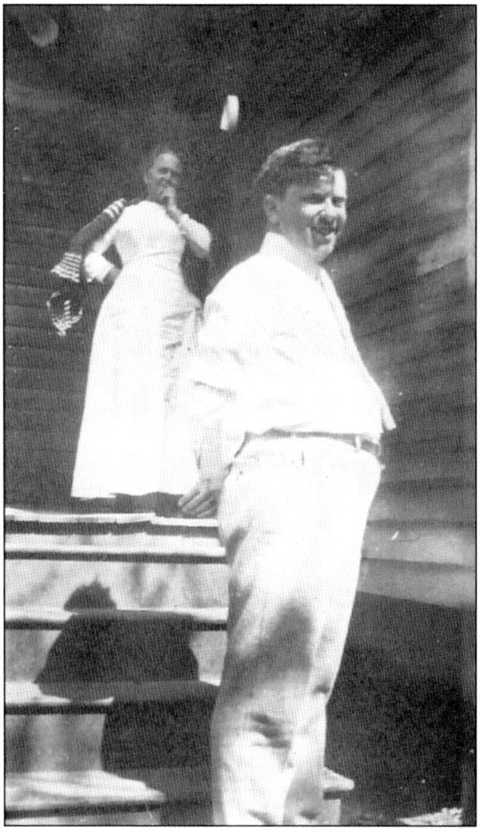

Southland Hotel Owners, 1914. J.B. Litesey and his wife, Georgia, operated the hotel for commercial men on Newnan Street. Woodfin "Hall" Carmical, who took this photograph, was a graduate of the Fourth District A&M School and stayed at the hotel during the summer of 1914 while he played baseball for the Carrollton Baseball Club. (Courtesy of UWG Special Collections.)

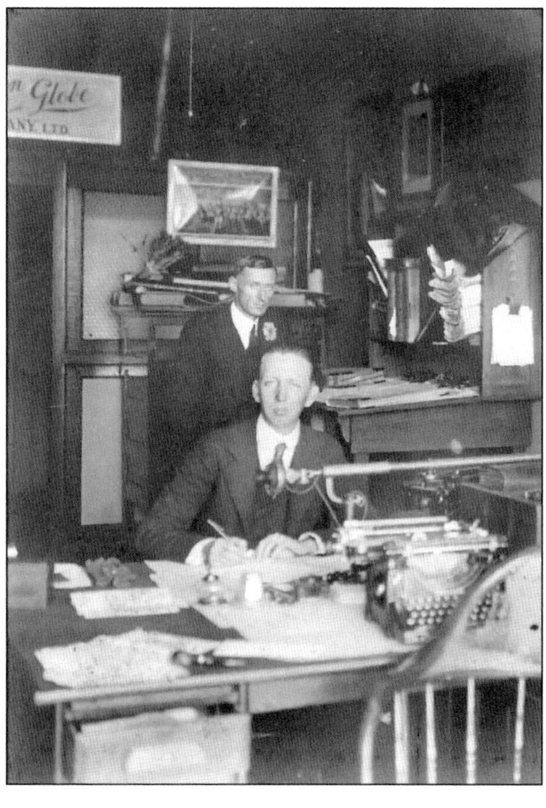

Benjamin "Mann" Long, 1919. At the rear of this photograph is Benjamin Long, who was an insurance agent in Carrollton. With him is Jim Coleman, presumably in Long's office, which was on the upper floor of the Boykin Building in the northeast quadrant of the square. Long opened his business in 1917. (Courtesy of Marion McNamara Dobbs.)

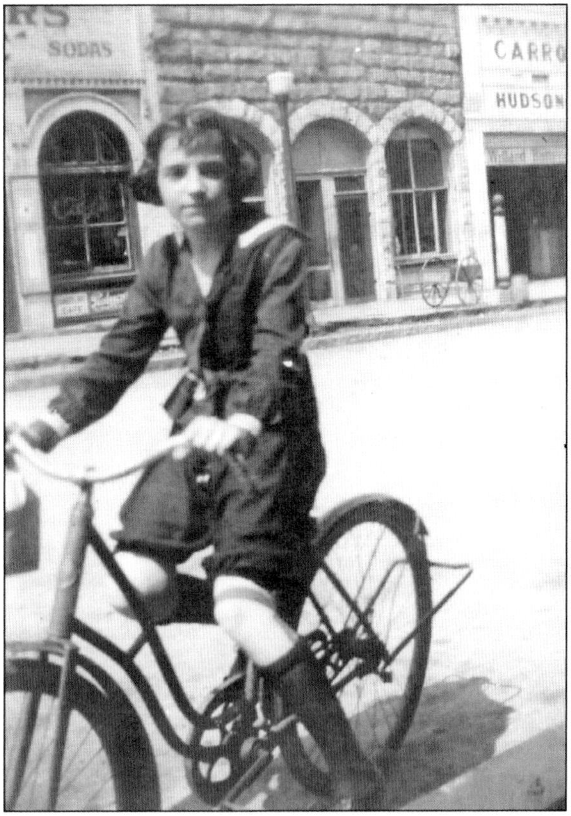

Newnan Street, 1921. Viola Bass (right) poses on her bicycle while a group of school-age boys (below) poses for the camera in downtown Carrollton. Behind them is the Hudson-Essex automobile dealership. The Essex was a low-cost brand of the Hudson car company that was first introduced in 1919. In that year, there were fewer than 500 automobiles in Carroll County. Despite this, the county approved a bond to improve rural roads. Some of the dealerships represented in Carrollton at this time were Ford, Dodge, Chalmers, Buick, and Overland. Once World War I was over and gasoline was available to consumers, locals organized the Carrollton Automobile Club. (Both, courtesy of UWG Special Collections.)

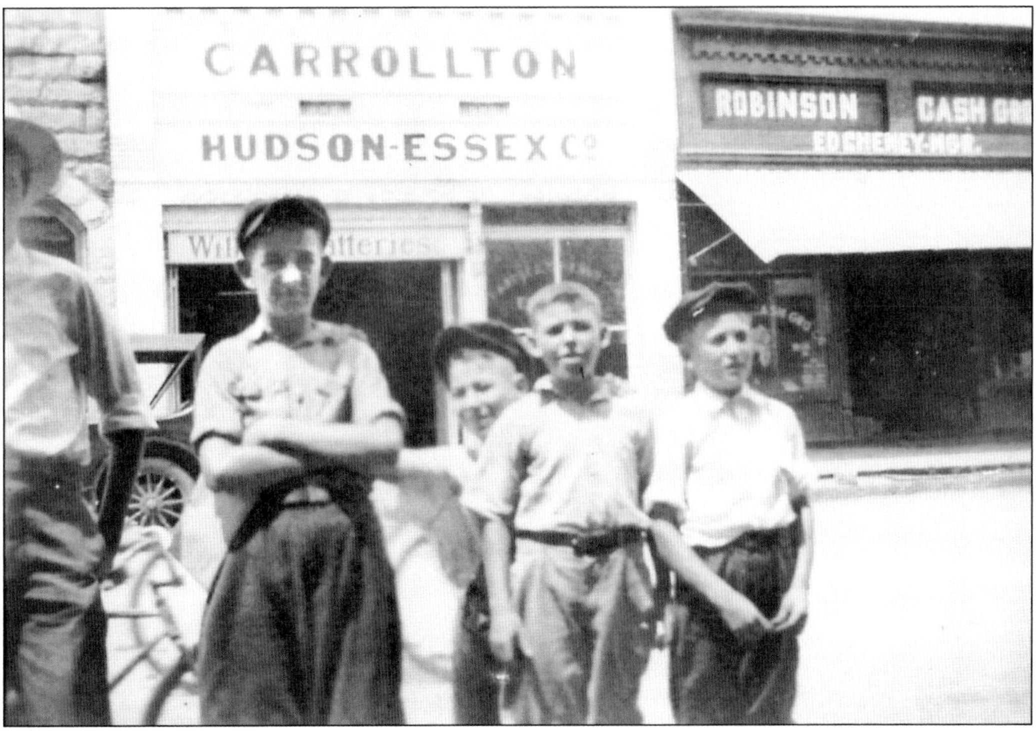

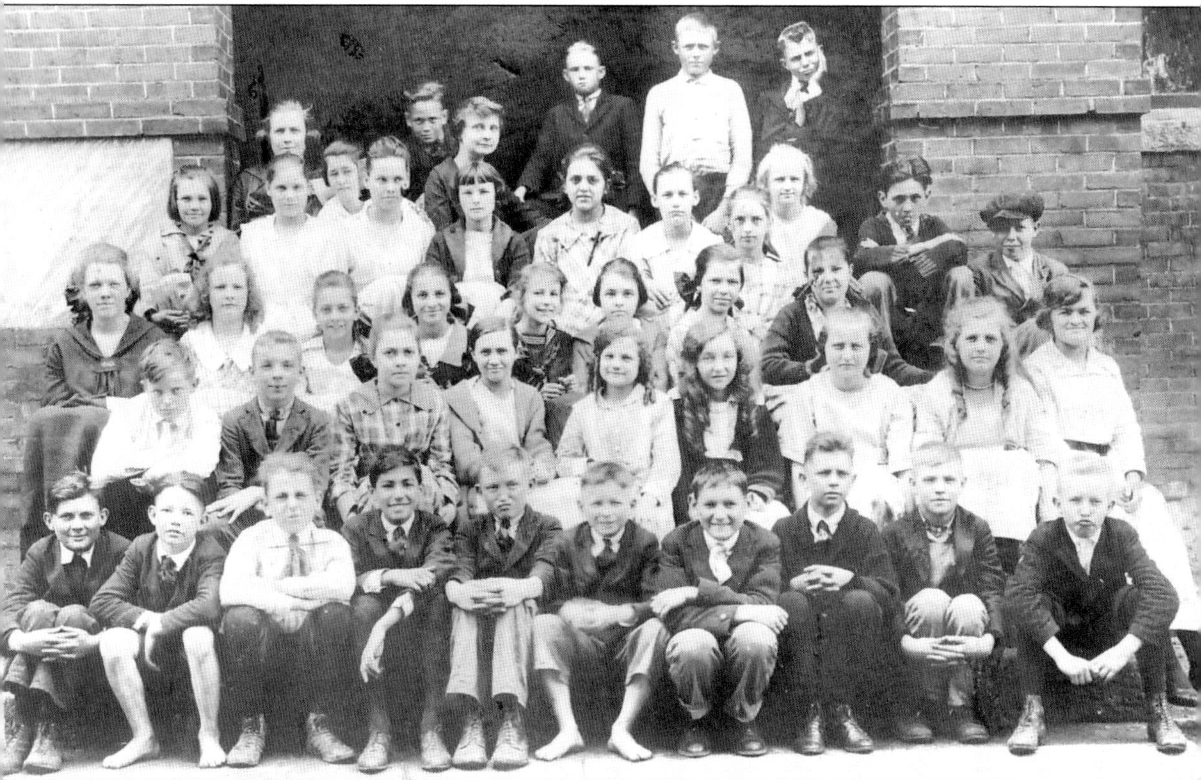

The Sixth Grade, c. 1920. This photograph was taken at the Carrollton Public School on College Street, which was built in 1898. The city's first public school was organized in 1887 for a term of five months, later extended to two semesters totaling 10 months. Some citizens petitioned the state legislature to repeal the school tax levied for the public school because they did not want to pay to educate other people's children. When this measure failed, the same group went back to the legislature complaining that citizens did not have a say in what kinds of teachers were hired, implying that the school board was recruiting the least-qualified teachers. This effort to repeal the school tax failed as well, due in large part to the efforts of US congressman and Carrollton native W.C. Adamson. In 1954, the College Street building was replaced by a new elementary school. Today, that building houses county offices. (Courtesy of UWG Special Collections.)

Myrtle Goodwyn and Friend, c. 1925. Myrtle Goodwyn, right, was born in 1909 in Roopville and grew up in Carrollton. Her father was physician Dr. Henry J. Goodwyn. They lived at 49 Dixie Street, which would be in the fourth block of Dixie south of Newnan Street today. (Courtesy of UWG Special Collections.)

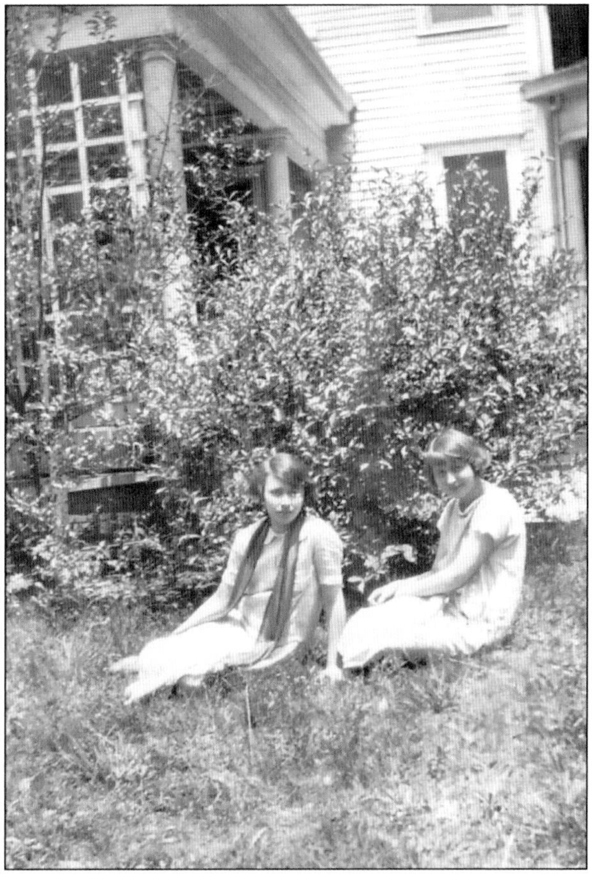

The Long Sisters, c. 1920. Celeste Long, at left, and her younger sister, Frances, pose in a wheelbarrow behind their home at 301 Dixie Street. The photographer was their father, Benjamin "Mann" Long, a Carrollton insurance agent whose photography documents half a century of Carrollton history. (Courtesy of Marion McNamara Dobbs.)

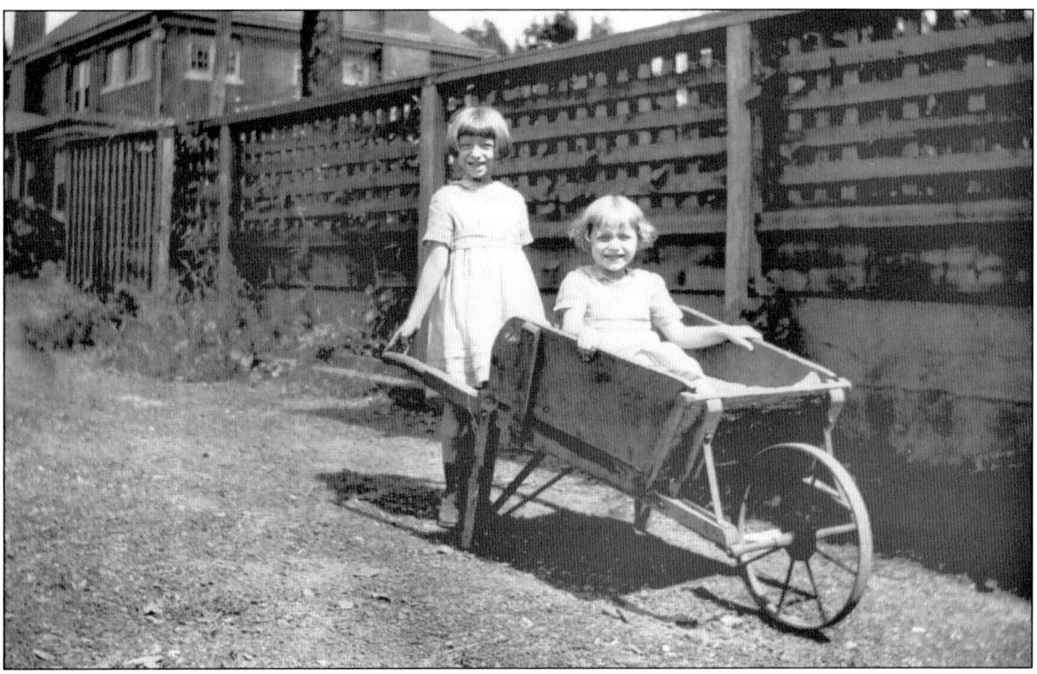

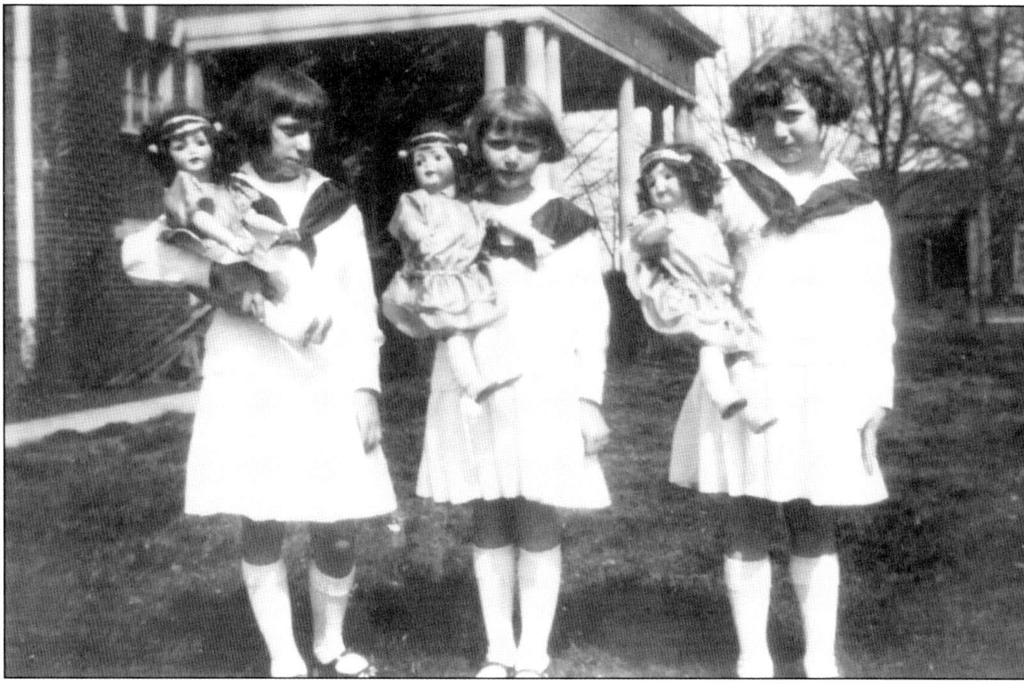

ROOP-LONG COUSINS, c. 1920. From left to right are sisters Celeste and Frances Long with their cousin Mary Helen Roop at the Roop home on Dixie Street. The Long girls' father and Roop's mother were siblings. The three girls grew up and were often pictured together, fondly referred to as the triplets. (Courtesy of Marion McNamara Dobbs.)

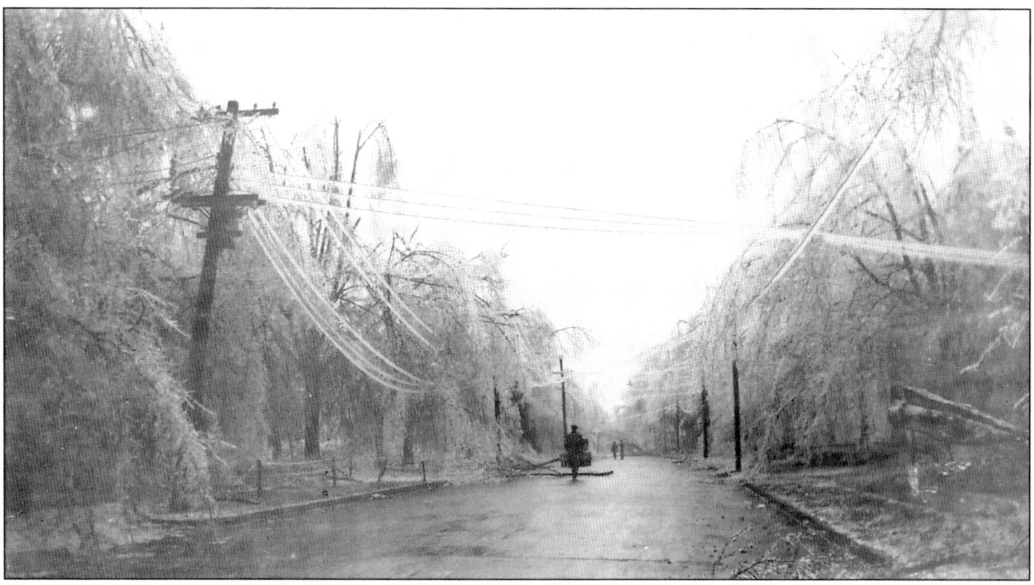

ICE STORM, 1935. Carrollton was hit with a rare ice storm in the last week of December 1935. The newspaper reported that trees bent and broke under the weight of the ice, water lines burst in the frigid temperatures, and electric lights flickered as utility lines were weighed down with ice. This is a view looking north from 43 Dixie Street. (Courtesy of Marion McNamara Dobbs.)

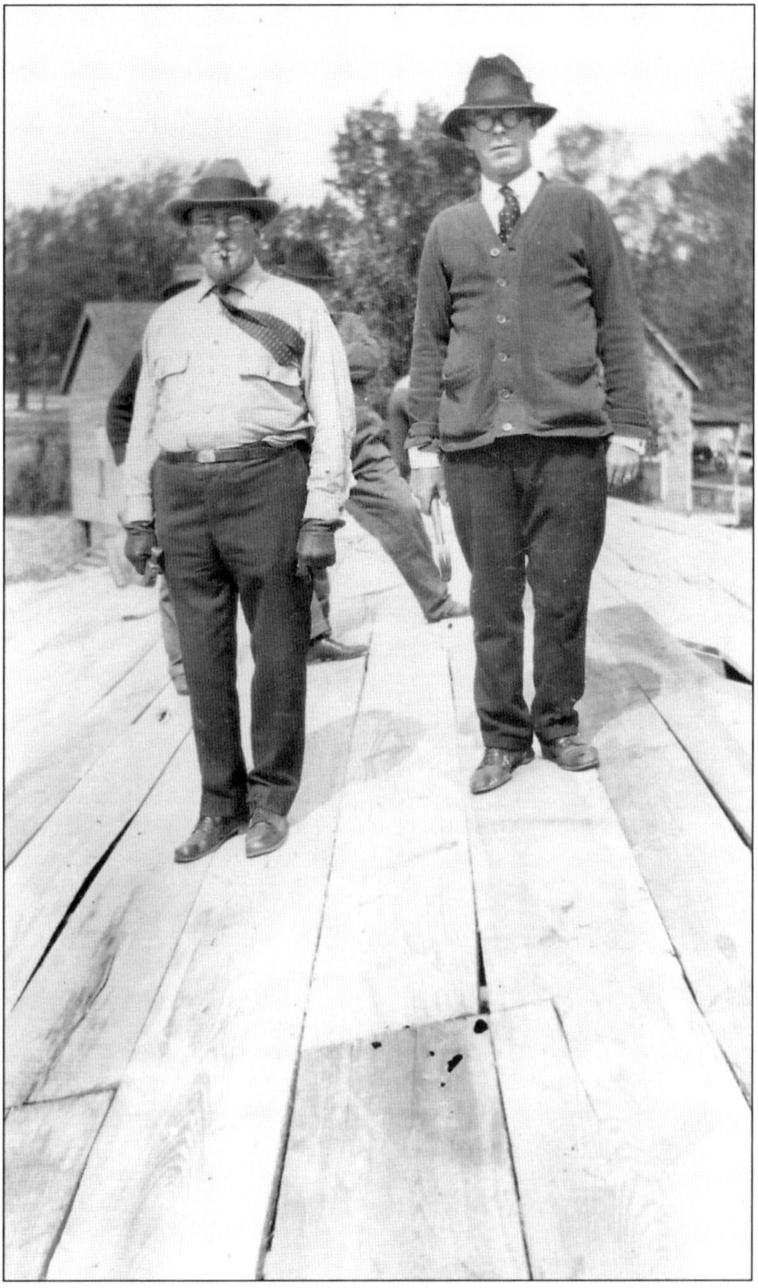

GYPSY SMITH REVIVAL, 1925. Carrollton's two most prominent Baptist ministers are pictured on the roof of a tabernacle under construction for a revival. Dr. Gilbert Dobbs, at left, was pastor of First Baptist Church from 1921 until 1927. Dr. John Milford was pastor of the Tabernacle Baptist Church from 1923 until 1926. They were only two of many citizens who helped erect the tented tabernacle, on Rome Street near the site of the Service Supply Company, in one day. It was reported to seat 3,000. While the men worked all day, the ladies provided basket lunches. The crusade was called Carroll County for Christ and was led by nationally renowned evangelist Gypsy Smith for one month, in October. Carroll County was home to more than 5,000 Baptists belonging to many churches large and small. (Courtesy of Marion McNamara Dobbs.)

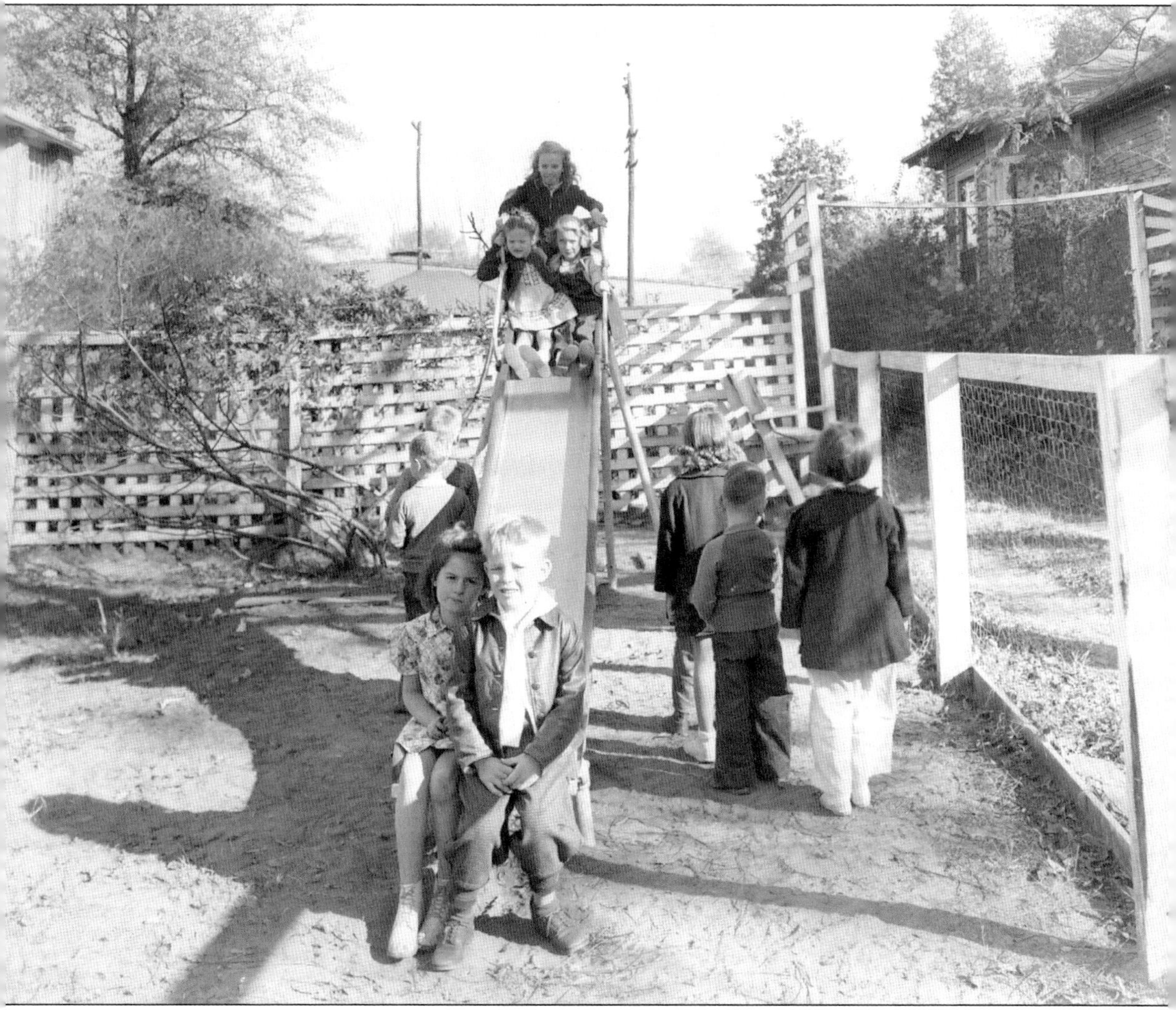

MANDEVILLE CHILDREN, C. 1945. In 1939, the Carrollton Presbyterian Church and Mandeville Mills opened a center for children and adults of the mill community, located on the southwest side of Carrollton. The Mandeville Center offered an outdoor playground, a library, crafts, sewing, pet shows, and community singing on Wednesday nights, among other activities. When the United States entered World War II, men who normally worked in the mills were called to military service. As with industry all over the nation, women stepped in to keep production going. The Mandeville Center offered child care tailored to the work schedules of mothers. It was also a source of uplift for a low-income population that in many ways was as segregated as African Americans had been. For years, the mill children attended the West View School in their community, even though the more substantial Maple Street School operated a few blocks away. (Courtesy of UWG Special Collections.)

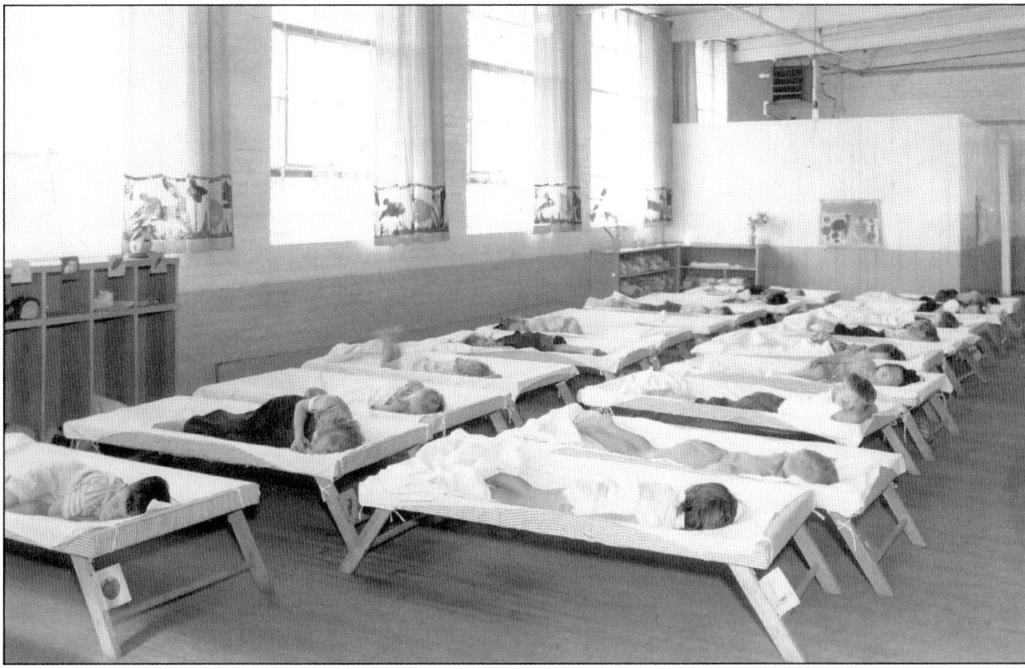

Mandeville Mills Nursery, c. 1943. A nursery school was provided so that mothers could work in the Mandeville Mills to produce more war goods. The school was open from 5:30 a.m. to 6:00 p.m., six days a week. The nursery was intended for "war working mothers in order to release more manpower" for military service. (Courtesy of UWG Special Collections.)

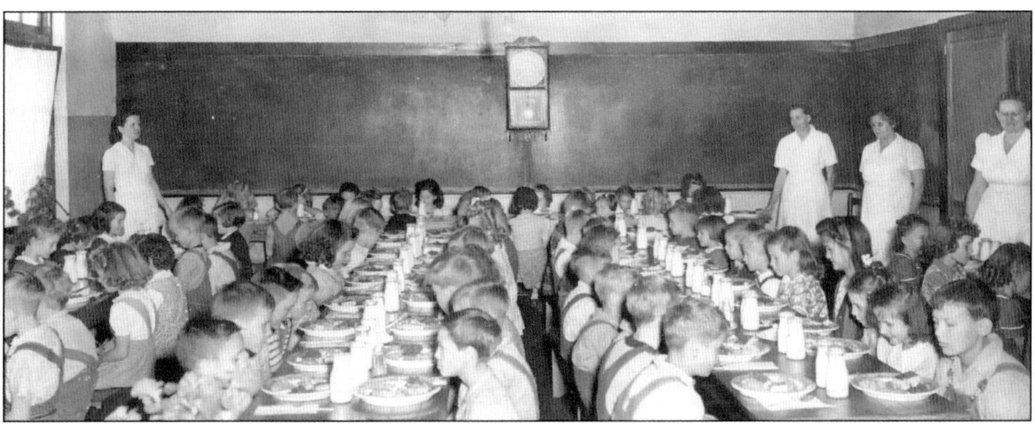

Balanced Meals and Milk, c. 1945. The Carroll Service Council provided milk, and the Mandeville Center gave students nutritious lunches. These children came from working-class homes with few opportunities. The social programs of the federal, county, and city agencies addressed nutrition as well as recreation, religion, health, welfare, and agriculture. (Courtesy of UWG Special Collections.)

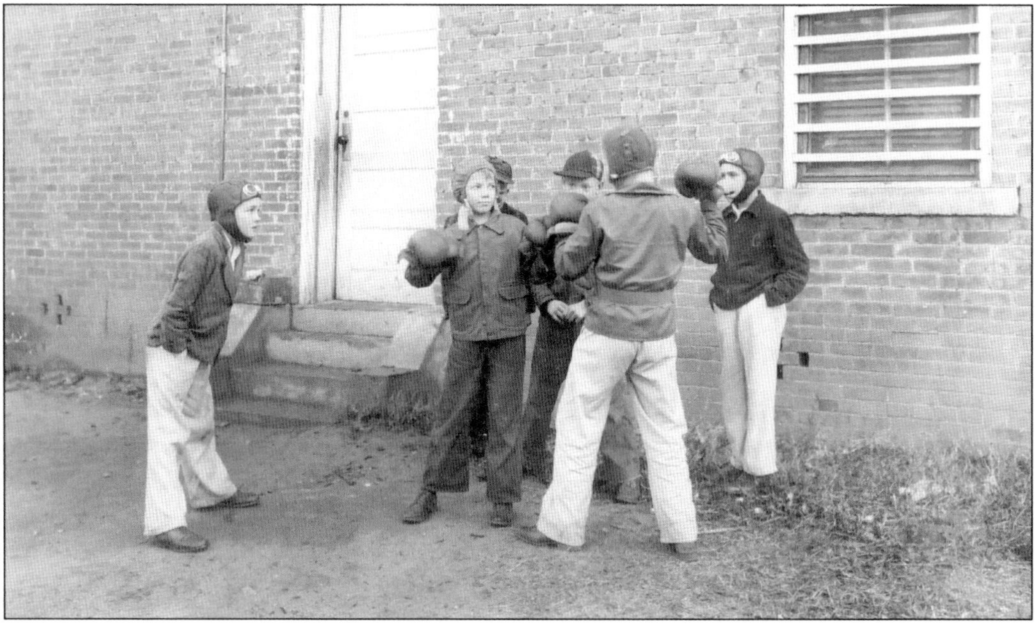

Mandeville Community Center, c. 1945. Recreation programs and equipment for the city's youth were part of the charge of the Carroll Service Council. In 1945, the Mandeville center had over 200 children enrolled. The Mandeville community, defined by the various mill buildings and adjacent mill workers' houses, is still visible today on the southwest side of the city. (Courtesy of UWG Special Collections.)

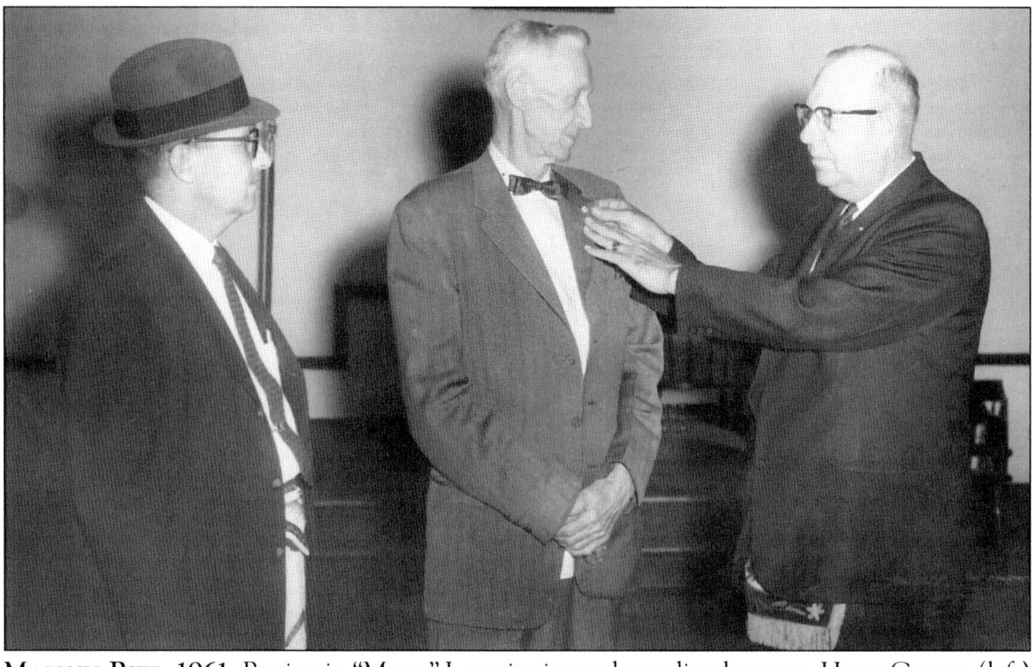

Masonic Rite, 1961. Benjamin "Mann" Long is pictured standing between Harry Cooper (left) and R.B. Muse during a Masonic ceremony. Long would have been 80 years old at the time of this photograph. He belonged to the Masonic Lodge No. 69, which was built in 1931 at the corner of Mill and Tanner Streets. (Courtesy of Marion McNamara Dobbs.)

Two

AROUND THE COUNTY

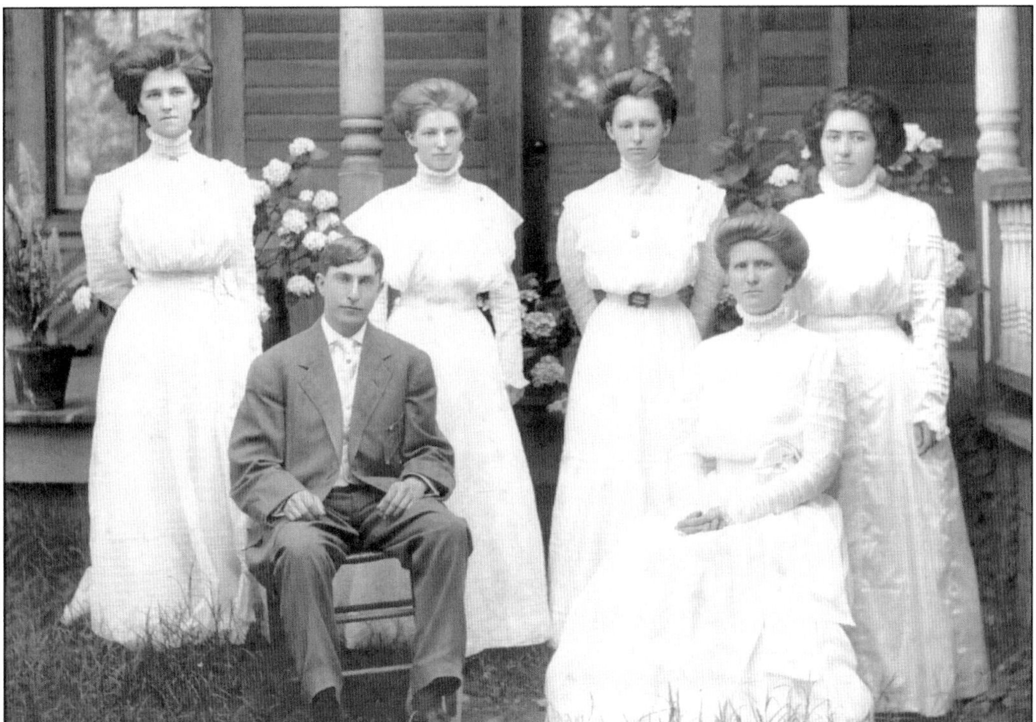

BOWDON COLLEGE GRADUATES, 1909. The young man pictured is R.H. Davis, and the seated woman is Annie Marlow. Emma Farmer is standing at far right. The other women are not identified. Bowdon College was opened in 1855 by Charles A. McDaniel in the southwestern part of Carroll County. It began as an upper-grade school but soon offered college courses. The school ceased operating in the mid-1930s after West Georgia College was chartered. (Courtesy of UWG Special Collections.)

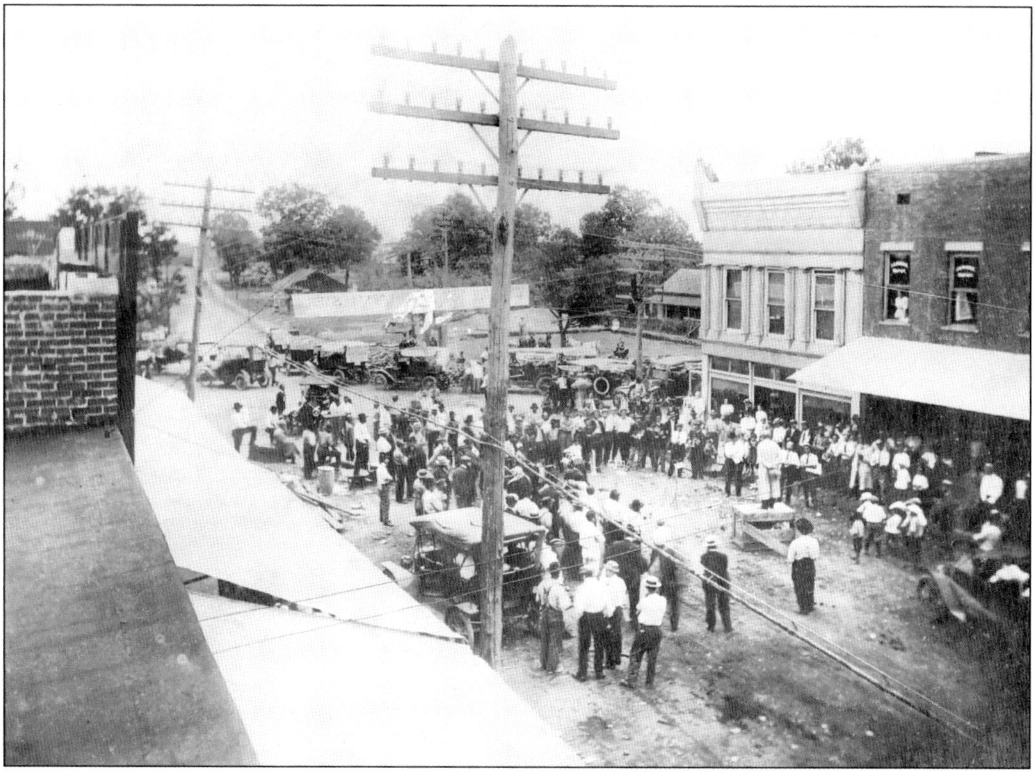

BOOSTER CLUB IN BREMEN, 1913. The Carrollton Booster Club visited locations around the county to promote its businesses. In the photograph above, former Carrollton mayor H. Whitfield Long is standing on a soapbox to address the citizens of Bremen, a city at the northern edge of Carroll County. The photographer was Long's son, Benjamin "Mann" Long. Below, it is not clear if this is the same visit by the Carrollton Booster Club. It appears to be a car rally organized for the occasion. A well-known Carrollton photographer, O.V. Fowler, took this photograph at Bremen. (Both, courtesy of Marion McNamara Dobbs.)

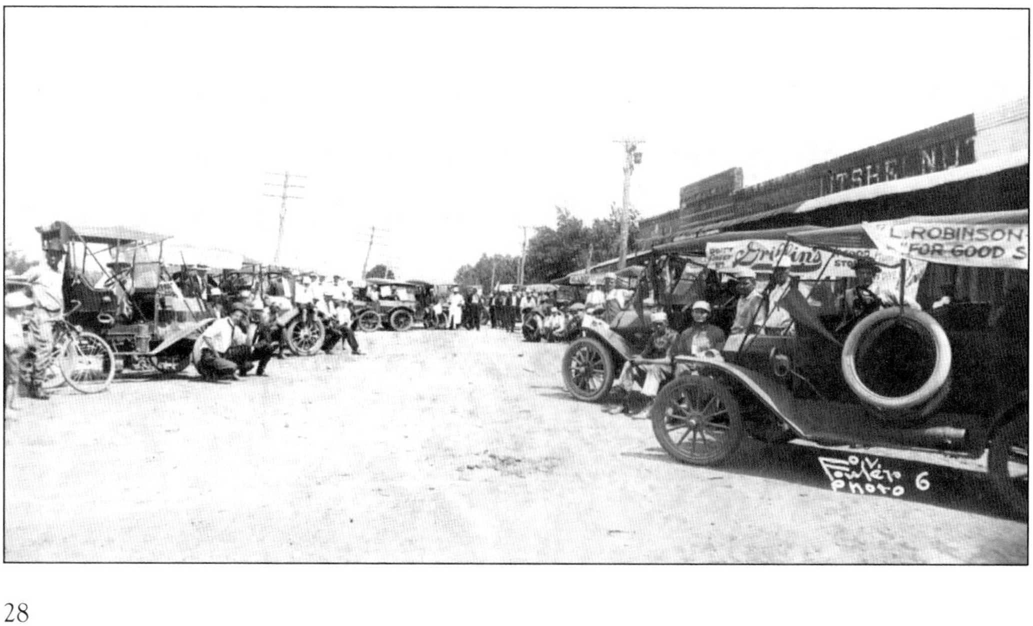

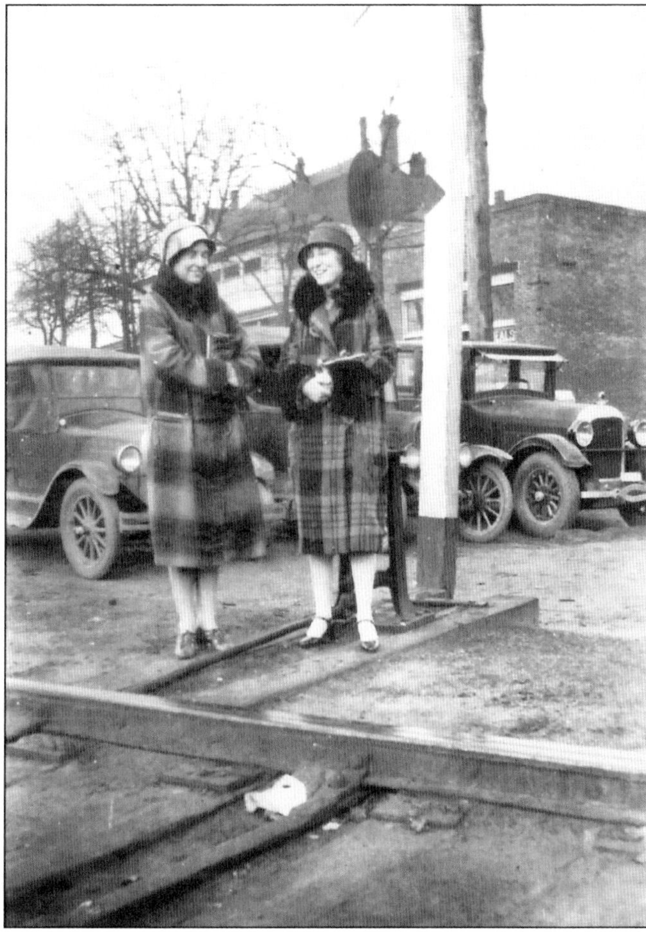

Sisters in Bremen, c. 1920. At left is Stella Long with her sister Helen posing in Bremen for their brother, insurance agent Benjamin "Mann" Long. The Long family was descended from one of the earliest settlers of Carroll County, John Long, who came from Tennessee in 1827. (Courtesy of Marion McNamara Dobbs.)

Bremen Railroad Station, c. 1920. Two fashionably dressed women bundled against the cold are pictured waiting for a train at the Bremen station. Bremen straddles Carroll and Haralson Counties, though its citizens report to the county seat of Buchanan in Haralson for public matters. (Courtesy of Marion McNamara Dobbs.)

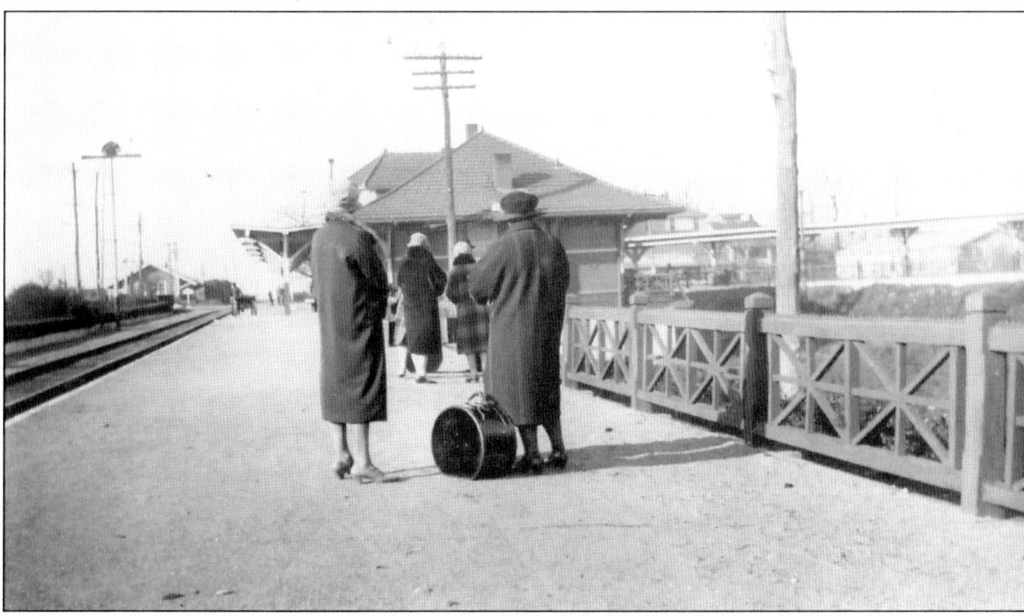

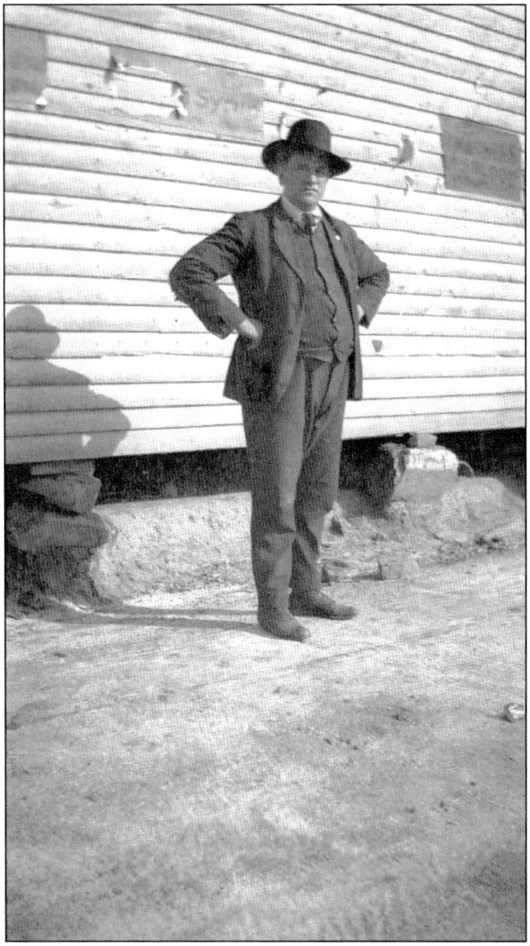

Luther Robinson, c. 1930. Luther Robinson and his brother operated a store in the community of Burwell just west of Carrollton. It was said that the store went bankrupt during the Depression because the Robinsons extended too much credit to their customers during hard times. (Courtesy of UWG Special Collections.)

Customers of Luther Robinson, c. 1930. The ubiquitous Coca-Cola sign that hung in every commercial establishment, no matter how humble, can be seen on Luther Robinson's store in Burwell. The store also featured the traditional front porch bench where regulars could sit and gossip. (Courtesy of UWG Special Collections.)

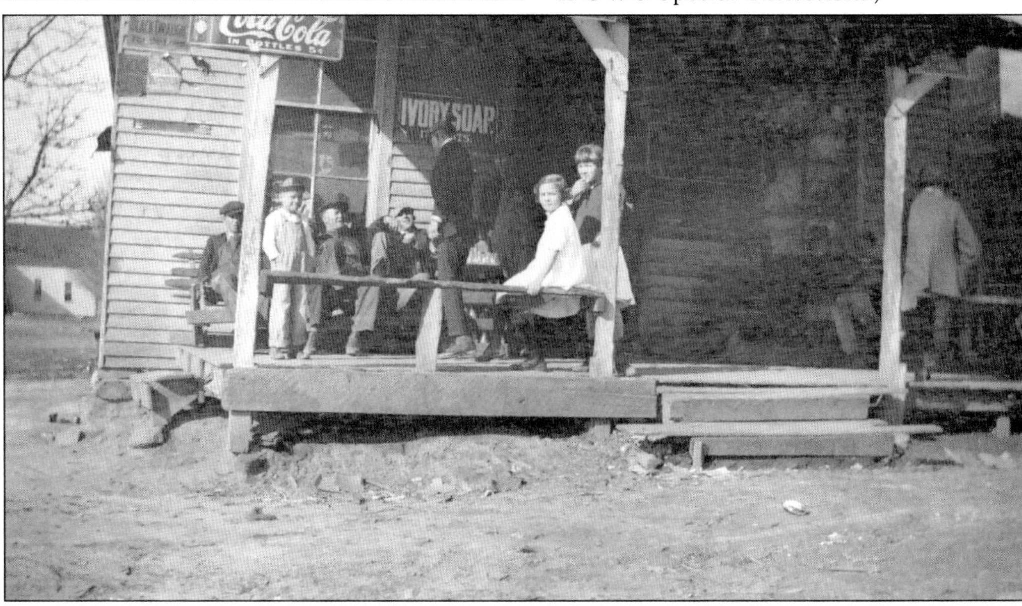

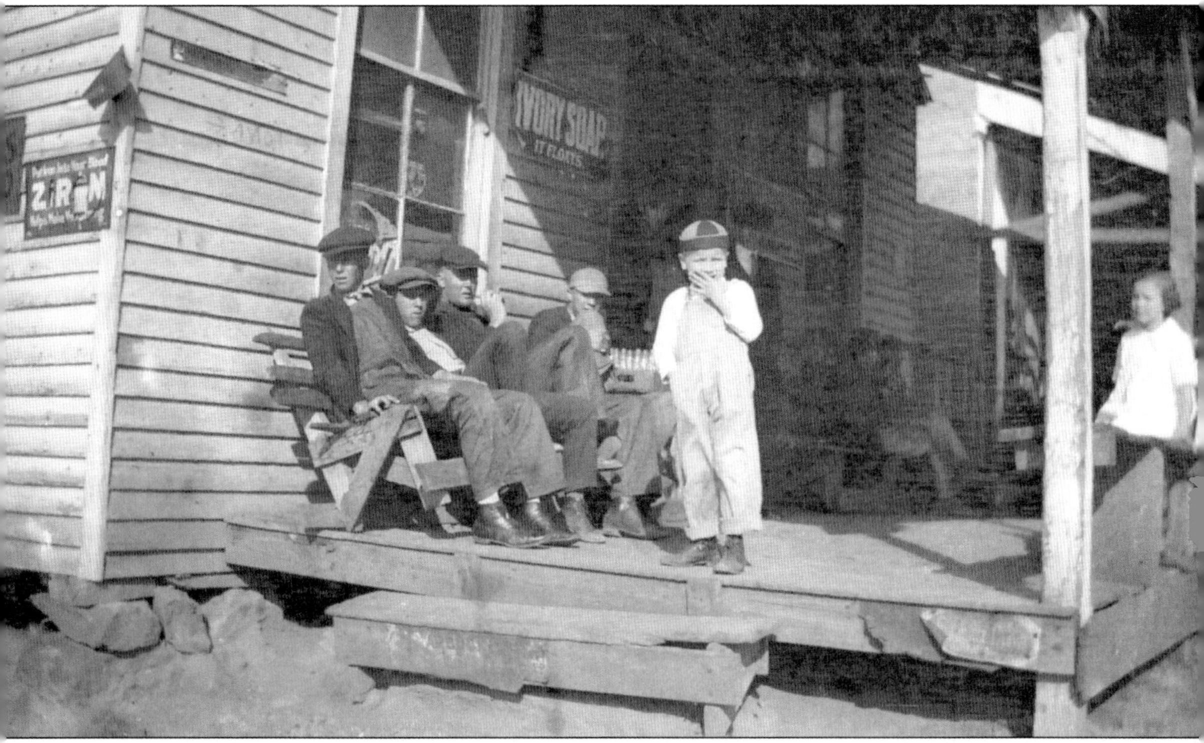

IVORY SOAP, IT FLOATS, c. 1930. Luther Robinson's store attracted children as well as these young men, who might be without jobs due to the Depression. The community of Burwell had a church and a public elementary school, the latter made possible after state legislators passed a local school tax. By the early 1940s, Burwell had become one of several Carroll County communities used by college educators to gain field experience while teaching children and adults how to improve their living conditions. More recently, in August 1995, an Atlantic Southeast Airlines plane flying from Atlanta to Biloxi, Mississippi, crashed into a field in this farming community, killing nine of the 29 passengers. The accident was blamed on propeller failure, which caused a rapid descent that the pilot could not correct. The nearby Shiloh United Methodist Church has created a memorial to the nine victims. (Courtesy of UWG Special Collections.)

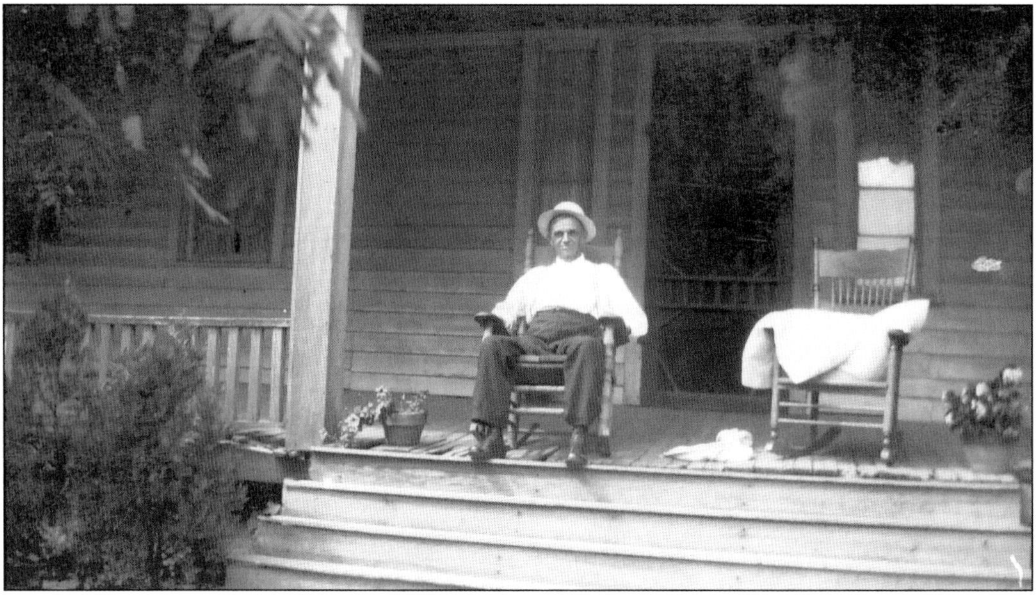

Jesse Orville Long, 1874–1937. In this c. 1935 photograph, Long is looking relaxed on the front porch of what was known as the Samuel Hart House. The house was where Long's father, Benjamin McFarland Long, was born in 1827. The elder Long was said to be the first white child born in Carroll County, part of former Creek Indian property. (Courtesy of Marion McNamara Dobbs.)

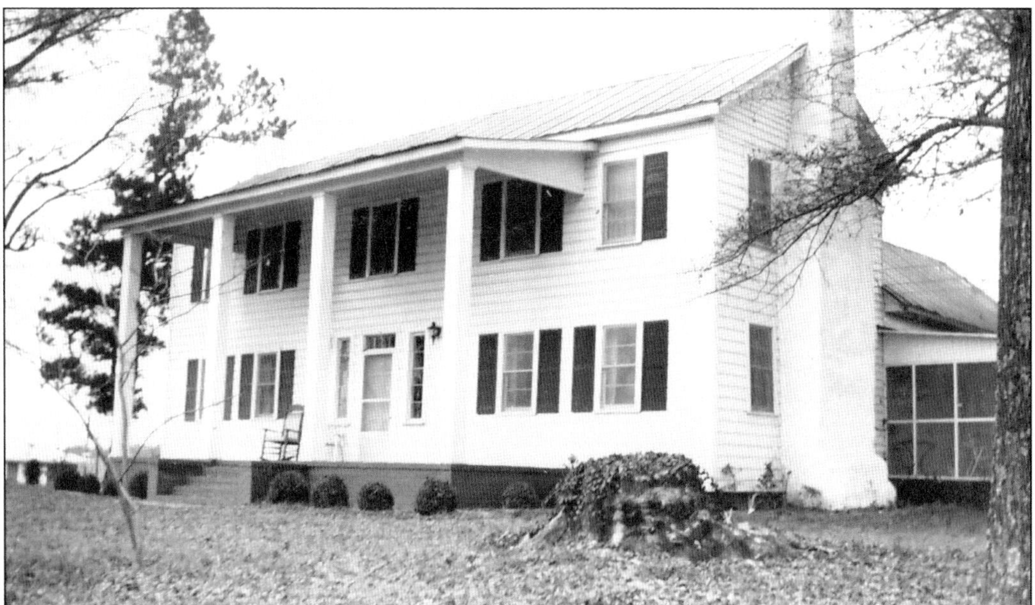

Hart House Remodeled. In 1961, the old homestead was remodeled, having passed out of the Long family. The porch design was largely changed, but the front door and its surrounding windows remained the same. The house was located about three miles southwest of Villa Rica on Highway 78. (Courtesy of Marion McNamara Dobbs.)

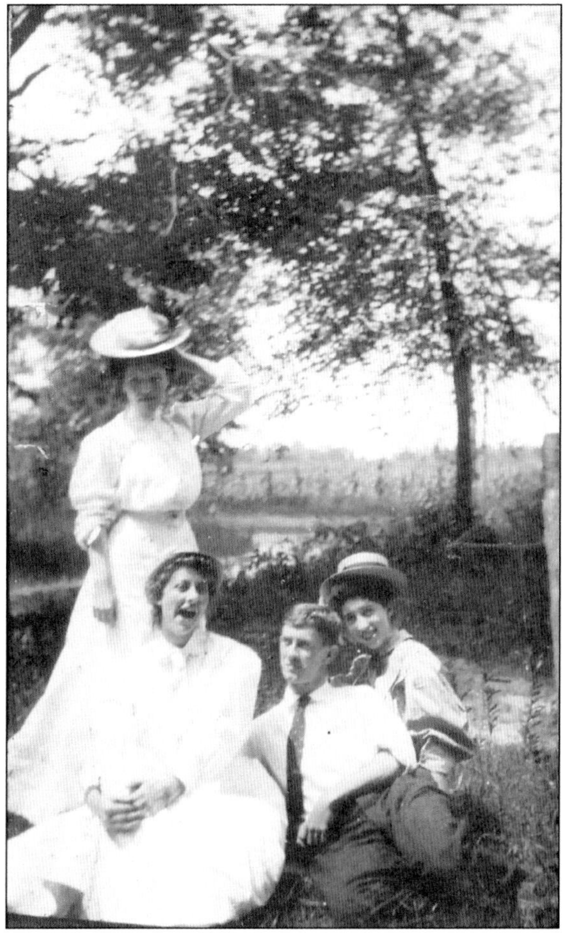

SIMONTON'S MILL, C. 1910. This was a popular spot on the Little Tallapoosa River for picnics and other outings. Standing in this photograph is Marion West, great-granddaughter of Appleton Mandeville, whose descendants defined Carrollton industry. Seated are, from left to right, Willie Erminger, Roy Mandeville, and Marion's sister Helen West. (Courtesy of Marion McNamara Dobbs.)

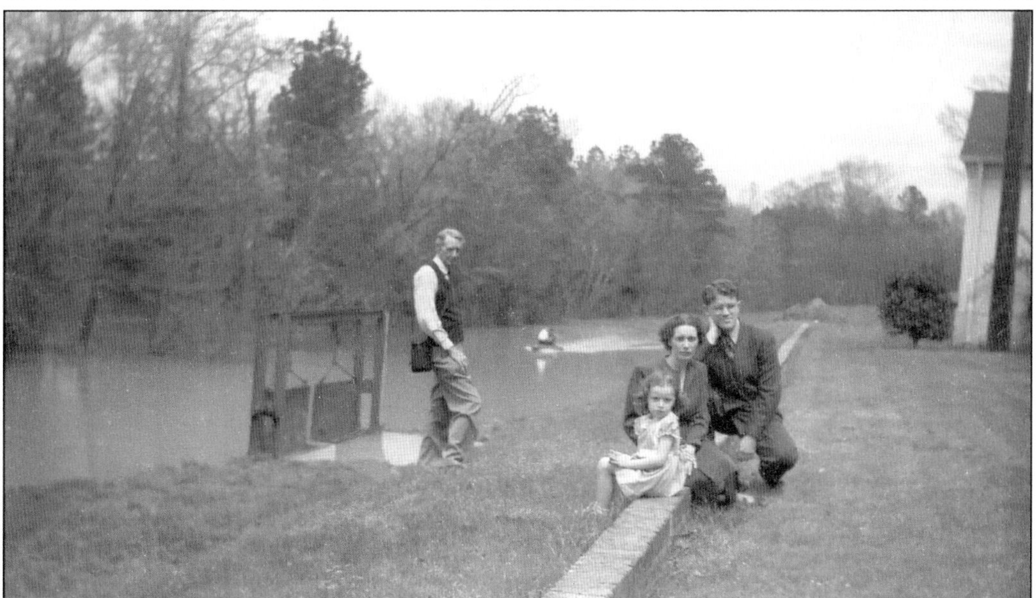

MCNAMARA FAMILY, C. 1945. Photographer and insurance agent Benjamin "Mann" Long is shown standing next to the Little Tallapoosa River, possibly near the city waterworks on the north side of Carrollton. Seated are his daughter, Frances McNamara, her husband, James, and their daughter Marion. (Courtesy of Marion McNamara Dobbs.)

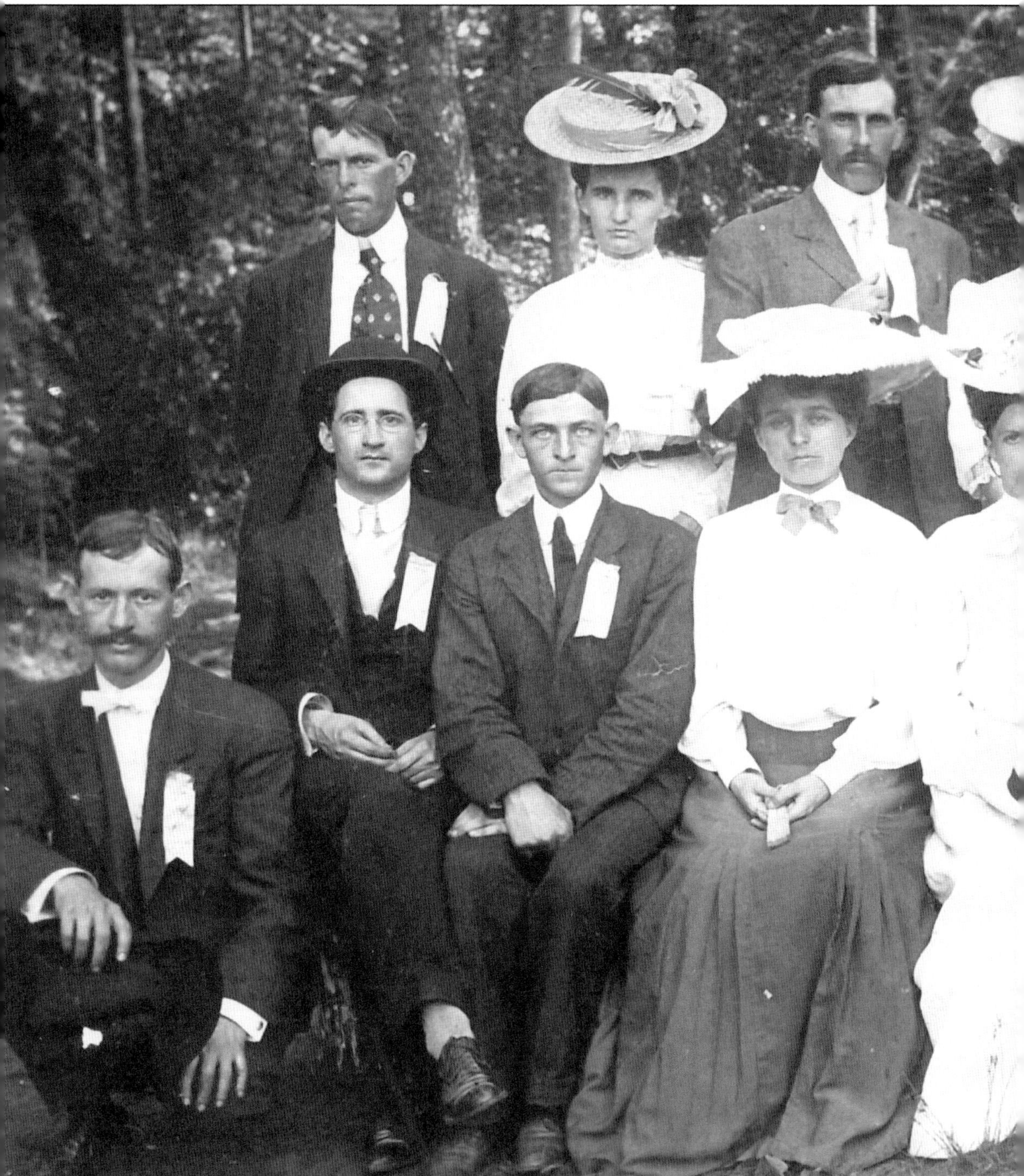

SIMONTON'S MILL, C. 1900. Originally known as the Espy Mill, it was built by E.W. Hibbler and later purchased by A.A. Simonton. Simonton was born in Alabama in 1849 and died in Carrollton in 1919. He was a successful miller and cotton gin operator. He and his wife, Margaret, had five children and lived in a large home on Maple Street. Simonton's elder brother, Charles, also lived

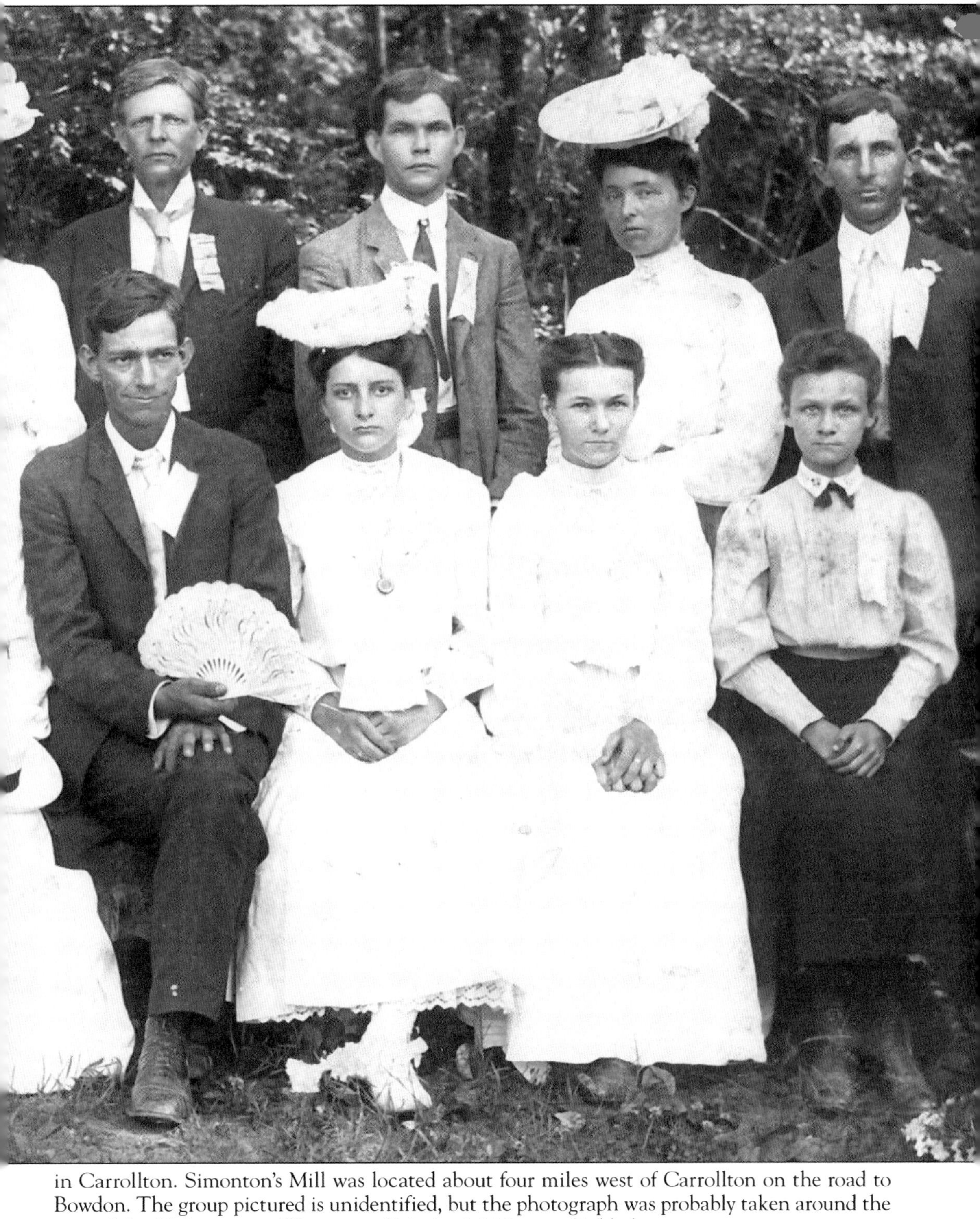

in Carrollton. Simonton's Mill was located about four miles west of Carrollton on the road to Bowdon. The group pictured is unidentified, but the photograph was probably taken around the turn of the 20th century. (Courtesy of Marion McNamara Dobbs.)

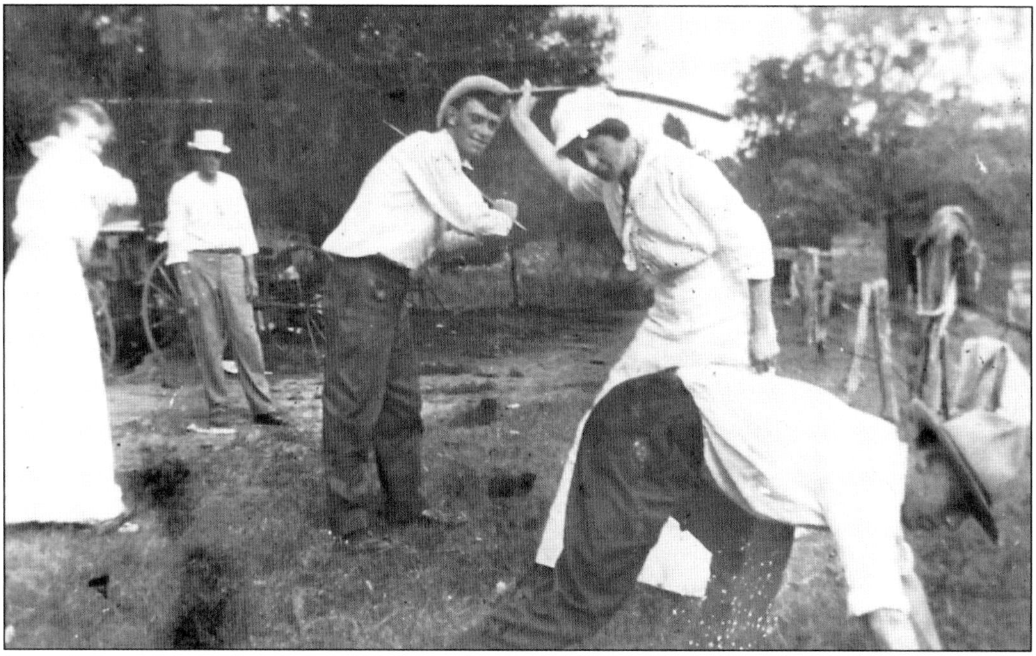

Leap Frog, 1914. These students from the Fourth District A&M School in Carrollton are pictured having a picnic and playing games at Camp Chattahoochee in Carroll County. It very likely was in the area today called the McIntosh Reserve, named for Chief William McIntosh, a Creek Indian whose father was a Scots settler. (Courtesy of UWG Special Collections.)

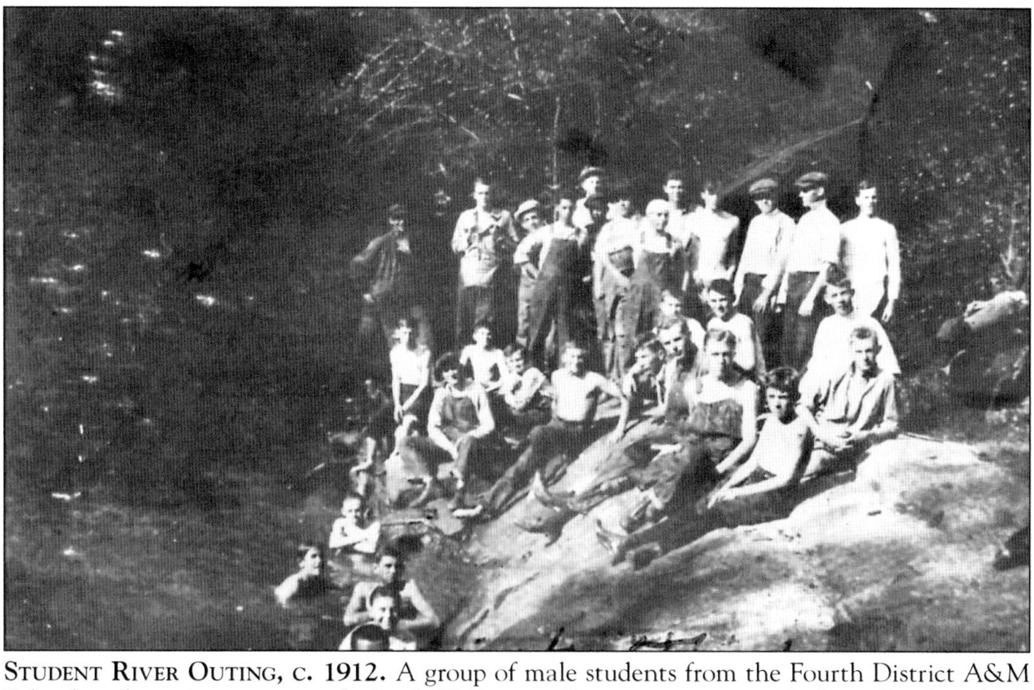

Student River Outing, c. 1912. A group of male students from the Fourth District A&M School made a trip to swim in the Little Tallapoosa River near campus. Technically, the school was not in the Carrollton city limits at this time, and the river was not far from campus. (Courtesy of UWG Special Collections.)

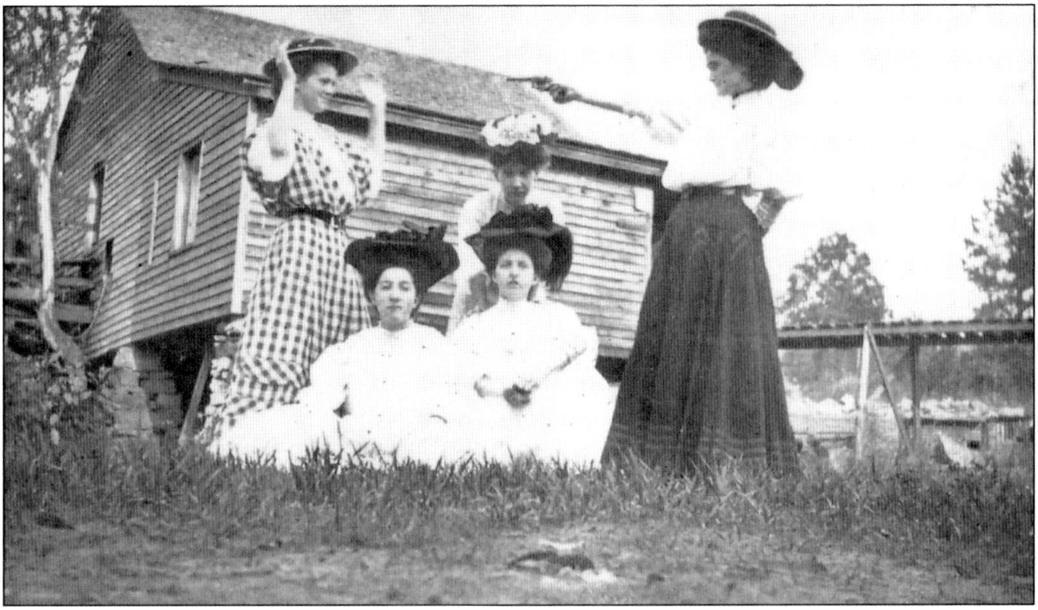

HAY'S MILL, C. 1910. Another popular picnic spot in Carroll County was Hay's Mill, located just southwest of the city. Hay's Mill Road runs today between Maple Street and the 166 Bypass around Carrollton. Mugging for the camera and standing from left to right are Nettie Tumlin, Maggie Tanner, and Charligne Vickers. Seated are Helen West and Mary Camp. (Courtesy of Marion McNamara Dobbs.)

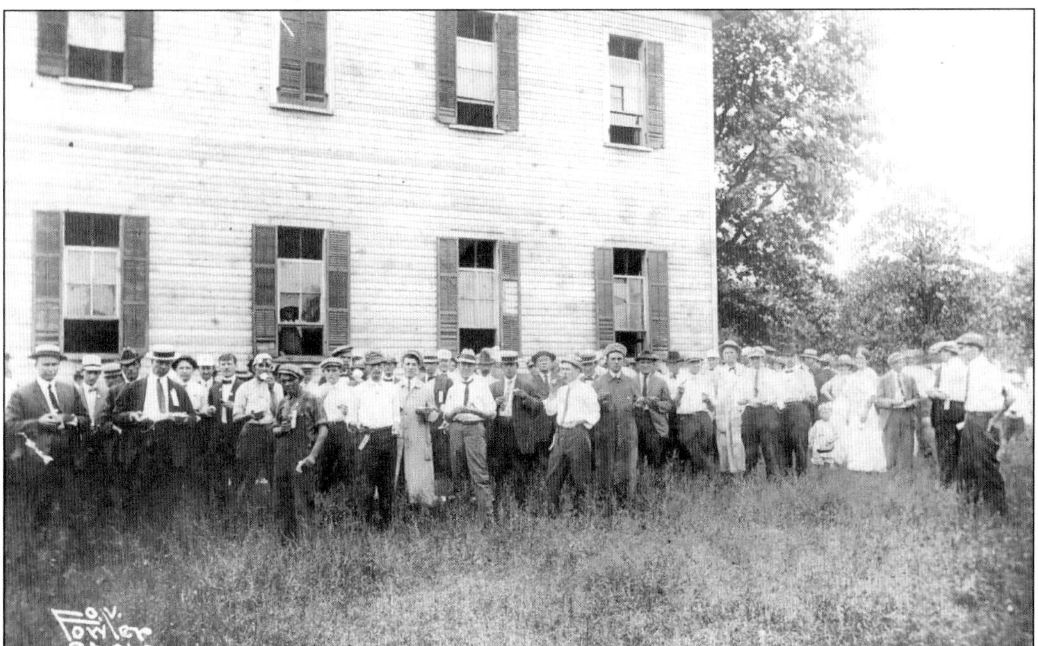

BOOSTER CLUB AT ROOPVILLE, SEPTEMBER 4, 1913. The Carrollton Booster Club visited Roopville and had a dinner on the grounds of the Henry Grady Institute. This school was erected in the 1880s and featured three classrooms on the first floor and an auditorium on the second floor. It was named for the famous Atlanta newspaperman. (Courtesy of Marion McNamara Dobbs.)

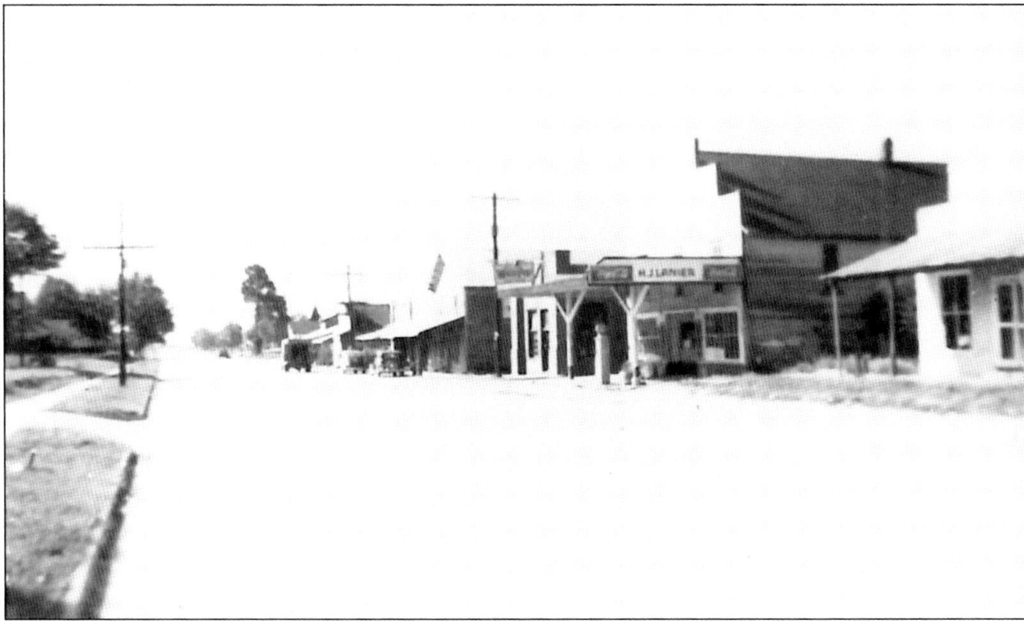

Roopville's Main Street, c. 1940. J.A. Veal owned Veal and Company, and his family was one of several that settled early in this district 10 miles south of Carrollton. The town was established on a high ridge, said to be the highest point in the county. Roopville was laid out by John K. Roop, a civic leader in Carroll County who served on the county school board and the board of roads and revenues. He was a leader of the Farmers Alliance in Carroll County, an outgrowth of the Populist Movement. The Alliance opened Georgia's first cooperative retail store, called the Carroll Cooperative Company, on the square, with Roop as its business manager. (Both, courtesy of Marion McNamara Dobbs.)

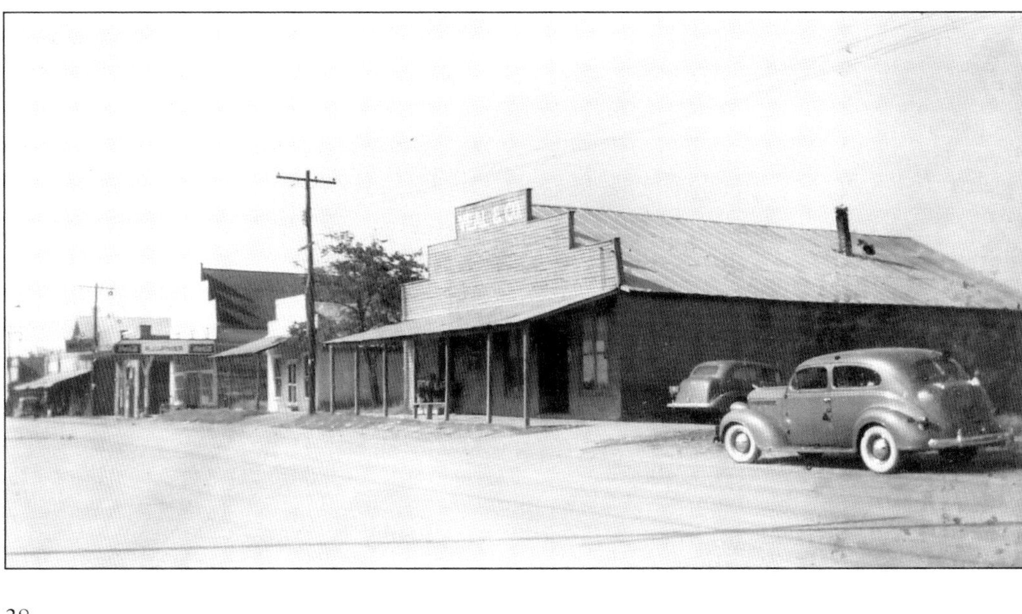

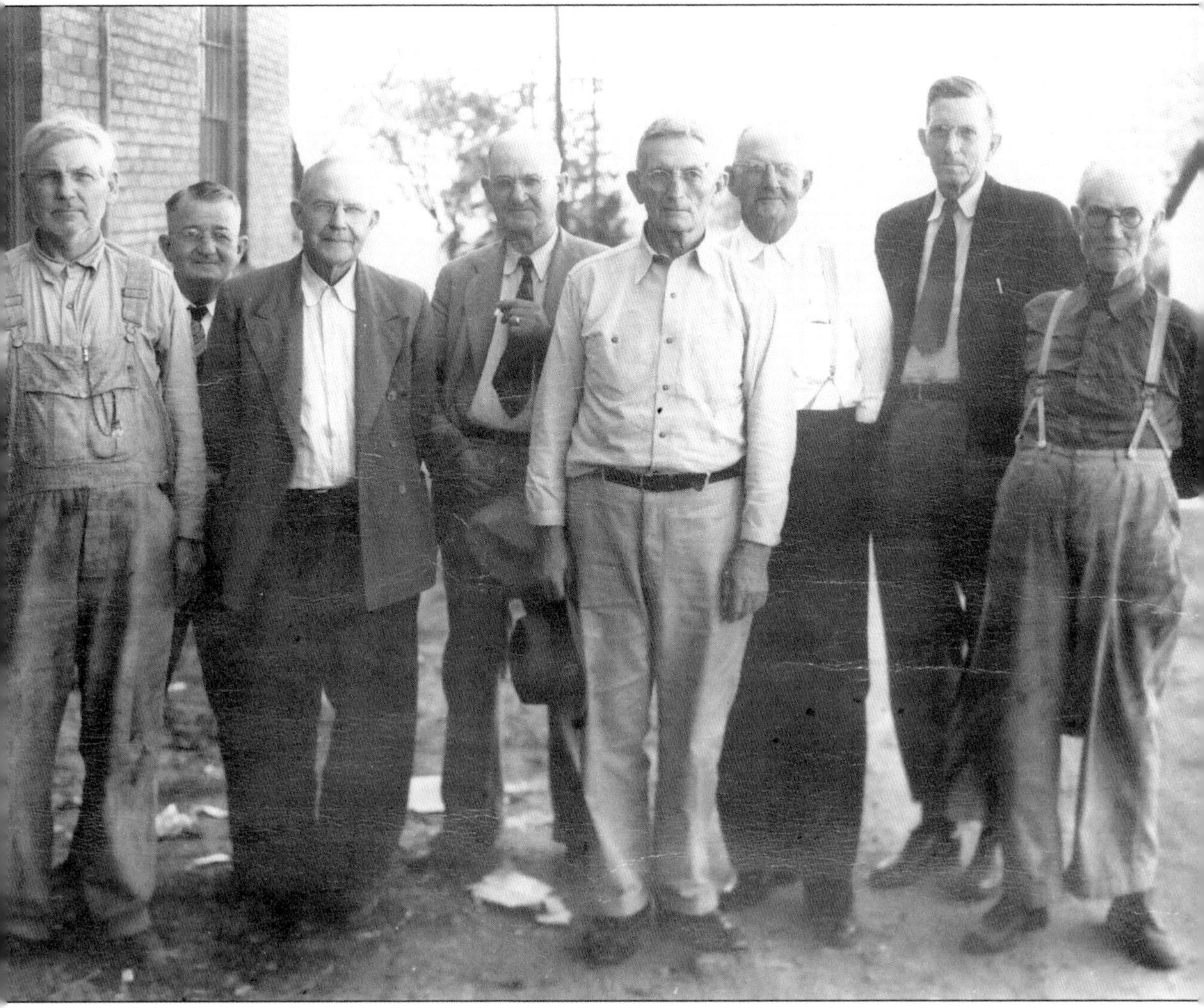

ROOPVILLE BUSINESS ASSOCIATION, C. 1930. These gentlemen are prominent citizens and merchants in Roopville during the early 20th century. Pictured, from left to right, are ? Monroe, J.T. Broadwater, Arthur Garrett, B.F. "Frank" Roop, Pelham P. Staples, J. Lee Garrett, James A. Veal, and L.A. Ware. Broadwater ran a barbershop, and Frank Roop was a teacher-turned-merchant who also served on the Carroll County Board of Education. Staples owned a grocery and general merchandise store. He also was said to have built a swimming hole in the 1930s, redirecting a creek to fill it after putting boards around the walls to keep it from caving in. J. Lee Garrett was town treasurer in 1905, as well as a farmer and furniture dealer, while Veal was town clerk for many years. Roopville was incorporated in 1885. (Courtesy of Marion McNamara Dobbs.)

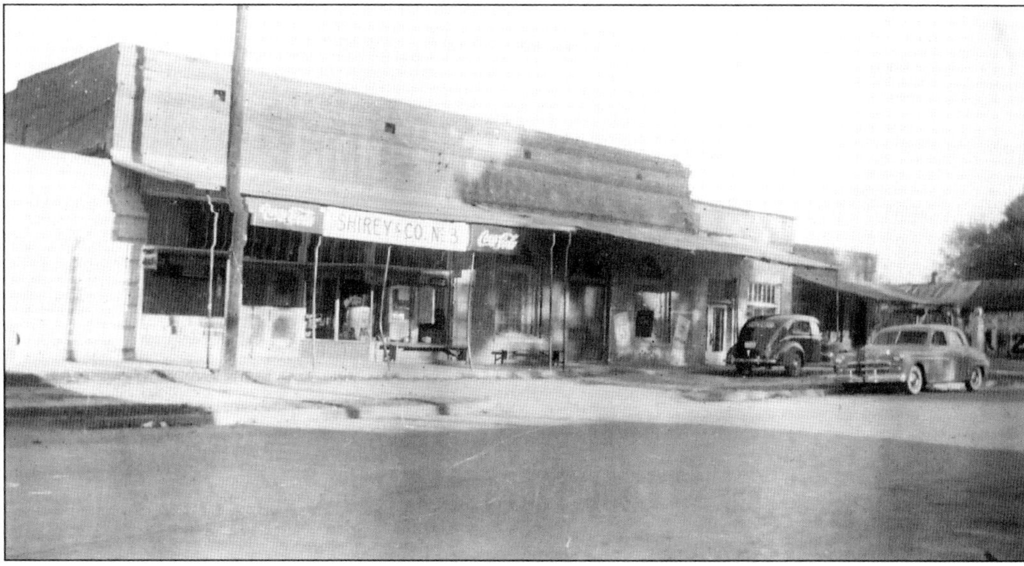

CITY OF WHITESBURG, C. 1940. Named for A.J. White, president of the Savannah, Griffin, and Alabama Railroad, this city is 12 miles southeast of Carrollton. At one time, it boasted a thriving industry for paper and textiles, a flourishing lumber trade, and a Methodist college. (Courtesy of Marion McNamara Dobbs.)

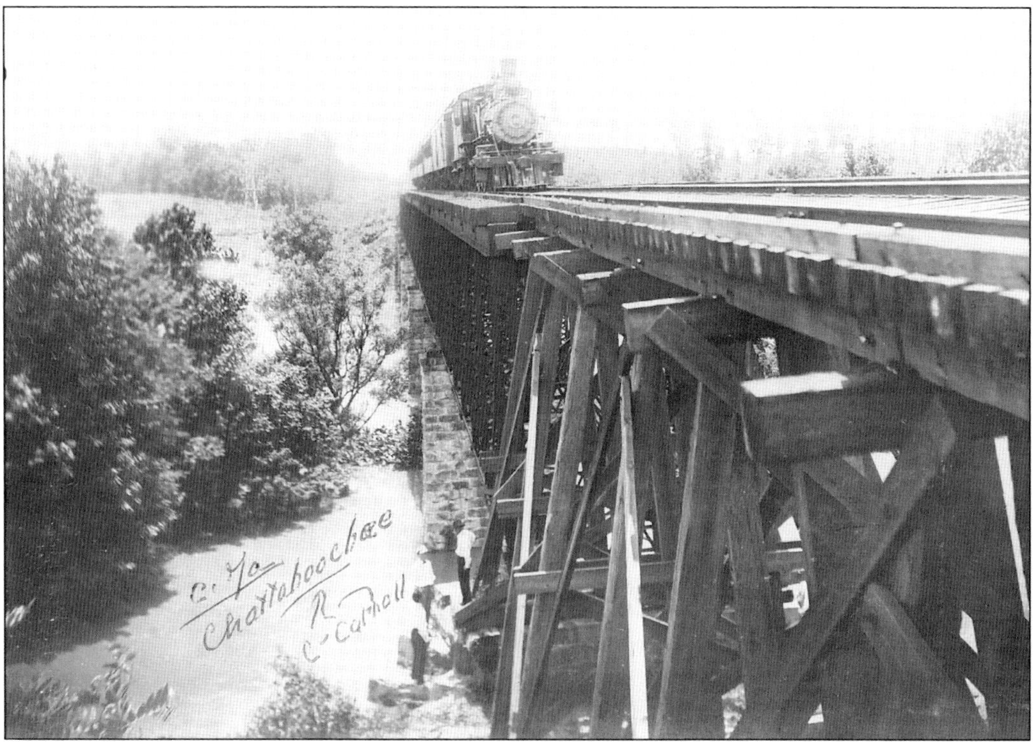

CENTRAL OF GEORGIA RAILROAD BRIDGE, C. 1914. This bridge crossed the Chattahoochee River near Whitesburg. Pilings from the bridge can still be seen today. The town is said to owe its existence to the laying of track in the 1870s because of the work delays associated with removing layers of rock there. (Courtesy of UWG Special Collections.)

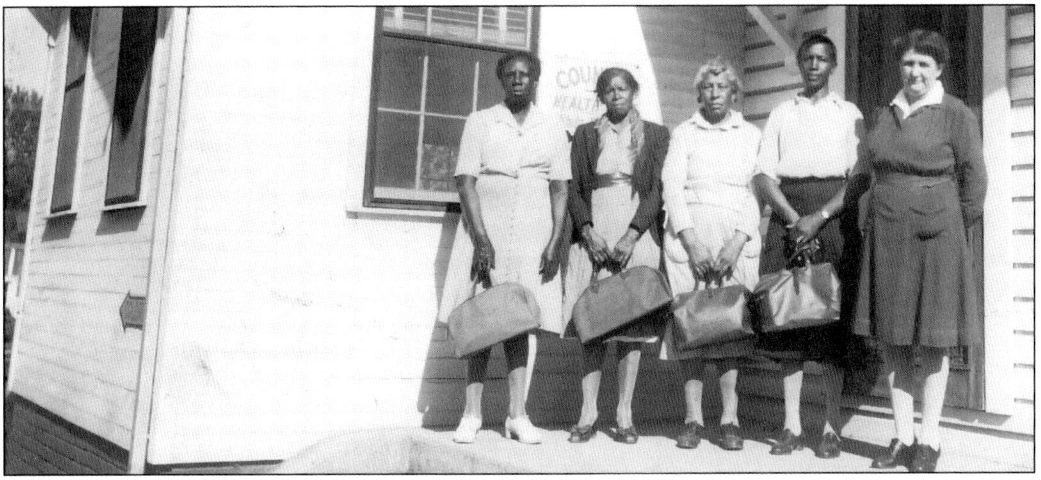

MIDWIVES, c. 1944. The Carroll Service Council formed in 1943 as a community action organization, creating an alliance of charitable programs already operated by churches, civic groups, and public services. One of the council's missions was health care for expectant mothers. In this photograph, the public health nurse poses with a group of African American midwives who had received "scientific training." (Courtesy of UWG Special Collections.)

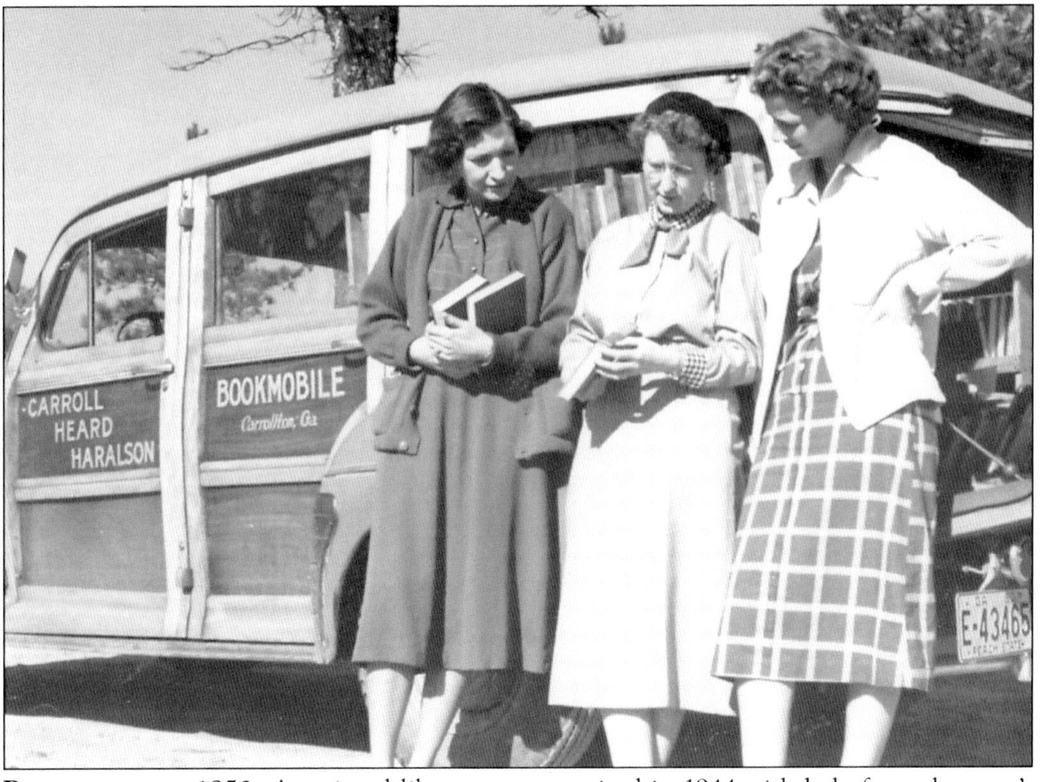

BOOKMOBILE, c. 1950. A regional library was organized in 1944 with help from the state's department of education. Edith Foster (center) spearheaded the effort aided by West Georgia College students. The program allowed far-flung county residents to have access to library books while making more coordinated library services available across counties. (Courtesy of UWG Special Collections.)

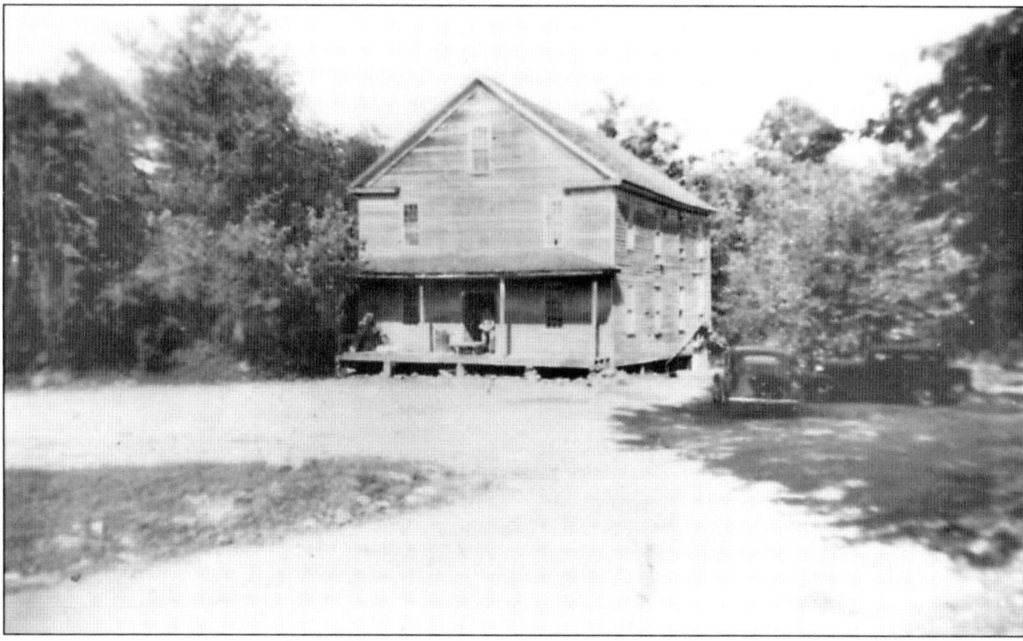

Lovvorn's Mill, 1940. The mill was situated on Indian Creek near Bowdon in western Carroll County. Gaines W. Lovvorn was the owner, according to the 1920 federal census for Bowdon. Lovvorn's son Len was the Bowdon postmaster in 1930. Another son, James, also worked at the post office, according to the 1930 census. (Courtesy of Marion McNamara Dobbs.)

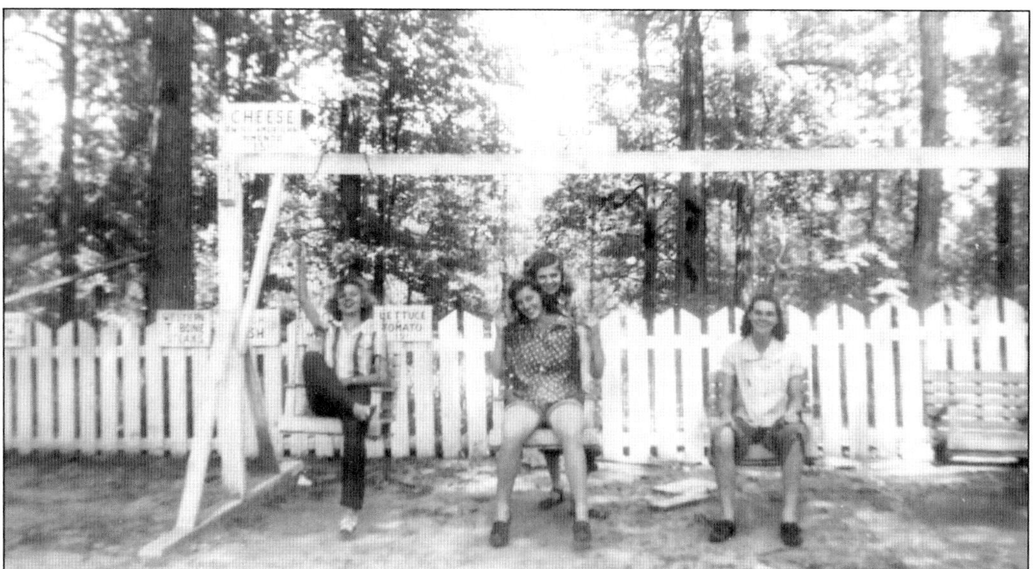

Sprayberry's, c. 1945. The well-known barbecue restaurant used to have a location north of Carrollton on what is now US 27, near the intersection with Route 113, or Temple Road. The restaurant still operates today in Newnan. These coeds from West Georgia College are taking a break from student teaching responsibilities. (Courtesy of UWG Special Collections.)

Three

Centennial

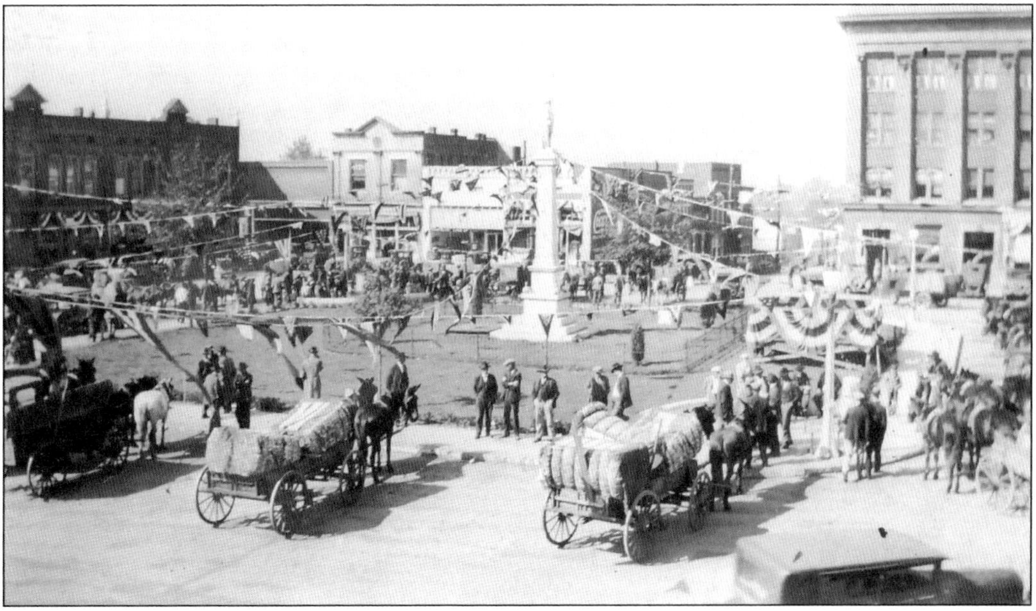

Centennial on the Square, 1927. This bird's-eye view of Adamson Square was taken from the northeast quadrant looking toward Alabama Street. The Confederate Monument had been erected over a decade earlier. Cotton wagons, representing the region's agricultural mainstay, line the square while flags flutter overhead. The celebration was a three-day event in October to mark Carroll County's first 100 years. (Courtesy of Marion McNamara Dobbs.)

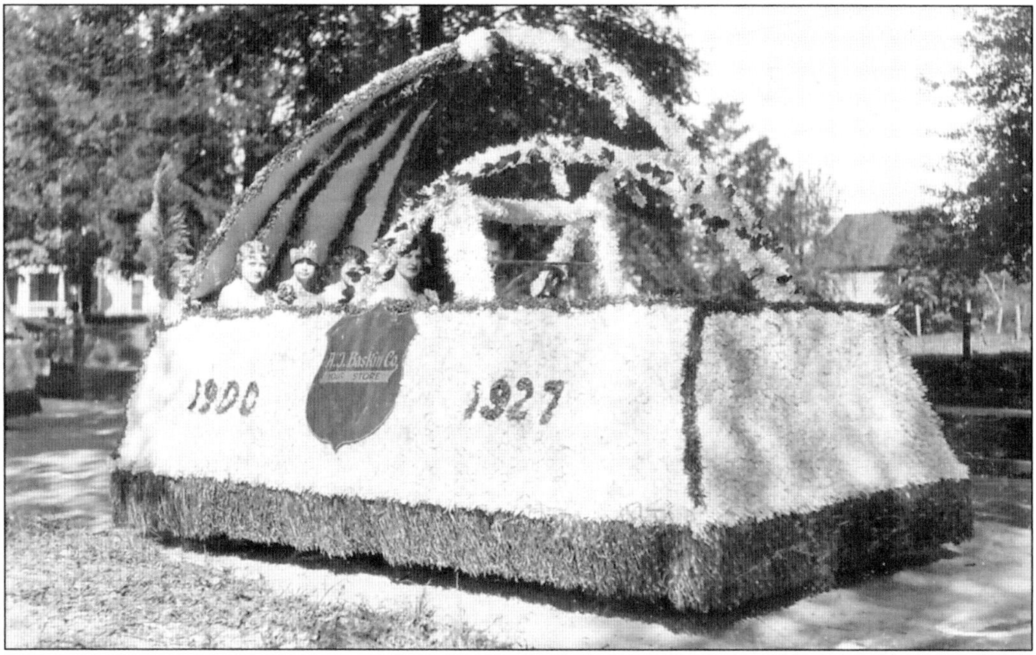

A.J. BASKIN COMPANY FLOAT. A grand parade of floats was featured on the first day of the celebration. The floats represented the county's leading industries, merchants, and educational institutions of the day. The celebration included exhibits of agricultural displays, livestock, "women's work," and historical relics. A.J. Baskin Company was a general merchandise store on the square, selling clothing, notions, and dry goods. (Courtesy of Marion McNamara Dobbs.)

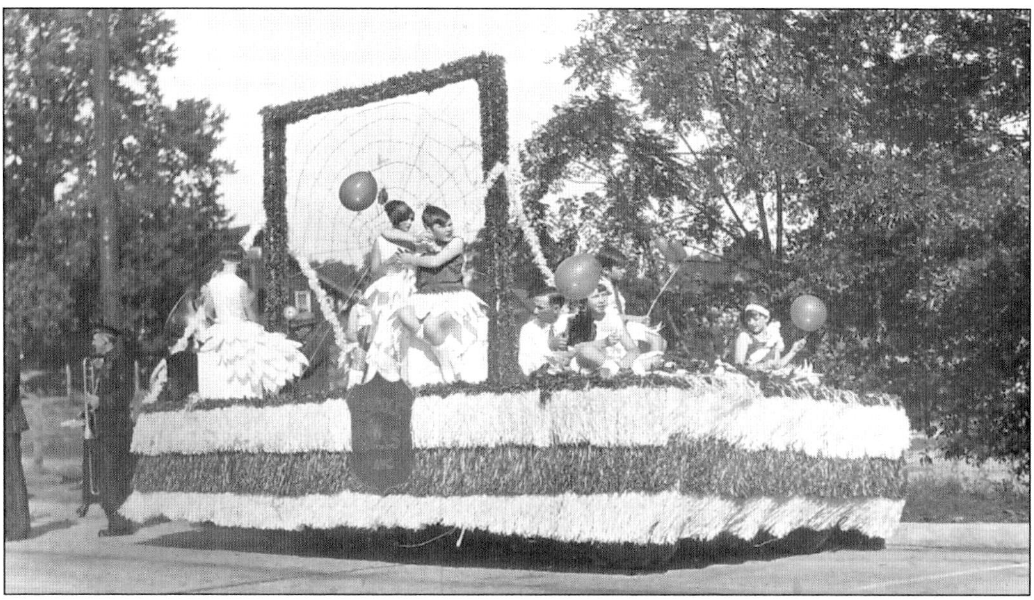

CARROLL MILLS INC. FLOAT. Carroll Mills opened on Depot (now Bradley) Street in 1921. The featured speaker on the first day of the centennial celebration was Thomas L. Long, a son of Benjamin McFarland Long, who had been made famous as the first white child born in Carroll County, which is former Creek Indian territory. The elder Long was born the year Carroll County was formed, and he died in 1903. (Courtesy of Marion McNamara Dobbs.)

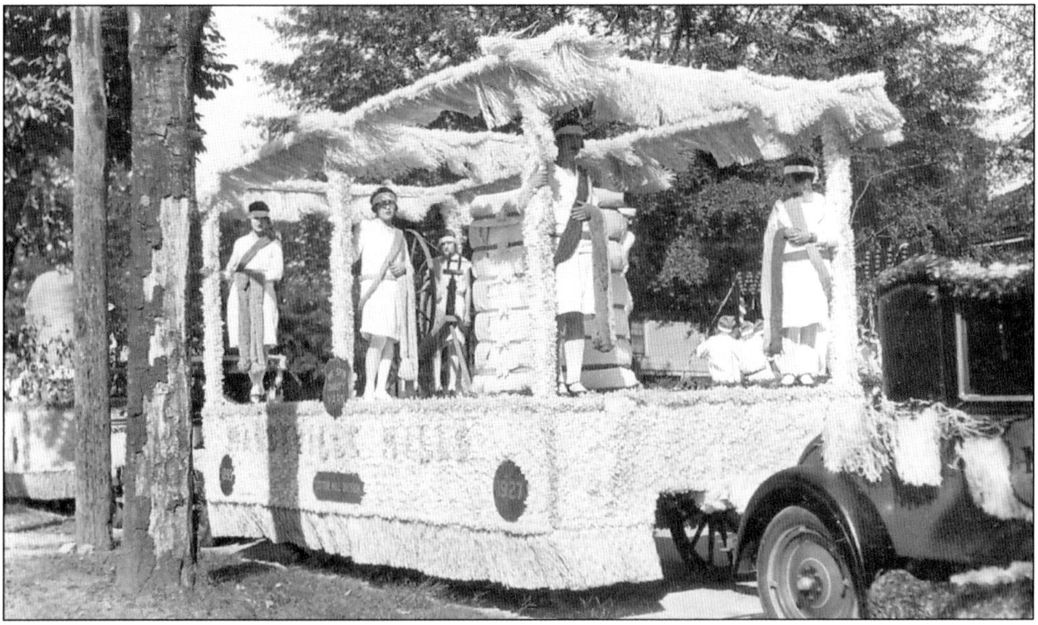

Mandeville Mills Float. "We Spin Quality Yarn" was the company's motto. The mill was named for the Mandeville family whose forbearer, Appleton Mandeville, moved to Georgia from New York. In 1833, he opened a mercantile business in Carrollton. His son L.C. Mandeville was a prosperous businessman and onetime mayor who opened the mill in 1902. (Courtesy of Marion McNamara Dobbs.)

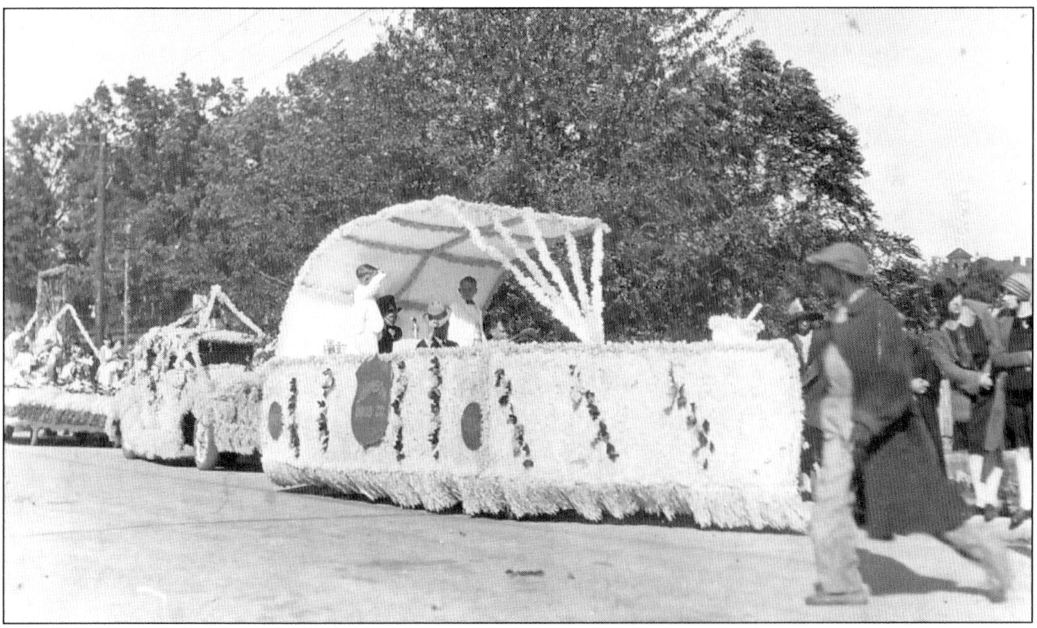

Johnson Drug Company Float. The drugstore occupied a storefront in the northeast quadrant of the square. The second day of the centennial celebration featured Home Coming Day, when citizens were urged to invite former residents. The speakers were judge and congressman W.C. Adamson, for whom the square was named, and Bishop Warren A. Candler of Atlanta, a noted Methodist minister and Villa Rica native. (Courtesy of Marion McNamara Dobbs.)

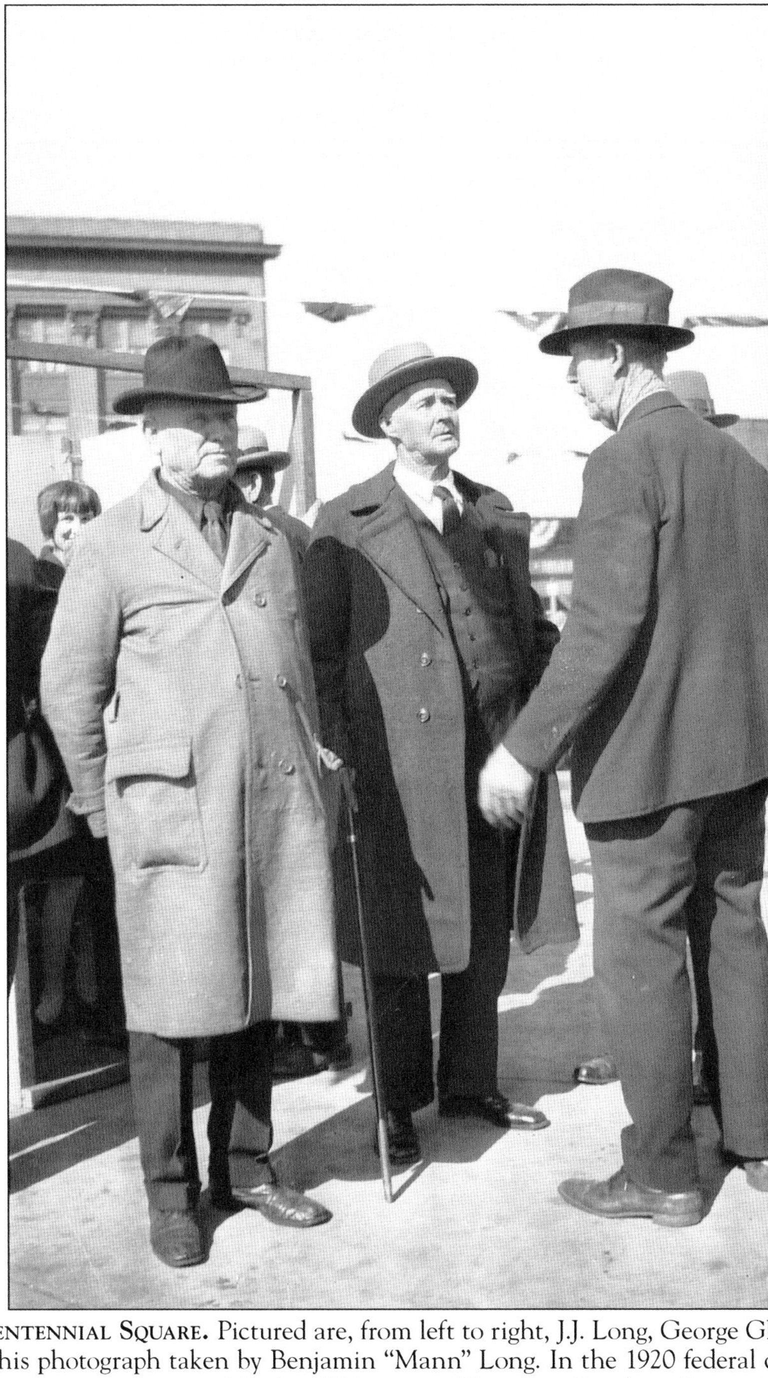

ON THE CENTENNIAL SQUARE. Pictured are, from left to right, J.J. Long, George Glass, and Ben Wager in this photograph taken by Benjamin "Mann" Long. In the 1920 federal census, Glass was listed as a house painter, and in the 1930 census, Wager was listed as a farmer. J.J. Long does not appear in either census, but he might have been related to the photographer. The centennial brochure promoted Carroll County by characterizing its people as "high class and dependable, with a complaisant and congenial attitude toward capital." According to the brochure, "Old fashioned Southern hospitality will cover the entire county like a blanket of softest down, and the latch-string of every home will hang on the outside." (Courtesy of Marion McNamara Dobbs.)

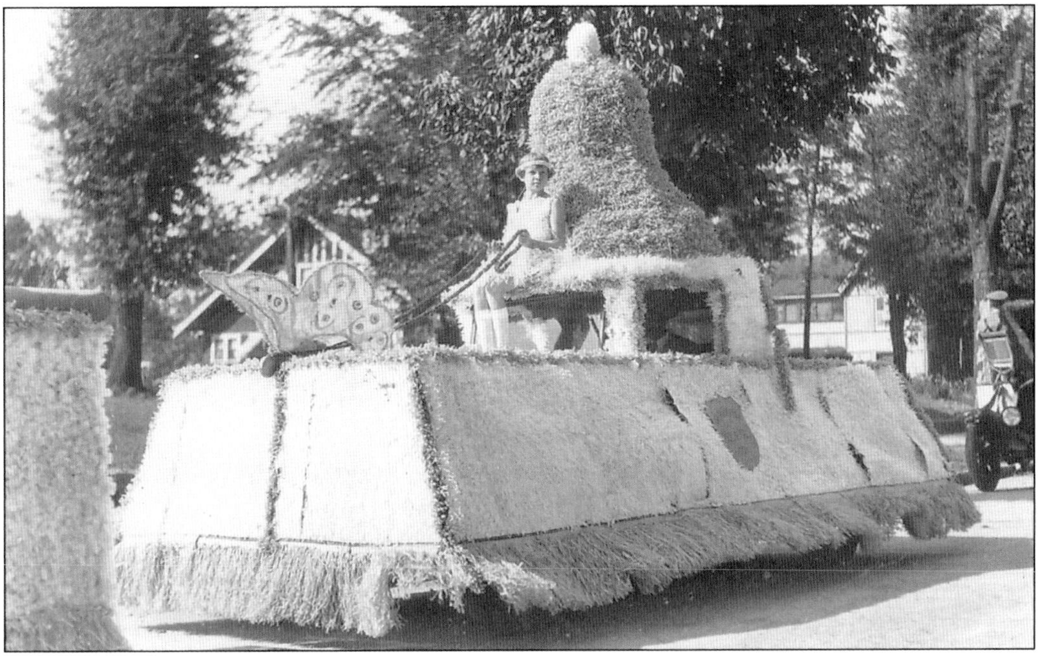

Gainesboro Telephone & Telegraph Company Float. The centennial brochure carried the slogan "Where Small Farms Produce Large Crops." New industries were exempt from taxes for five years, according to the flyer. The celebration was an unabashed effort at boosterism for the local industrial and agricultural economy. (Courtesy of Marion McNamara Dobbs.)

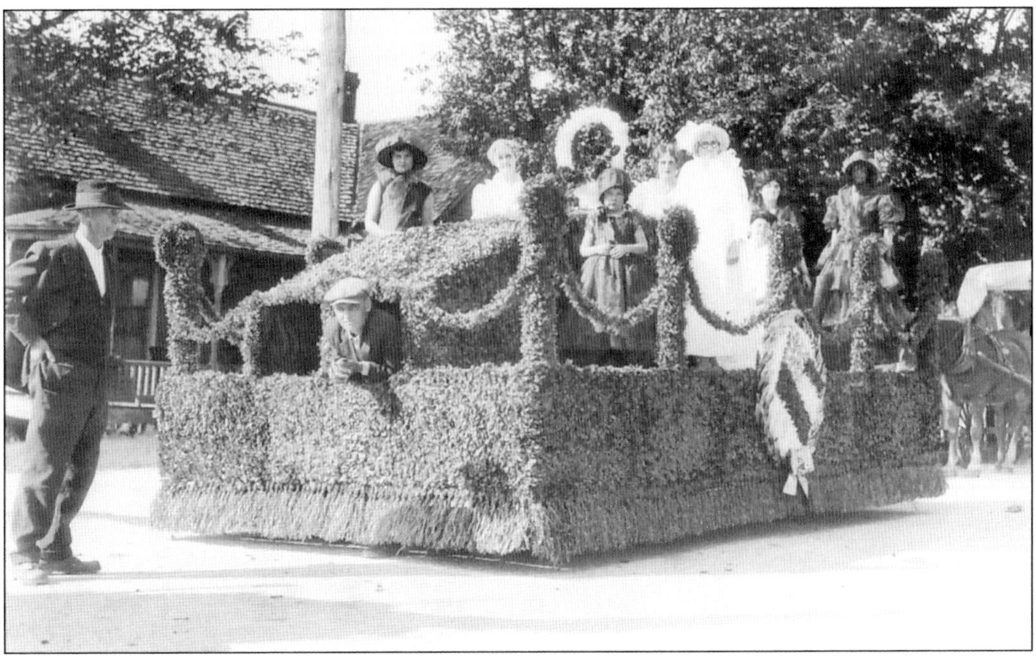

Float in Line. This float is not identified, but is one of about 80 that made their way around the square. The float parade ended at Centennial Grounds, which was located on Newnan Street and featured a midway. A pageant was performed by a cast of 1,000 on the third day, based on a script by Atlanta writer Helen Knox Spain. (Courtesy of Marion McNamara Dobbs.)

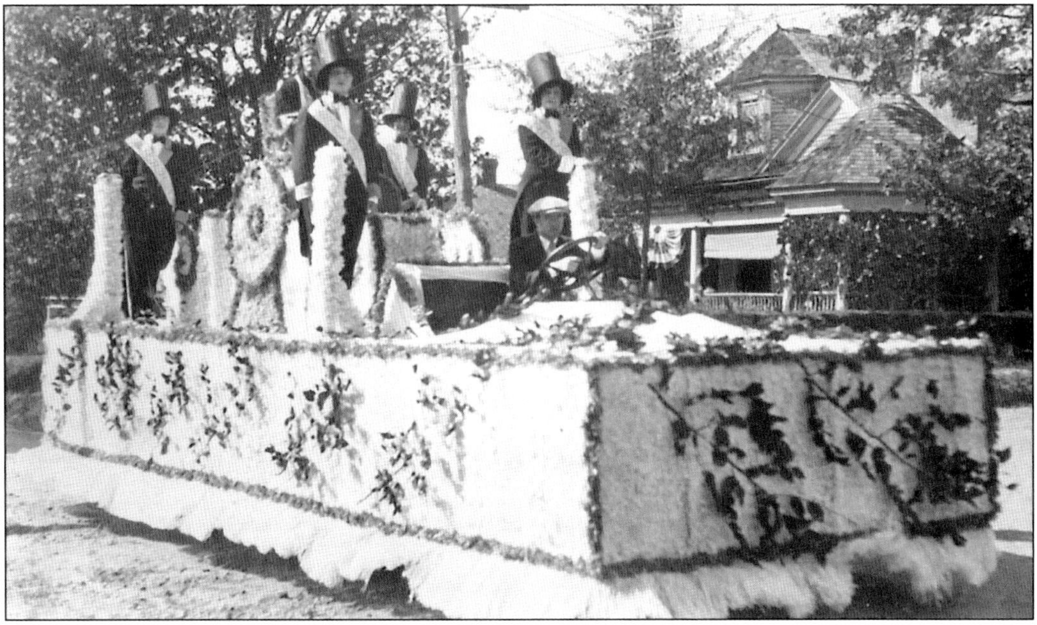

POULTRY, GRAIN, DAIRY, AND INDUSTRY FLOAT. According to the banners, this float proclaims the county's economic activities. It almost appears that "king cotton" might be seated on a throne amidst the other four. The centennial flyer points out that while agriculture still centered on cotton, the county's soil, grass, and water supplies also gave opportunities for dairying and livestock. (Courtesy of Marion McNamara Dobbs.)

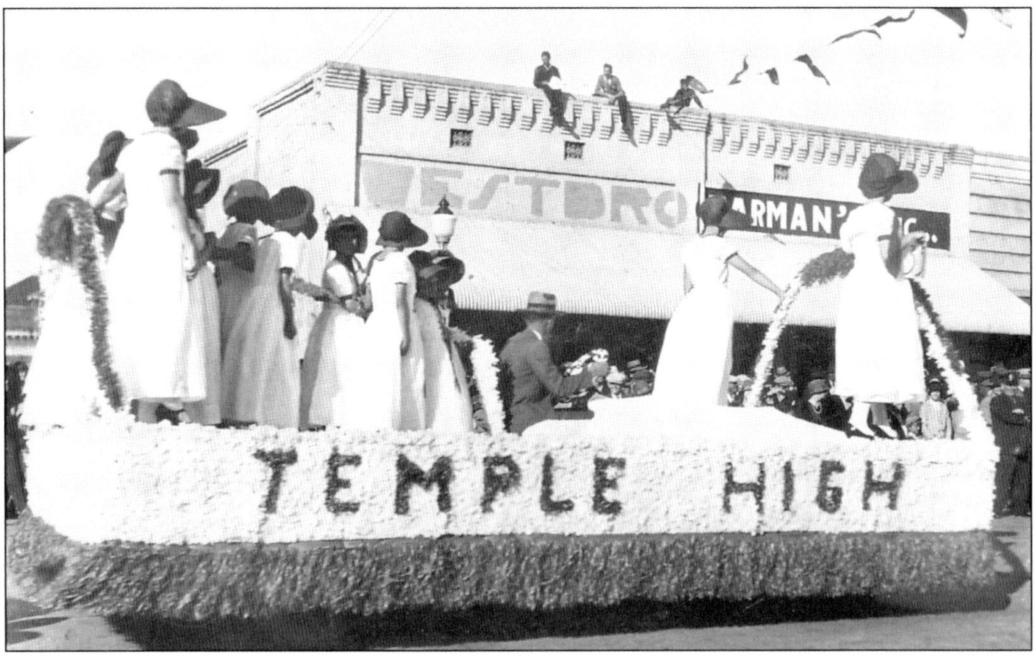

TEMPLE HIGH SCHOOL FLOAT. This float is making its way around the northeast quadrant of the square as several viewers perch on top of storefronts to watch. The county had 16 high schools at this time. In the next decade, consolidation was adopted as a more efficient model for providing public education countywide. (Courtesy of Marion McNamara Dobbs.)

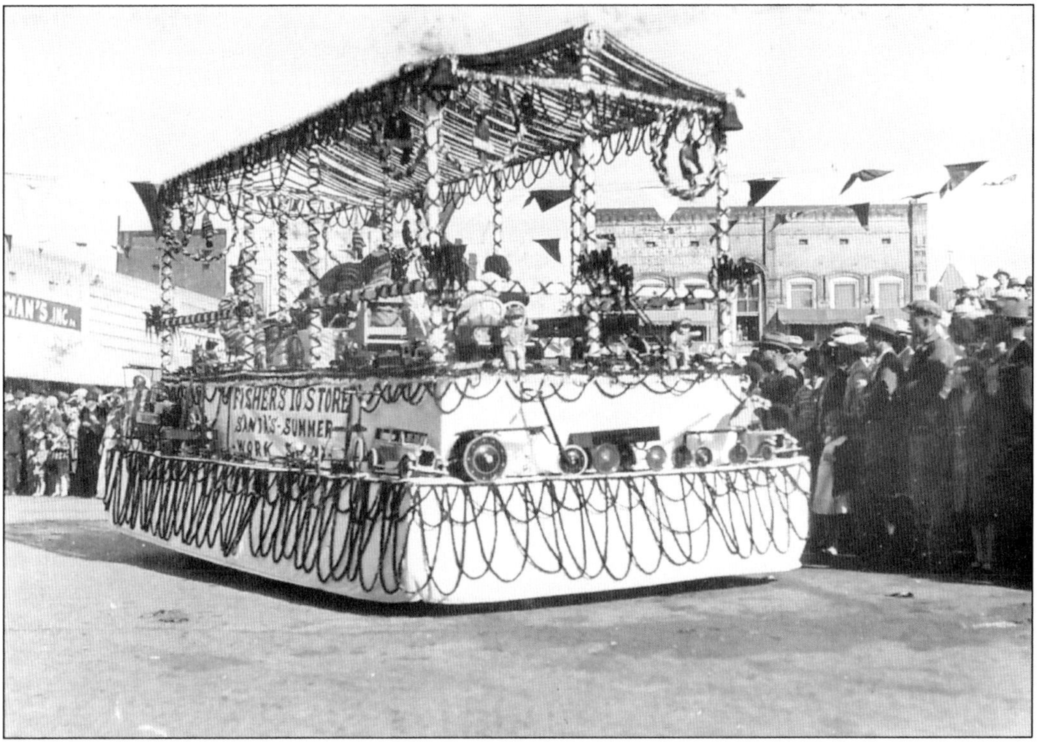

FISHER'S 10¢ STORE FLOAT. In association with the Kress Company, M.L. Fisher opened his five-and-ten on the square in 1923. Originally from Rome, Georgia, Fisher had two Carrollton stores and one in Cartersville at the time of the centennial. (Courtesy of Marion McNamara Dobbs.)

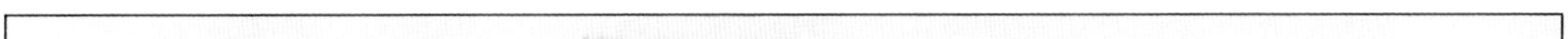

BESSIE TIFT COLLEGE FLOAT? According to newspaper reports of the day, local alumnae of the women's college in Forsyth, Georgia, entered a float in the Centennial Parade. It appears the parade route came up to the square on Rome Street, judging from the observers on the rooftops. (Courtesy of Marion McNamara Dobbs.)

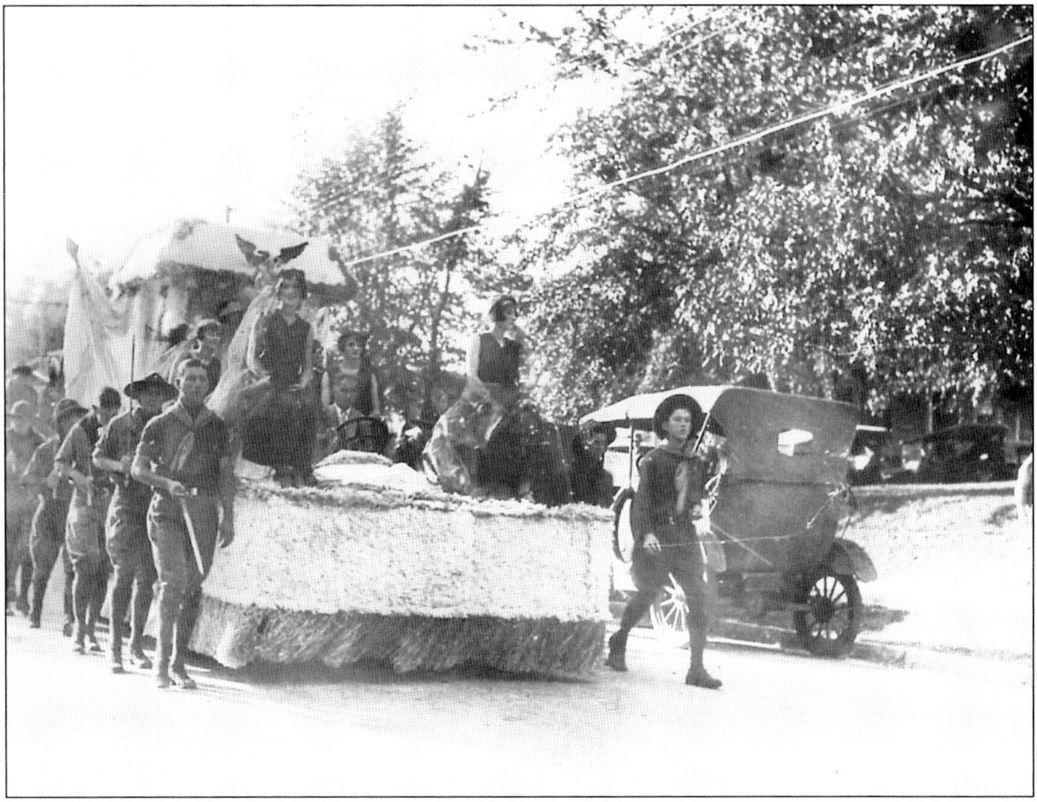

Boy Scout Escorts. These Scouts are escorting a float that is carrying the centennial queen and her entourage of six young women. Blanche Holloway is the queen. Speakers on the third day of the celebration included Edgar Watkins of Atlanta and B.F. Moore of Birmingham, both former Carroll residents. (Courtesy of Marion McNamara Dobbs.)

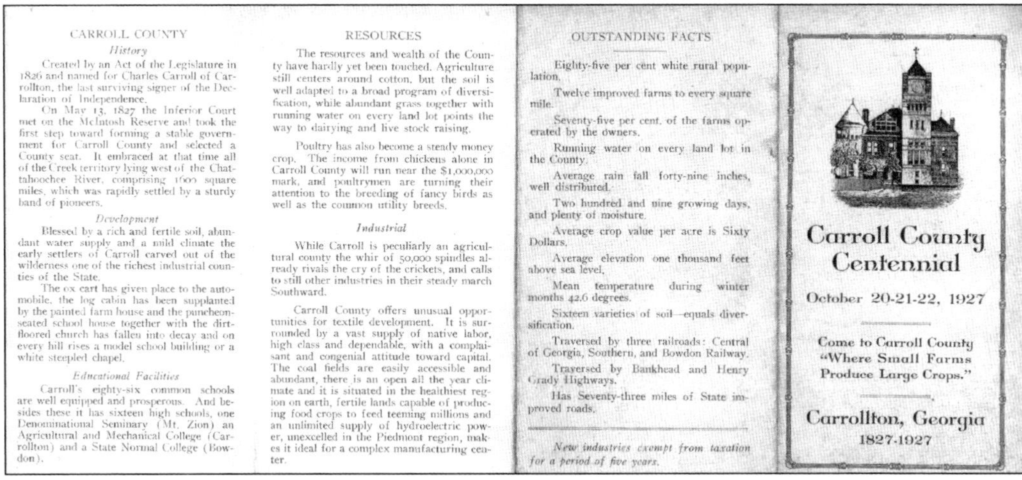

CARROLL COUNTY

History

Created by an Act of the Legislature in 1826 and named for Charles Carroll of Carrollton, the last surviving signer of the Declaration of Independence.

On May 13, 1827 the Inferior Court met on the McIntosh Reserve and took the first step toward forming a stable government for Carroll County and selected a County seat. It embraced at that time all of the Creek territory lying west of the Chattahoochee River, comprising 1600 square miles, which was rapidly settled by a sturdy band of pioneers.

Development

Blessed by a rich and fertile soil, abundant water supply and a mild climate the early settlers of Carroll carved out of the wilderness one of the richest industrial counties of the State.

The ox cart has given place to the automobile, the log cabin has been supplanted by the painted farm house and the puncheon-seated school house together with the dirt-floored church has fallen into decay and on every hill rises a model school building or a white steepled chapel.

Educational Facilities

Carroll's eighty-six common schools are well equipped and prosperous. And besides these it has sixteen high schools, one Denominational Seminary (Mt. Zion) an Agricultural and Mechanical College (Carrollton) and a State Normal College (Bowdon).

RESOURCES

The resources and wealth of the County have hardly yet been touched. Agriculture still centers around cotton, but the soil is well adapted to a broad program of diversification, while abundant grass together with running water on every land lot points the way to dairying and live stock raising.

Poultry has also become a steady money crop. The income from chickens alone in Carroll County will run near the $1,000,000 mark, and poultrymen are turning their attention to the breeding of fancy birds as well as the common utility breeds.

Industrial

While Carroll is peculiarly an agricultural county the whir of 50,000 spindles already rivals the cry of the crickets, and calls to still other industries in their steady march Southward.

Carroll County offers unusual opportunities for textile development. It is surrounded by a vast supply of native labor, high class and dependable, with a complaisant and congenial attitude toward capital. The coal fields are easily accessible and abundant, there is an open all the year climate and it is situated in the healthiest region on earth, fertile lands capable of producing food crops to feed teeming millions and an unlimited supply of hydroelectric power, unexcelled in the Piedmont region, makes it ideal for a complex manufacturing center.

OUTSTANDING FACTS

Eighty-five per cent white rural population.

Twelve improved farms to every square mile.

Seventy-five per cent. of the farms operated by the owners.

Running water on every land lot in the County.

Average rain fall forty-nine inches, well distributed.

Two hundred and nine growing days, and plenty of moisture.

Average crop value per acre is Sixty Dollars.

Average elevation one thousand feet above sea level.

Mean temperature during winter months 42.6 degrees.

Sixteen varieties of soil—equals diversification.

Traversed by three railroads: Central of Georgia, Southern, and Bowdon Railway.

Traversed by Bankhead and Henry Grady Highways.

Has Seventy-three miles of State improved roads.

New industries exempt from taxation for a period of five years.

Carroll County Centennial

October 20-21-22, 1927

Come to Carroll County "Where Small Farms Produce Large Crops."

Carrollton, Georgia

1827-1927

Carroll County Centennial Brochure. Featured on the front cover is a drawing of the county courthouse at the time. In 1929, it burned and was replaced with the current courthouse at the same location. As noted here, the county was named for Charles Carroll, who was the last living signer of the Declaration of Independence at the time Carroll was organized in 1827. (Courtesy of Marion McNamara Dobbs.)

Four

Cotton and Canneries

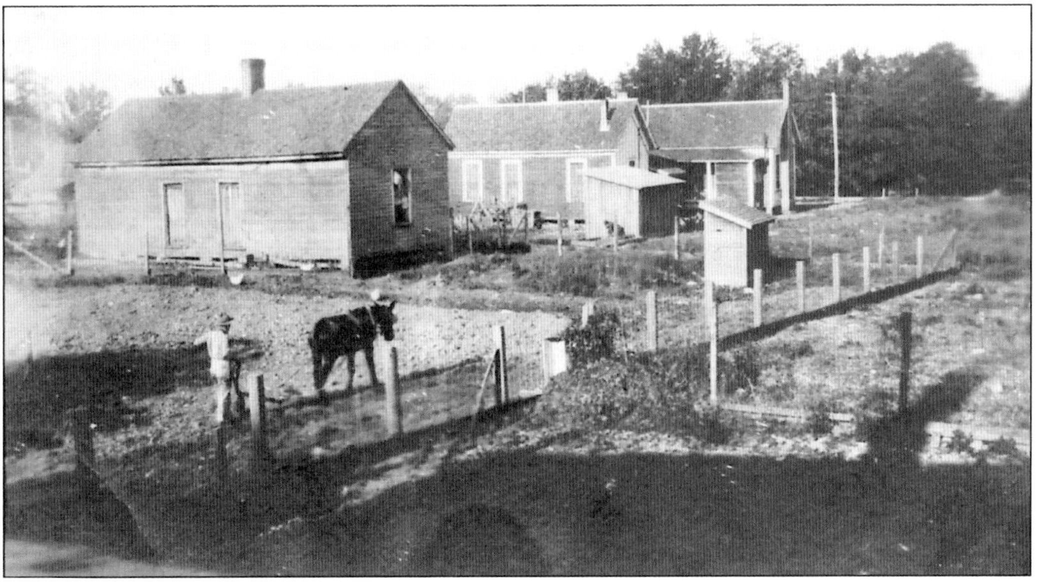

Mule and a Plow. The long shadows of late afternoon fall across this farmer as he finishes plowing a field in Carroll County. Farm population in the county was at its peak by 1920. By the end of the Depression, however, the economy had forced many of these people off the land and into urban centers for war industry–related jobs. (Courtesy of Marion McNamara Dobbs.)

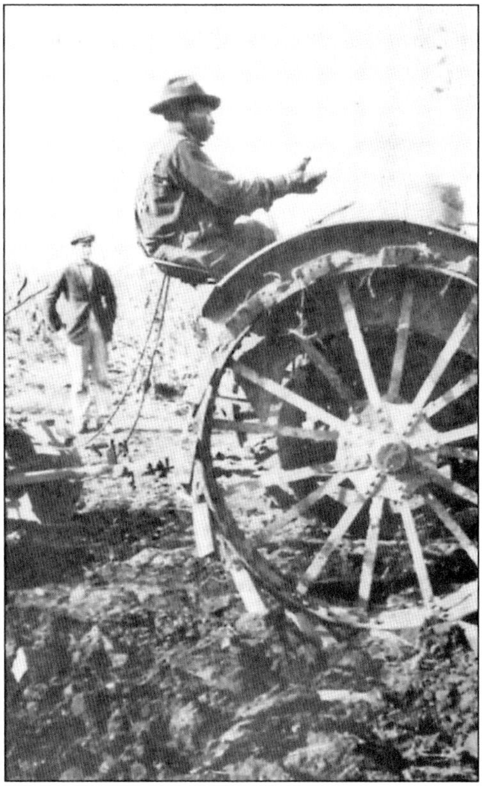

Early Tractor, c. 1915. An African American worker is pictured riding a tractor that appears to be pulling a field tiller. The ratio of whites to blacks in Carroll County did not change significantly in the century between Reconstruction and 1965, with the African American population averaging about 20 percent. (Courtesy of UWG Special Collections.)

Subsoiling with Dynamite, 1920. Students at the Fourth District A&M School had to help break up the heavy clay soil in order to allow cultivation. One rather primitive method was to place explosives in holes dug in the soil, and the explosives' impact would break up the soil. Mechanized farm equipment was prohibitively expensive and not generally available until the 1940s. (Courtesy of UWG Special Collections.)

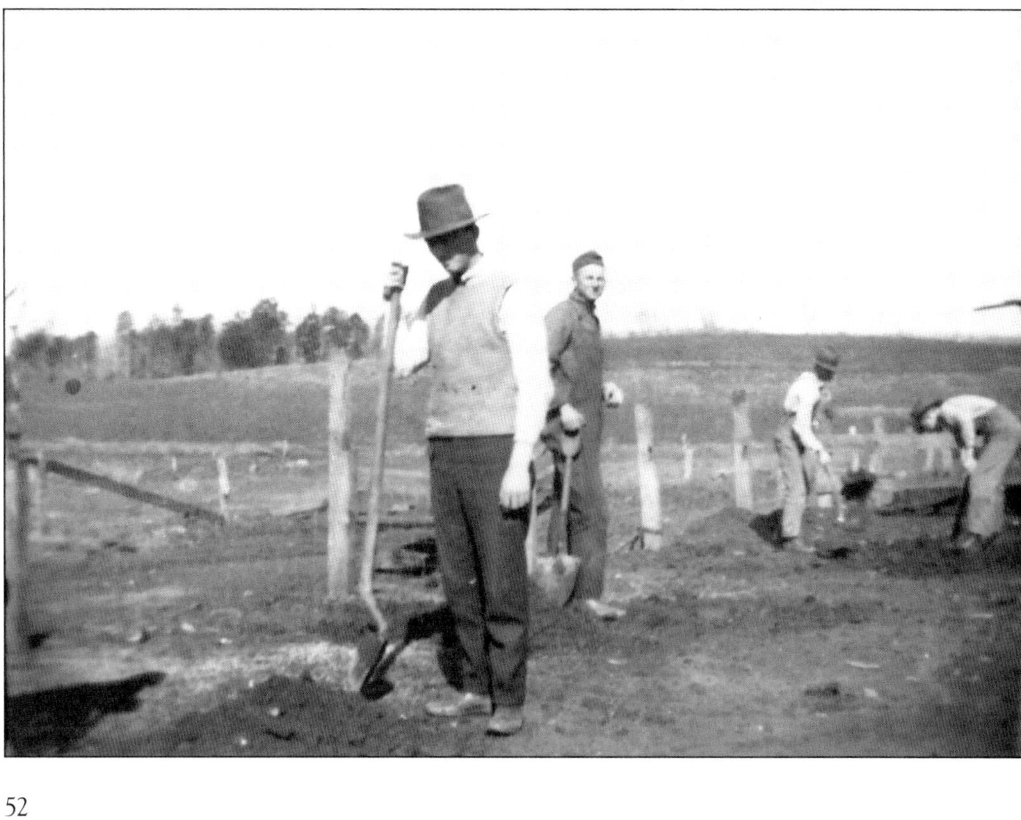

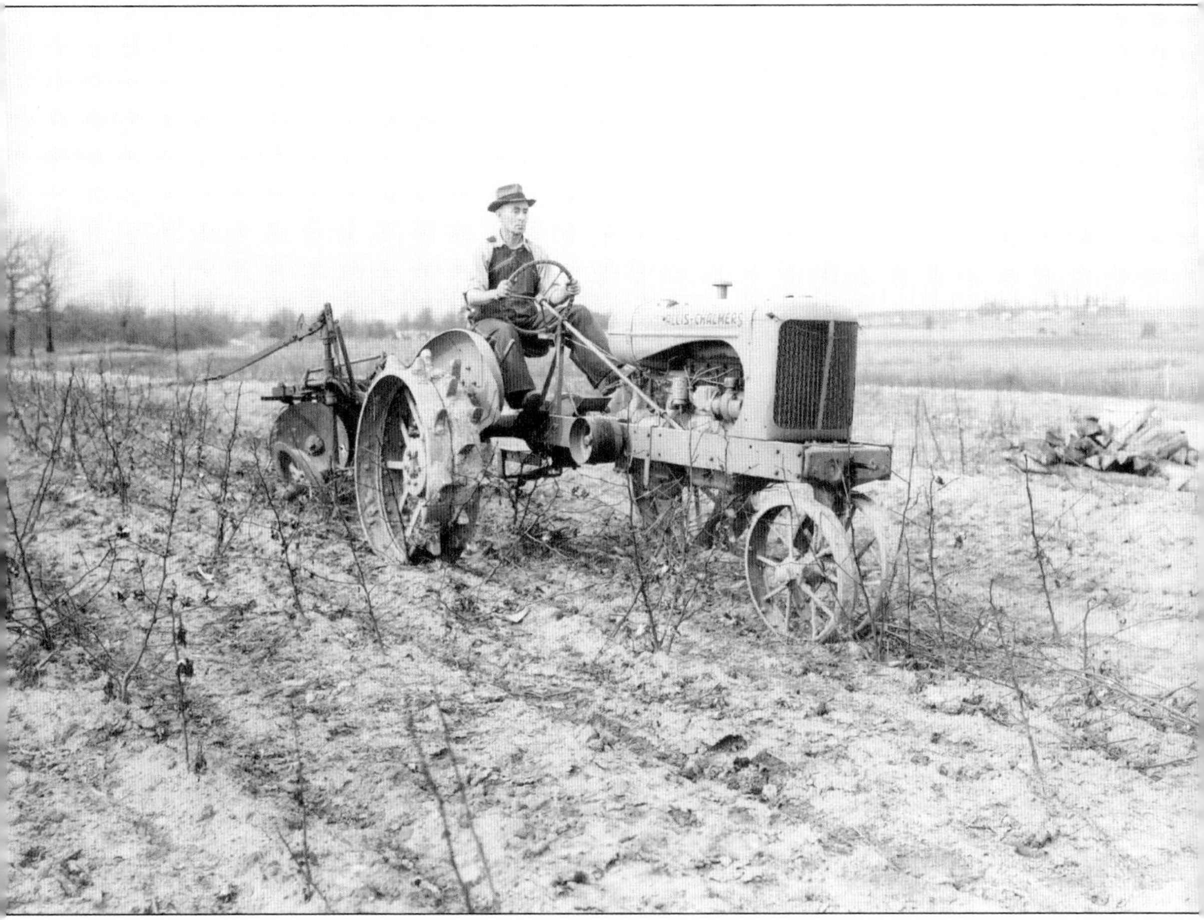

DISKING A FIELD, c. 1940. In 1942, the Carroll County Cooperative Federation was organized across 12 communities and allowed farmers to share the expenses of farming. The success of each cooperative project gave farmers money to invest in further projects—from canneries, which preserved food for home use and school lunchrooms, to grist and feed mills. The cooperative earned enough money to purchase equipment such as harrows, plows, and tractors. This Carroll County farmer drives an Allis-Chalmers tractor that probably dates from the late 1930s. The Wisconsin-based manufacturing company started making tractors and other agricultural equipment in 1914. Without the cooperative effort, individual farmers could not have afforded the machinery and facilities needed to profit from farming. (Courtesy of UWG Special Collections.)

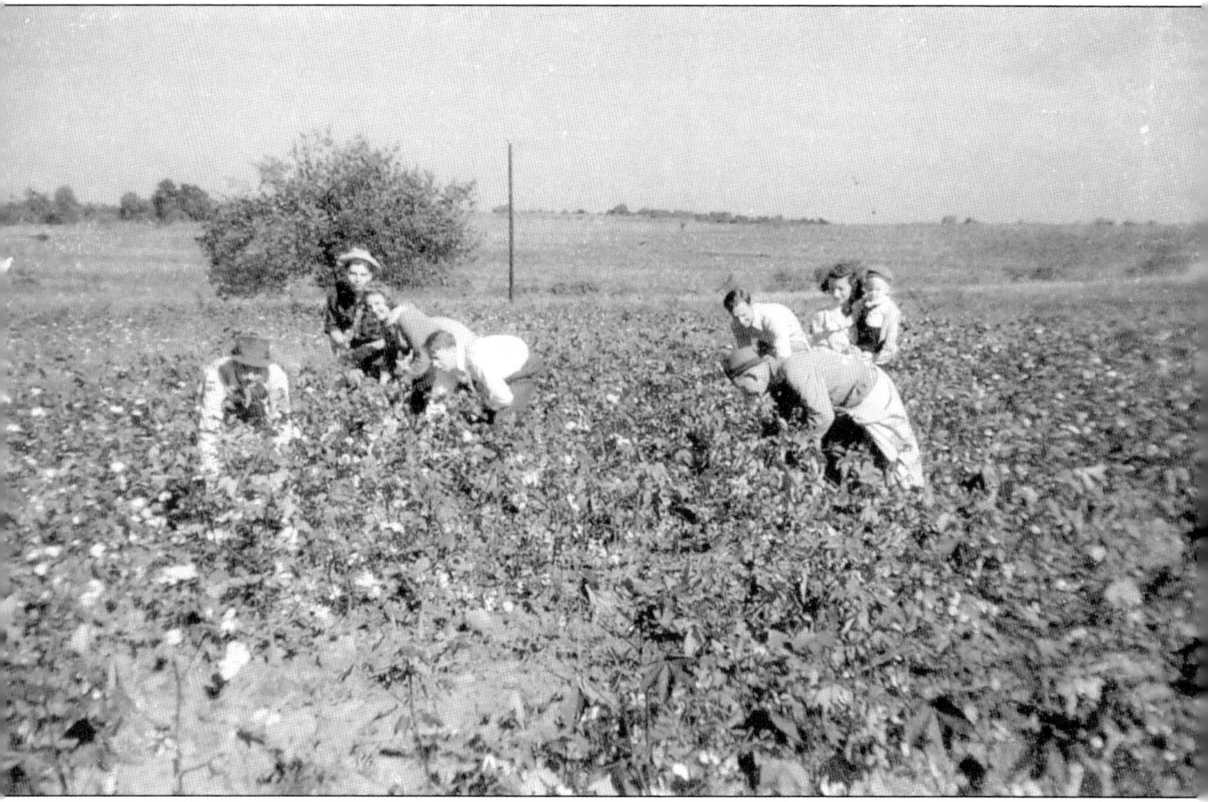

T.R. Griffin Farm, 1942. During World War II, much of the county's supply of farm labor was sent to military service. The farming at home could not stop, so college students and other young people not serving in the military offered their labor. Harvesting cotton was backbreaking work that could not be made easier with machinery in the hilly terrain of Carroll County. Georgia growers had competition from out west, where geography provided many advantages. The terrain was flatter, and new farming machinery could reduce the amount of labor needed to grow the crop. Just prior to the Depression, a Georgia farmhand might handle 35 acres, compared to his counterpart in the west, who might handle 100 acres. By the time some Georgia farmers had acquired the same farm equipment, many had already abandoned cotton for other crops. (Courtesy of UWG Special Collections.)

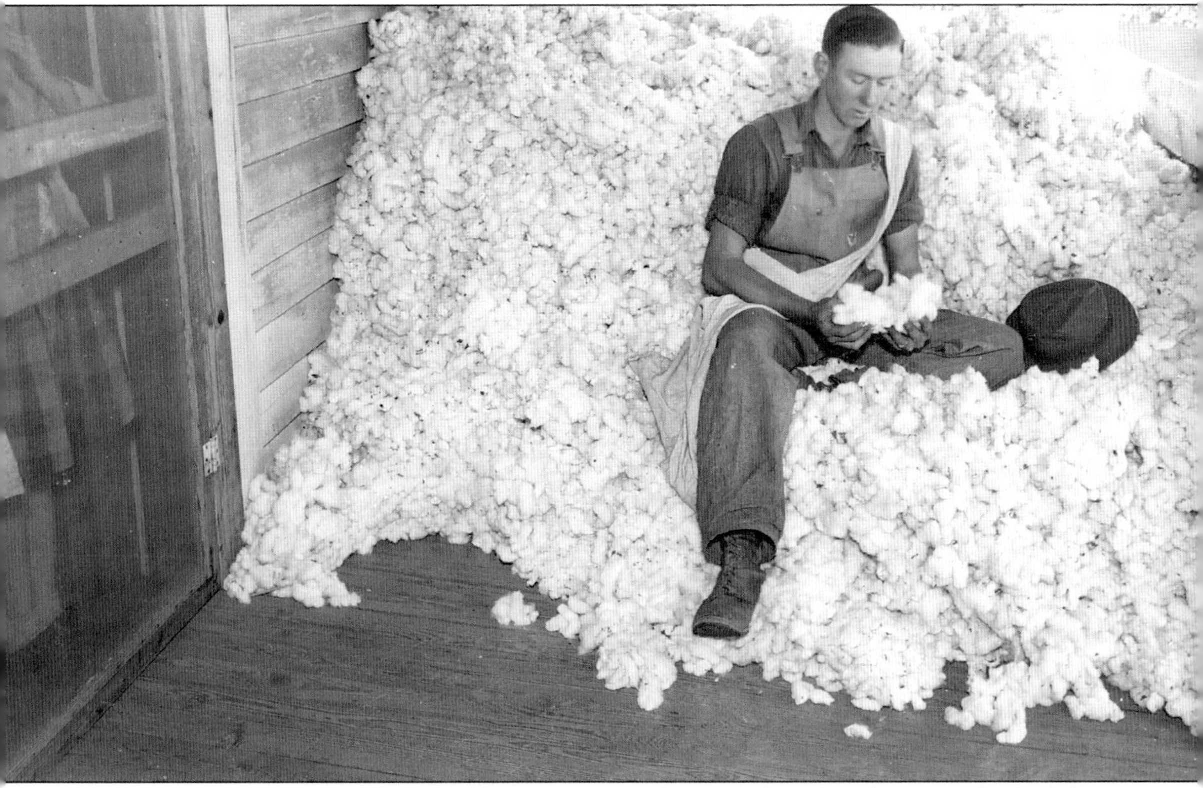

COTTON NOT KING, 1945. The Carroll Service Council's Agriculture Panel promoted 4-H clubs to teach the young farming generation how to diversify crops and get a better yield. Between 1930 and 1944, a third fewer acres in the county were planted in cotton, but the number of pounds of cotton produced rose by 50 percent. The boll weevil, the Depression, and World War II were all factors in unseating cotton as Georgia's main crop. The weevil literally destroyed the crop, cotton glutted Depression-era markets resulting in low profits, and the agricultural needs of a nation at war demanded production of food, not cotton. Diversification of crops took hold after the war, with hay, seeds, and field crops. In Carroll County, pimiento peppers and broiler hens were produced. (Courtesy of UWG Special Collections.)

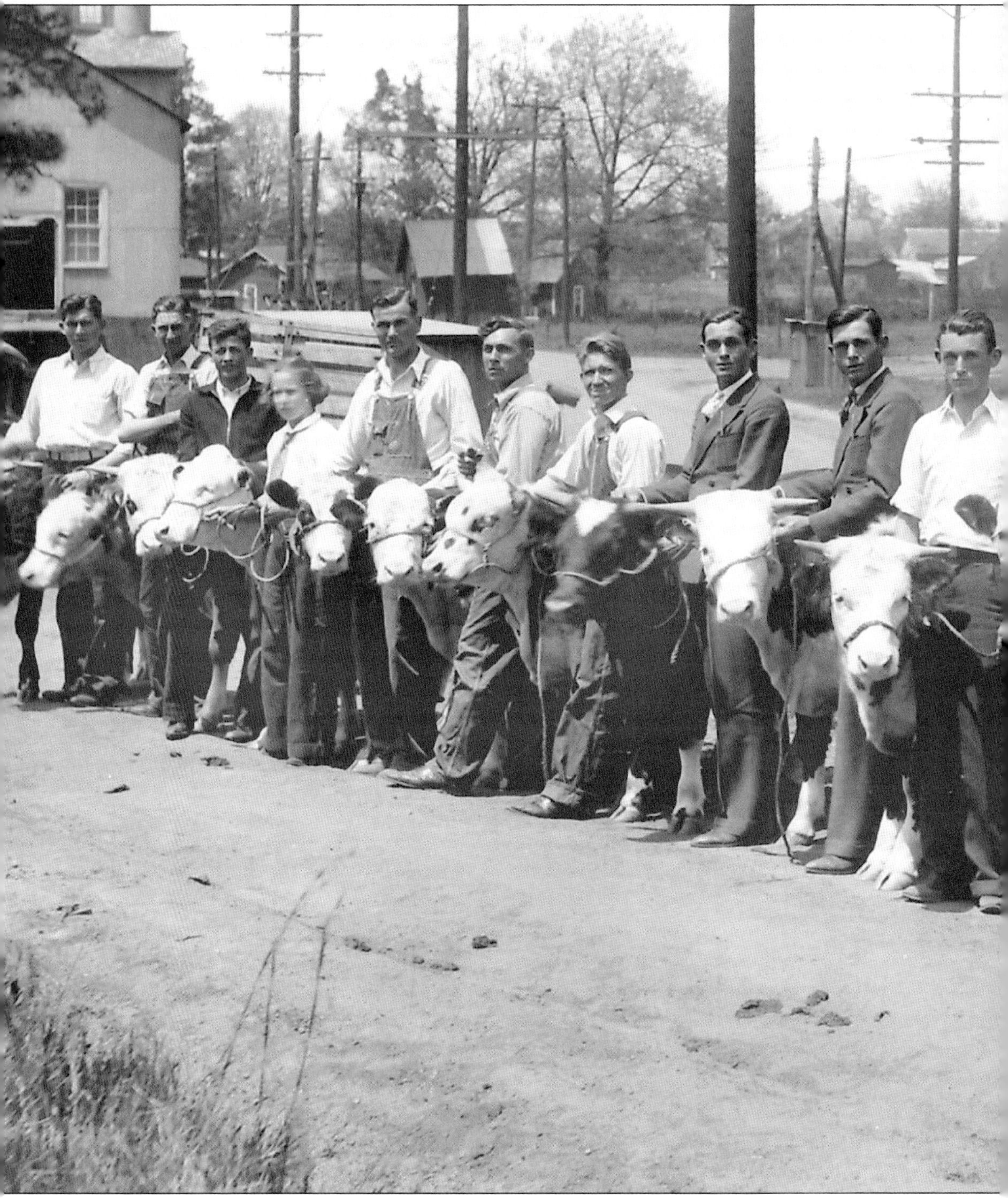

4-H CLUBS. The Carroll Service Council provided an assistant to the county extension agent who devoted his time to 4-H clubs. Calling Carroll County's youth its most important crop, the service council reported in 1945 that 28 clubs with more than 700 young people had been organized in the community. One purpose of the 4-H movement, according to the council, was to

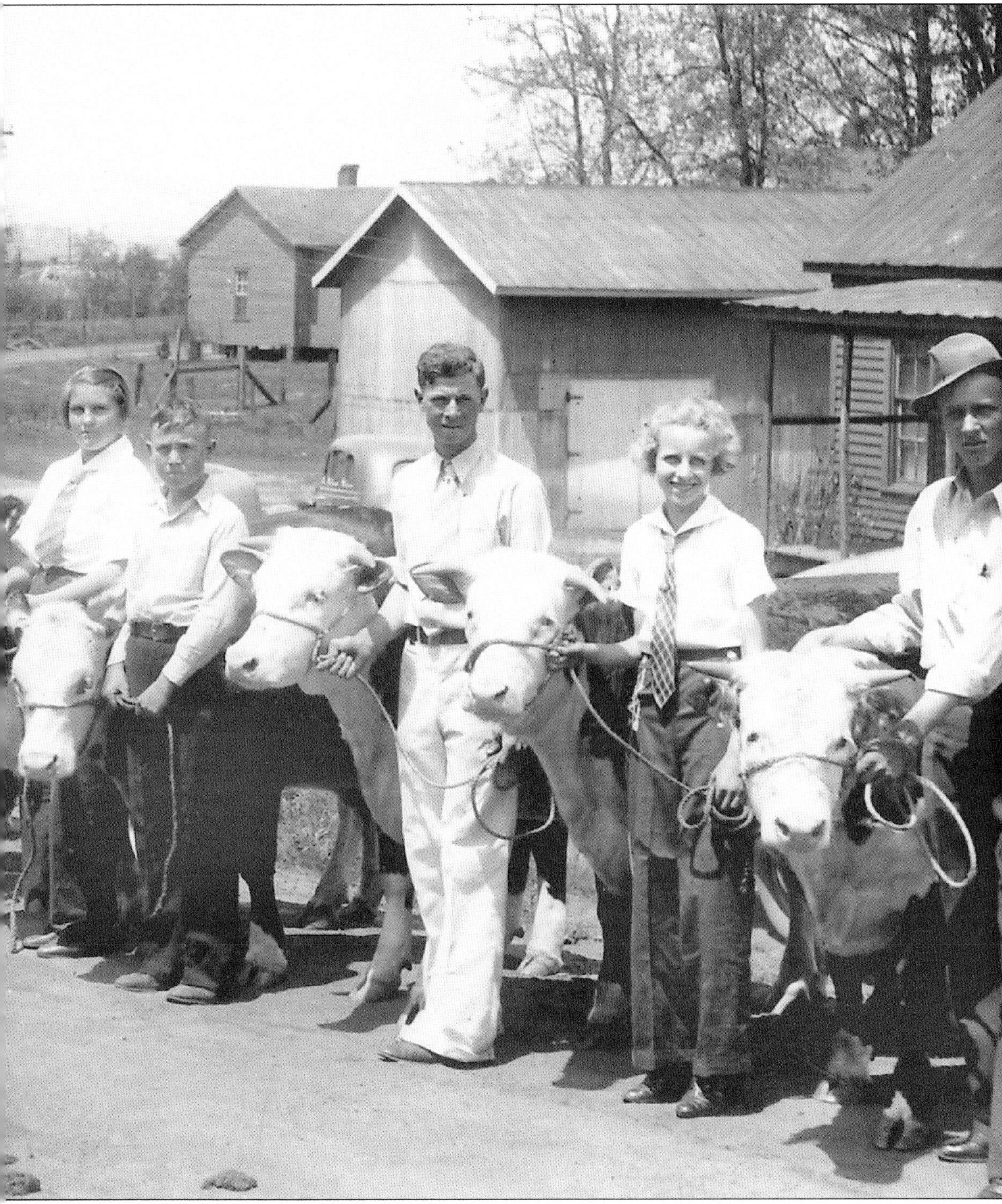

teach rural youth high standards and ideals for farming, community life, and citizenship. The 4-H clubs sponsored competitions in which Carroll County youth frequently took awards. The 1945 annual report of the council states that 89 boys participated in dairy cattle projects, and many were looking forward to establishing their own herds. (Courtesy of UWG Special Collections.)

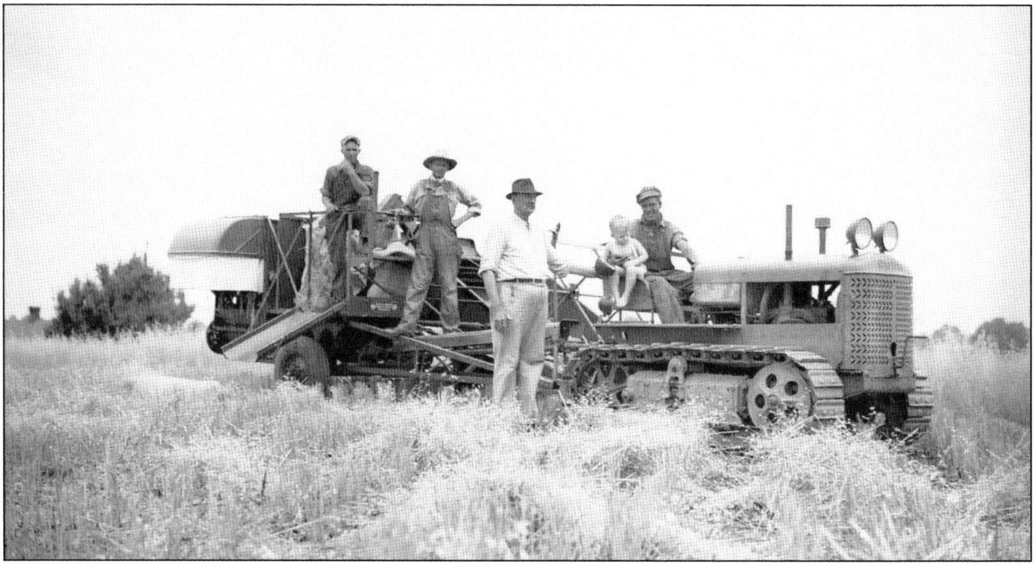

ECK STRICKLAND FARM, C. 1945. Ector Strickland was born in 1886 and was a successful Carrollton farmer and warehouse owner who lived at 144 South Coleman Street. In this photograph, it appears the farmhands have cut a field of hay for him. (Courtesy of UWG Special Collections.)

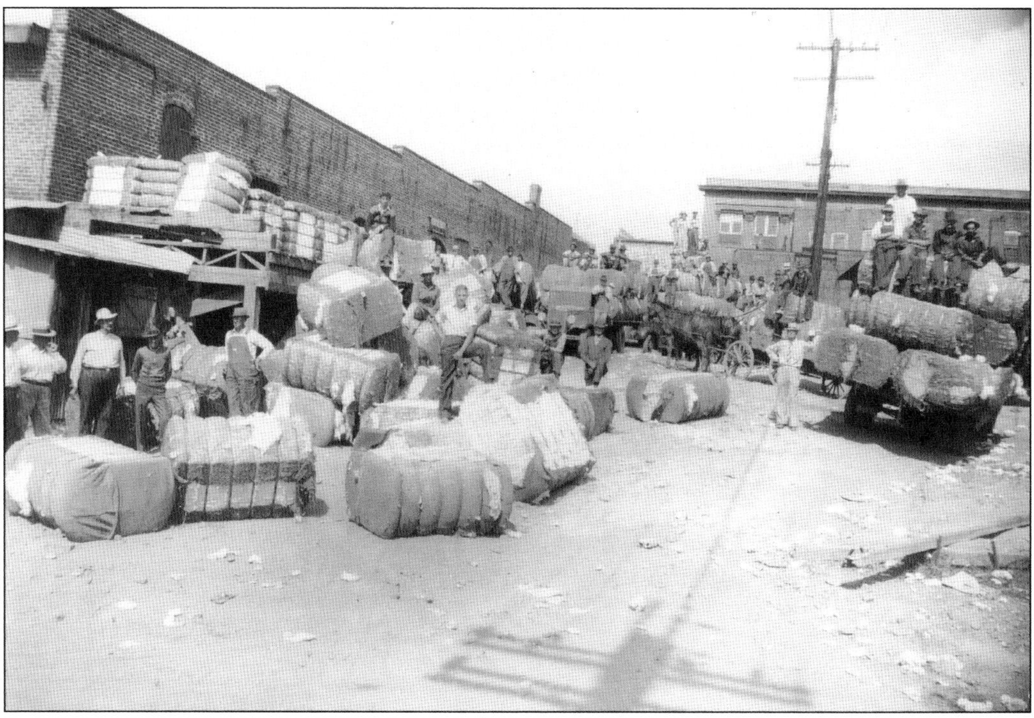

STRICKLAND COTTON WAREHOUSE, 1939. Eck Strickland was listed as a cotton buyer in the 1930 federal census. Besides his own farming operations, he owned a Carrollton cotton warehouse on Thomasson Avenue, which ran parallel to Bradley Street on the east. In this photograph, bales are being delivered to the warehouse. (Courtesy of Marion McNamara Dobbs.)

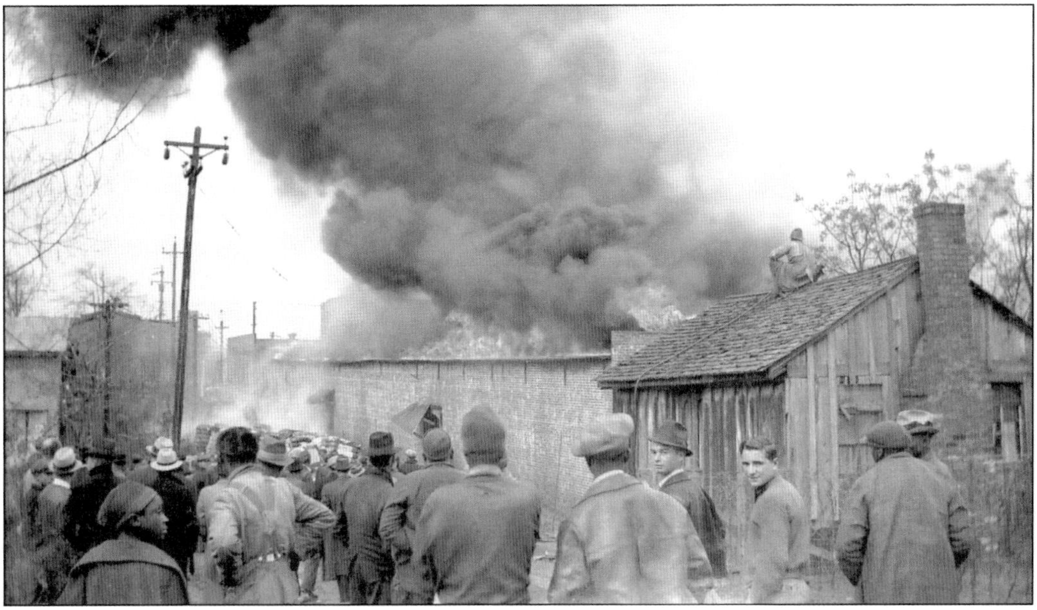

$300,000 Warehouse Fire, 1937. A fire of unknown origin is pictured burning at a cotton warehouse on Bradley Street in Carrollton. According to the newspaper, it damaged about 3,400 bales of cotton worth close to $300,000. A 60-foot section of wall collapsed, slightly injuring two West Georgia College students, Andy Floyd and R.L. Crawford. (Courtesy of UWG Special Collections.)

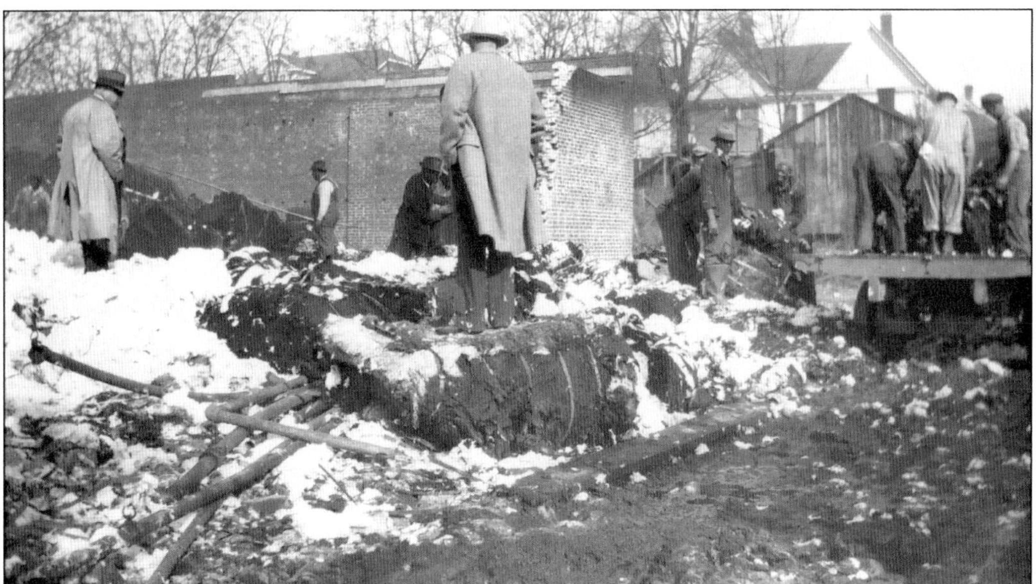

Cotton Fire Clean Up, 1937. The building was owned by Cedartown Cotton and Trading Company, which was fully insured, according to the newspaper. The Southeastern Compress and Warehouse Company leased the building to store about 9,000 bales of cotton. The fire was difficult to put out, and smoldered for days while workers tried to salvage undamaged bales. (Courtesy of UWG Special Collections.)

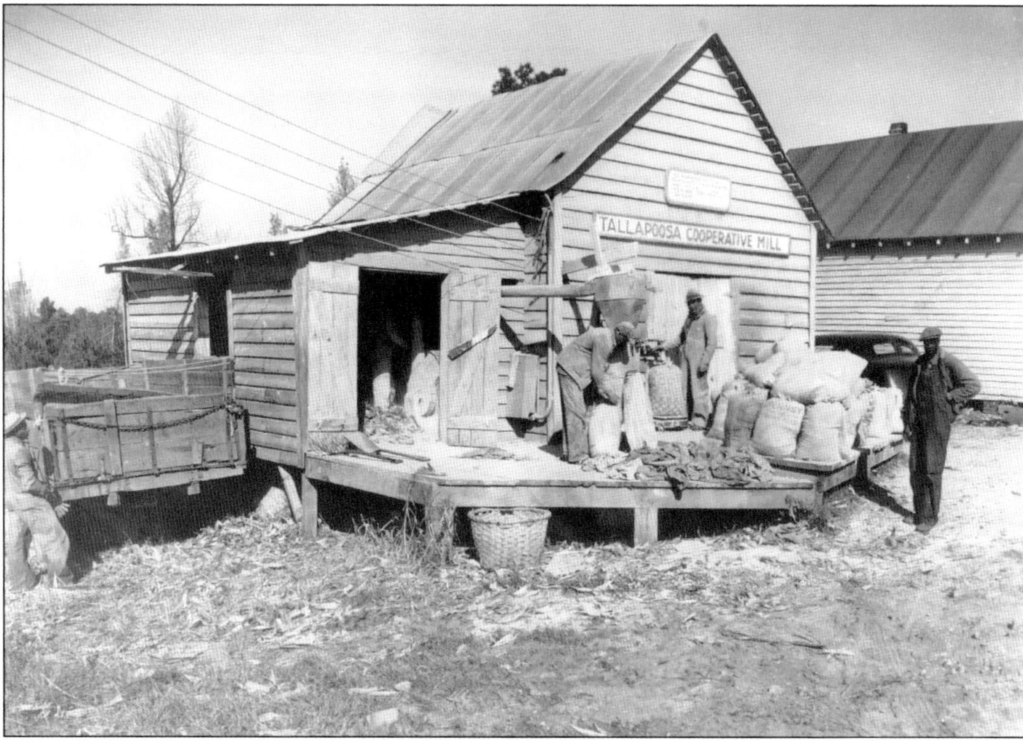

TALLAPOOSA COOPERATIVE MILL, C. 1945. The Tallapoosa community southwest of Carrollton was considered the model for a countywide farmers' cooperative, the Carroll County Cooperative Federation. Working with educators and agriculture specialists from West Georgia College, the Tallapoosa mill allowed farmers to process corn and grain with commonly owned equipment. (Courtesy of UWG Special Collections.)

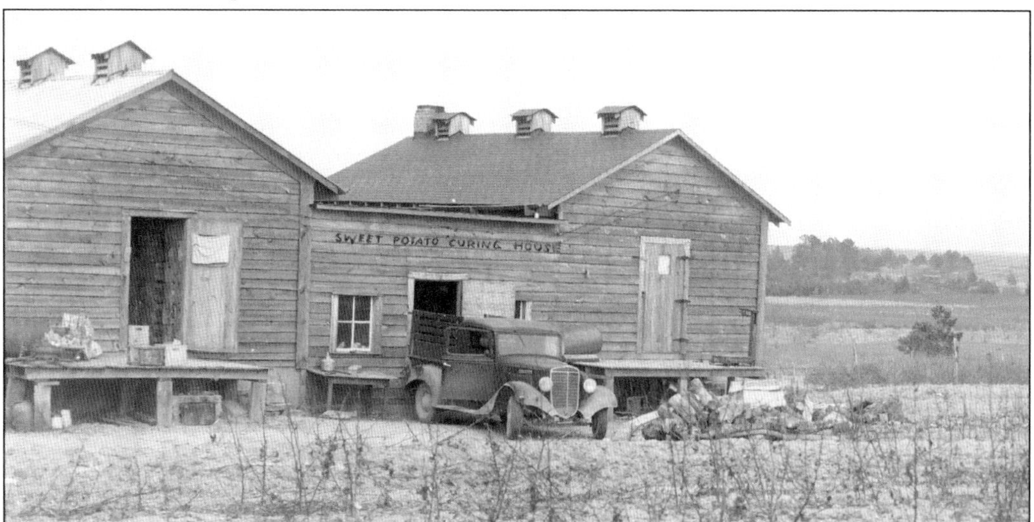

SWEET POTATO CURING HOUSE, C. 1945. Besides cooperative mills for grain and feed, the Carroll County Cooperative Federation promoted potato curing houses, canneries, and refrigerated storage lockers for the county's farmers. Farmers were able to plant a variety of crops and raise more livestock when these facilities were made available to them. (Courtesy of UWG Special Collections.)

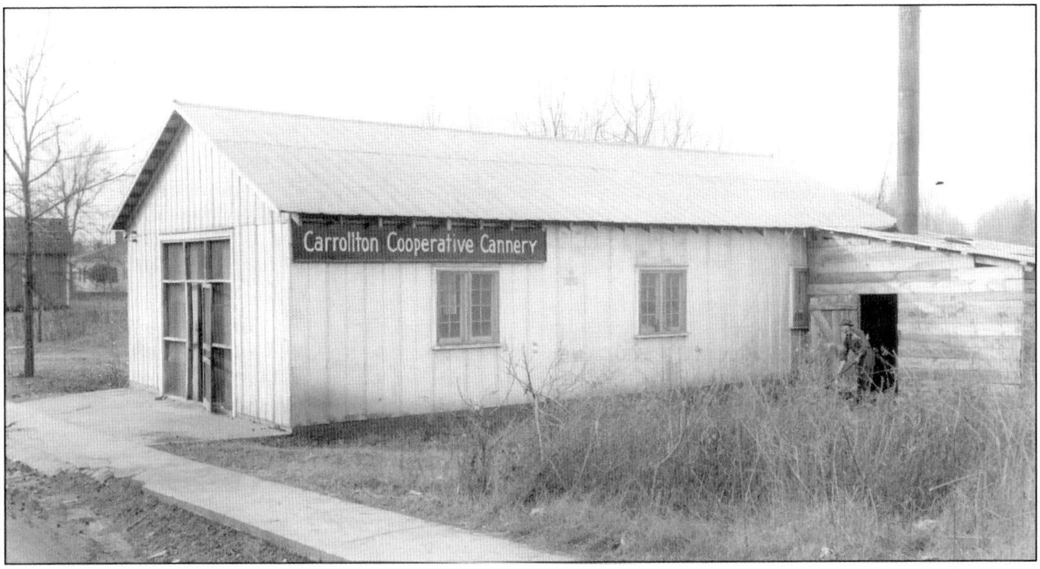

CARROLLTON COOPERATIVE CANNERY, c. 1943. About 50,000 pints of food were canned during the cooperative's first year under the management of R.L. McGuire, according to the Carroll County Cooperative Federation newsletter. The plant, located on South Cliff Street, was canning meat from as many as seven beefs a day. (Courtesy of UWG Special Collections.)

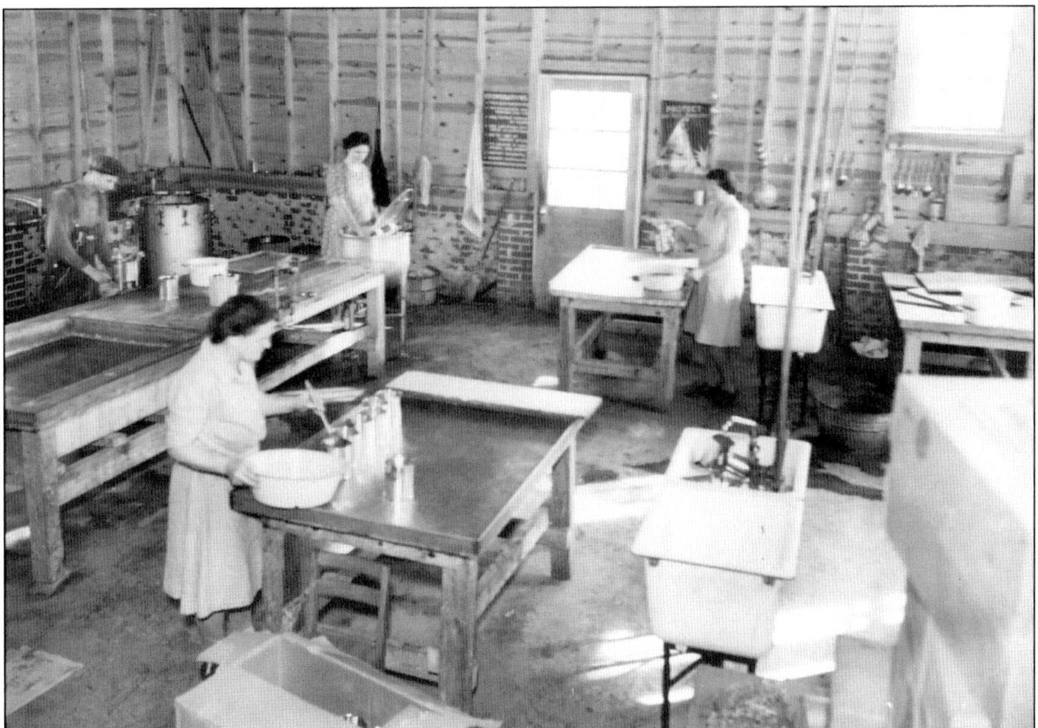

PRODUCE CANNING COOPERATIVE, c. 1943. This photograph shows the interior of the Carrollton Cooperative Cannery. The co-op movement was closely tied to the outlying school communities in Carroll County such as Sand Hill, Burwell, Smyrna, and Tallapoosa; and it grew to include community banks, stores, and credit unions. (Courtesy of UWG Special Collections.)

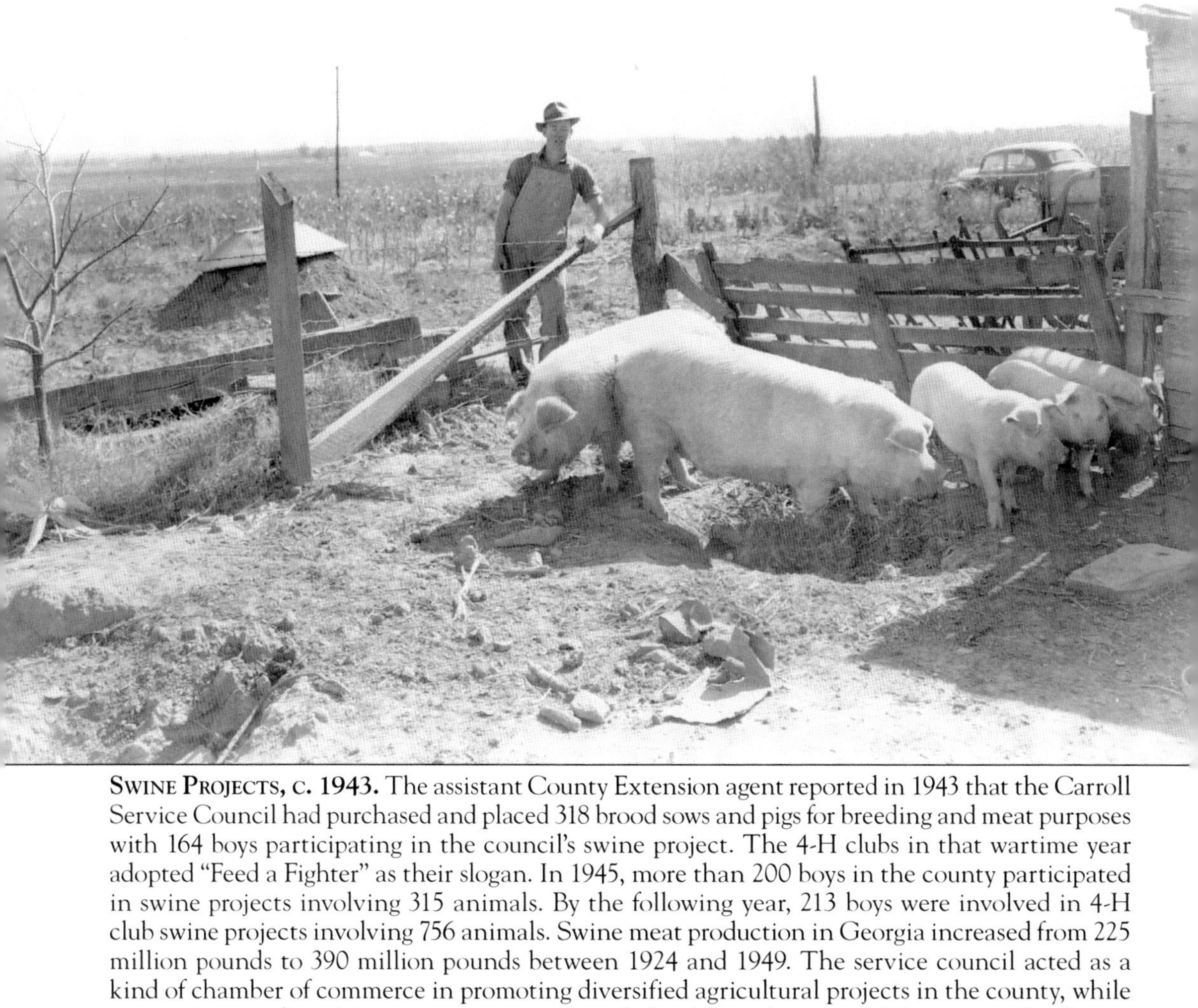

SWINE PROJECTS, C. 1943. The assistant County Extension agent reported in 1943 that the Carroll Service Council had purchased and placed 318 brood sows and pigs for breeding and meat purposes with 164 boys participating in the council's swine project. The 4-H clubs in that wartime year adopted "Feed a Fighter" as their slogan. In 1945, more than 200 boys in the county participated in swine projects involving 315 animals. By the following year, 213 boys were involved in 4-H club swine projects involving 756 animals. Swine meat production in Georgia increased from 225 million pounds to 390 million pounds between 1924 and 1949. The service council acted as a kind of chamber of commerce in promoting diversified agricultural projects in the county, while sponsoring youth training to create more knowledgeable and successful farmers in the future. (Courtesy of UWG Special Collections.)

Five

Sports

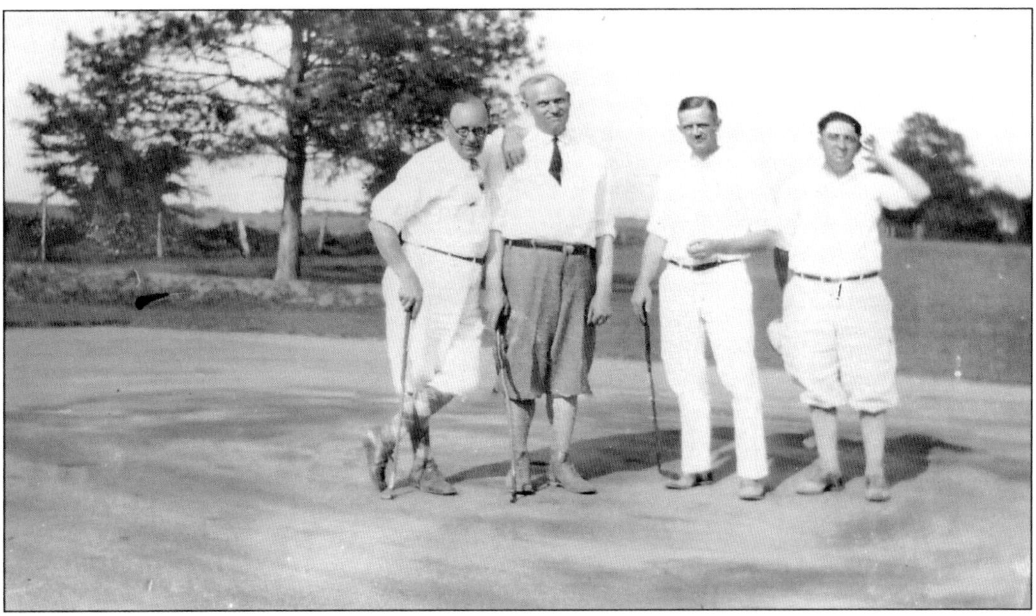

Gypsy Smith, Golfer and Evangelist, c. 1925. The evangelist Gypsy Smith (left) poses with several of Carrollton's notables during a golf outing. The locals are, from left to right, C.E. Roop, Pat Phelan, and Pomp Shaefer, who was the first president of Sunset Hills Country Club. (Courtesy of Marion McNamara Dobbs.)

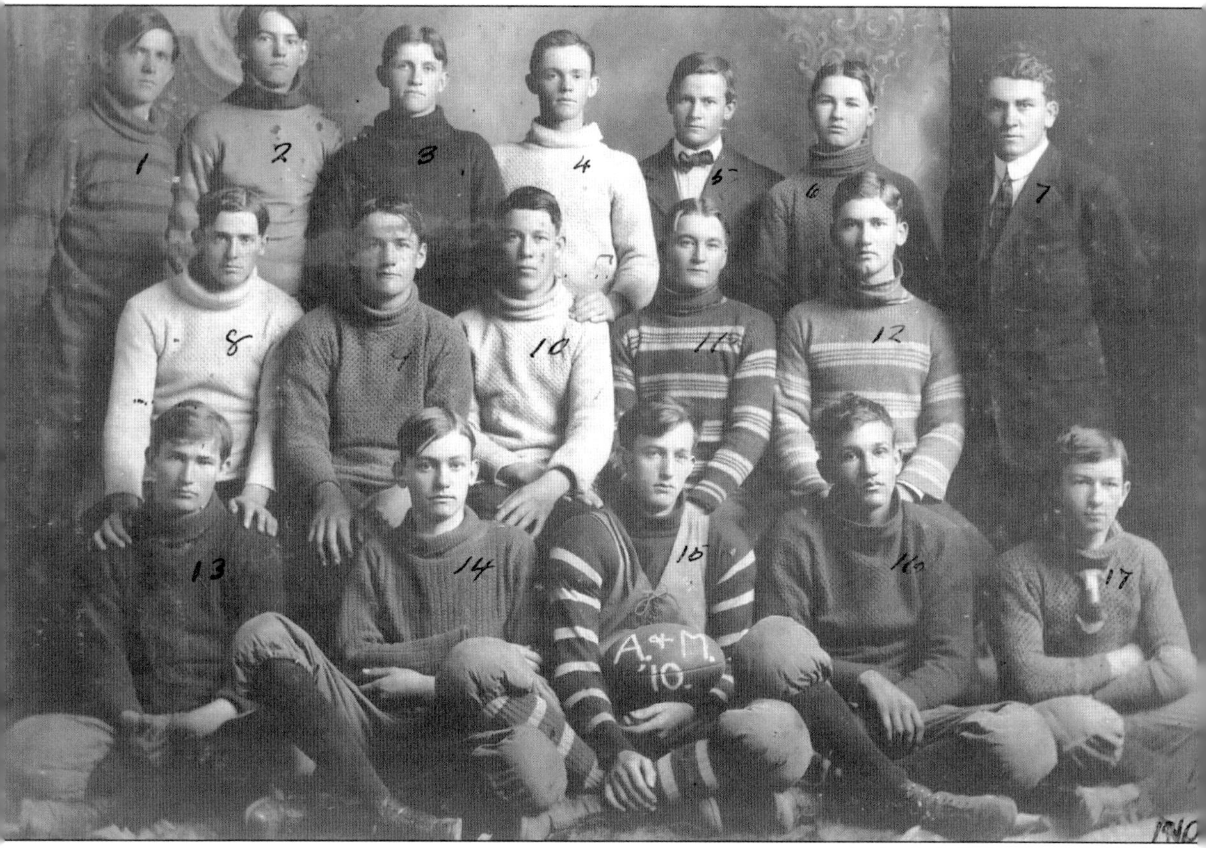

First Football Team, 1910. The Fourth District A&M School organized the county's first football team with Lander Lane of LaGrange as captain and student coach. A firsthand account from student J.C. Bonner—who later became a history professor at West Georgia College—at the time of the games described players who "stalked on the field with ungainly stride, and took their positions in much the same manner as they would settle down to the chore of milking a cow." It was common for spectators, who stood on the sidelines, to attack a player who had viciously tackled a favorite star. The A&M team was showered with brickbats at one LaGrange game, according to Bonner's recollections. He also remembered that most teams employed ringers, or "tramp athletes," before the rules tightened in 1920. (Courtesy of UWG Special Collections.)

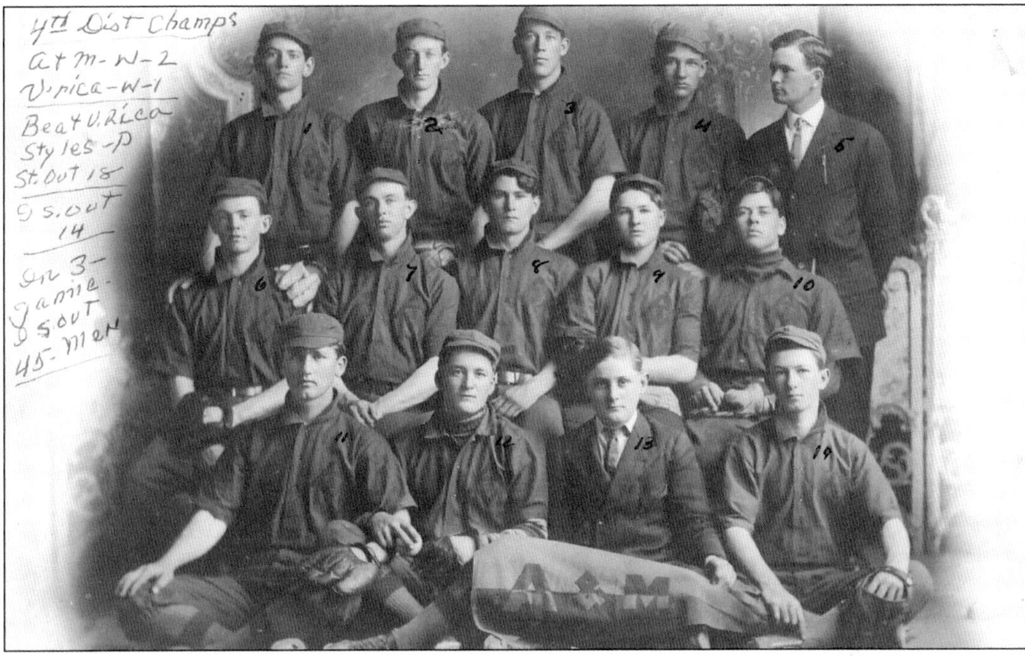

A&M Baseball, 1911. Adopting the new school colors of blue and red, the baseball team started playing in 1908. The uniforms were blue trimmed in red, and the caps were blue with the letters A&M in red. The voluntary team that formed in 1911 won 13 out of 14 games played. (Courtesy of UWG Special Collections.)

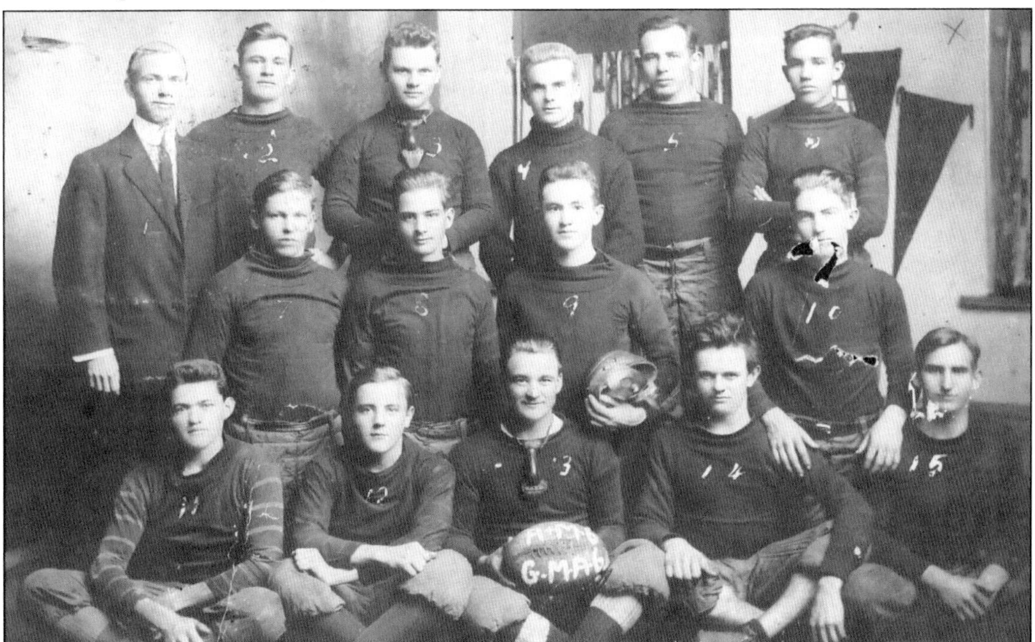

A&M Tigers, 1913. Mechanical teacher and former Auburn University player O.K. David led the football team. A gridiron was fashioned on the back campus, though it measured less than official width. Some nicknames for the players included "Runt," "Poote," "Lobster," and "Wild West." (Courtesy of UWG Special Collections.)

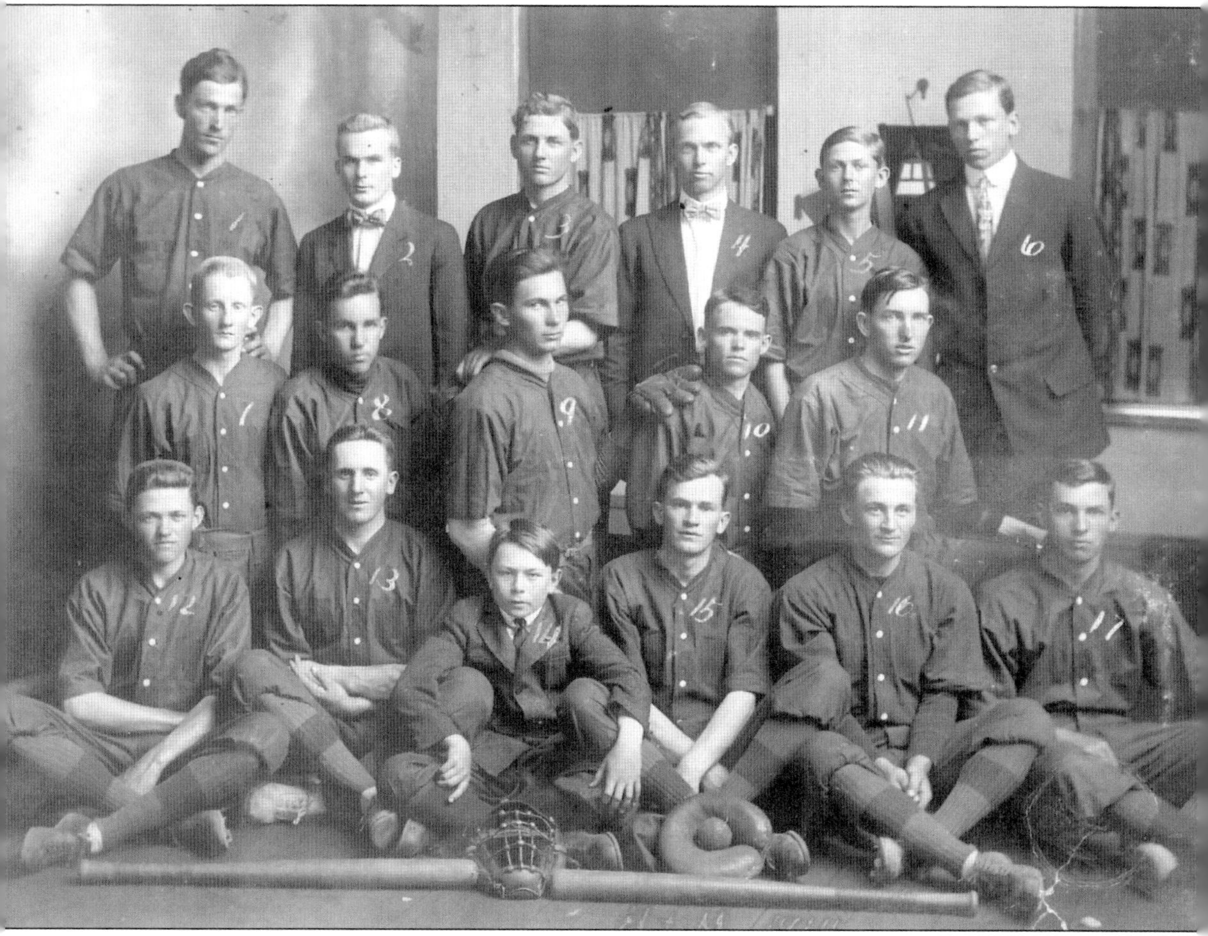

A&M Baseball, 1914. Seated second from right in the first row, Woodfin "Hall" Carmical was in his last year as a student at the Fourth District A&M School. He would come back to teach the following year, as well as to play baseball with the Carrollton city league. He was known for his ambidextrous pitching, so it was no surprise that one of his nicknames was "Pitcher." A native of Newnan, Georgia, Carmical came to the A&M school in the 1910–1911 school year. He began playing baseball in 1911 when an athletic association was formed, producing a championship team. Besides Carmical, the 1911 team included Joe Davis, Bill Jarrell, Lander Lane, Jess Craven, Norman Causey, Yuke Hay, Carl Almon, and Glenn Carter. In those early years, many athletes played more than one team sport. (Courtesy of UWG Special Collections.)

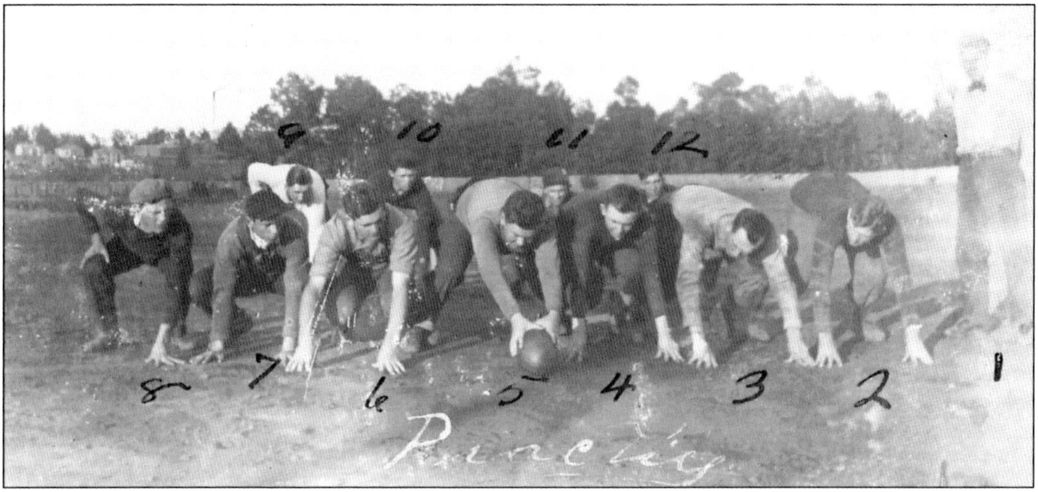

Tigers at Practice and Play, 1913. The score was decidedly in A&M's favor when the team beat Senoia (Brantley Institute) 81-0. The Tigers also played LaGrange, Newnan, Georgia Military Academy, Monroe A&M, Hearn Academy, and Columbus Industrial School. The Tigers tied the military academy, a school that had ranked first among Georgia's preparatory schools. It cost about $125 to equip the A&M team, and the players paid for all but $50 of that cost. Football games on campus were played about where the Martha Munro Building stands today. (Both, courtesy of UWG Special Collections.)

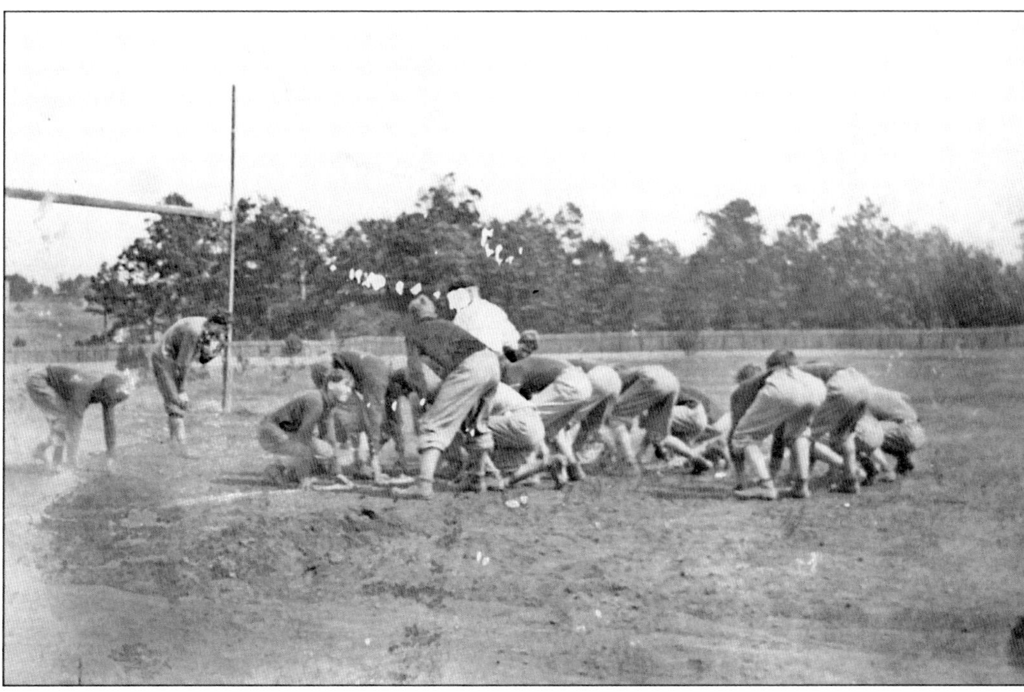

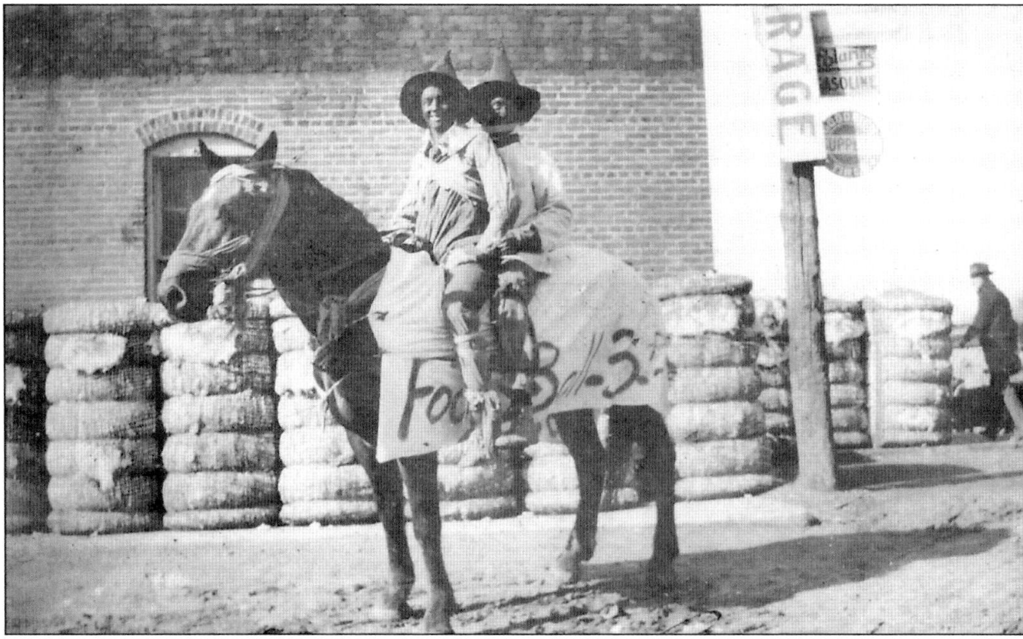

Victory Over Seventh District A&M, 1916. The Fourth District A&M School celebrated a win over a rival A&M school that was located in Powder Springs, Georgia, with a score of 20-12. The student clowns are Ernest Truitt (left) and Homer Cook. (Courtesy of UWG Special Collections.)

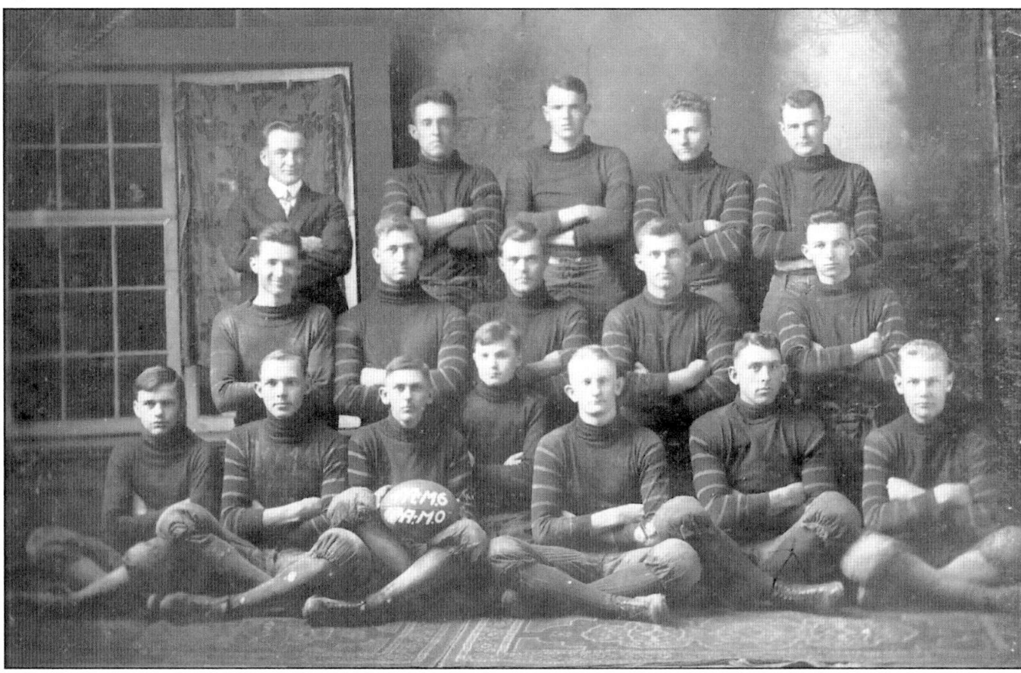

Disastrous Loss, 1916. Local news reporting termed Gordon High School's 54-7 win over the A&M school a disastrous loss for the Tigers in 1916. However, the A&M team could report a mostly successful season under coach Woodfin "Hall" Carmical, an A&M graduate who became a mechanical teacher at the school. (Courtesy of UWG Special Collections.)

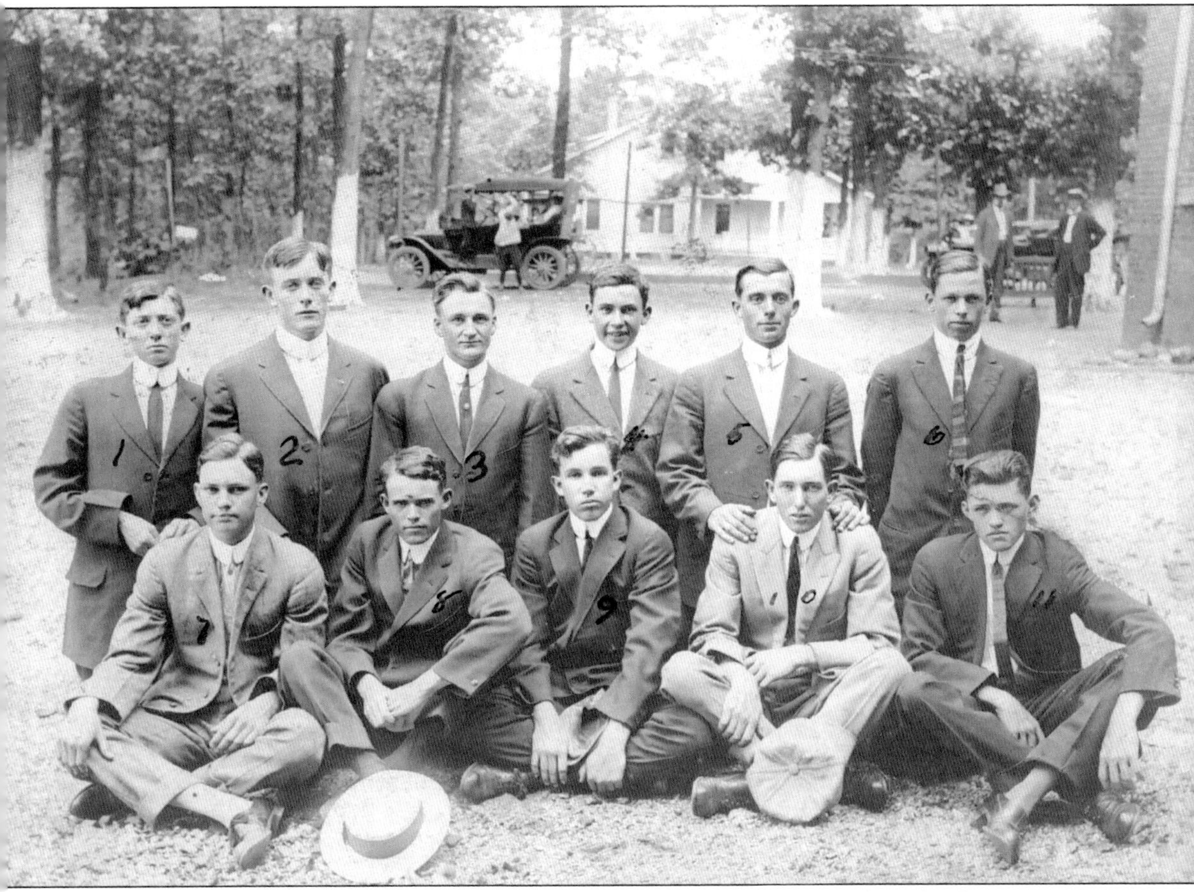

A&M Baseball Team Portrait, 1914. The baseball players are pictured on the front campus drive in their formal suits. From left to right are (first row) J.D. Bradfield, John Smith, Arnell Ware, Porter Brooks, and Fred Hallum; (second row) Arthur Hyde, Devanie Truett, Woodfin "Hall" Carmical, Charlie Ware, Will Cotton, and Robert Spearman. Carmical was pitcher and played third base for the A&M team. Hallum had a reputation as the best all-around athlete the A&M school ever produced. In the background is the president's home when it was located on the eastern side of campus, near where Cobb Hall is today. The house is now the Honors College, located at the corner of Maple Street and West Georgia Drive, where it was moved in the late 1950s. (Courtesy of UWG Special Collections.)

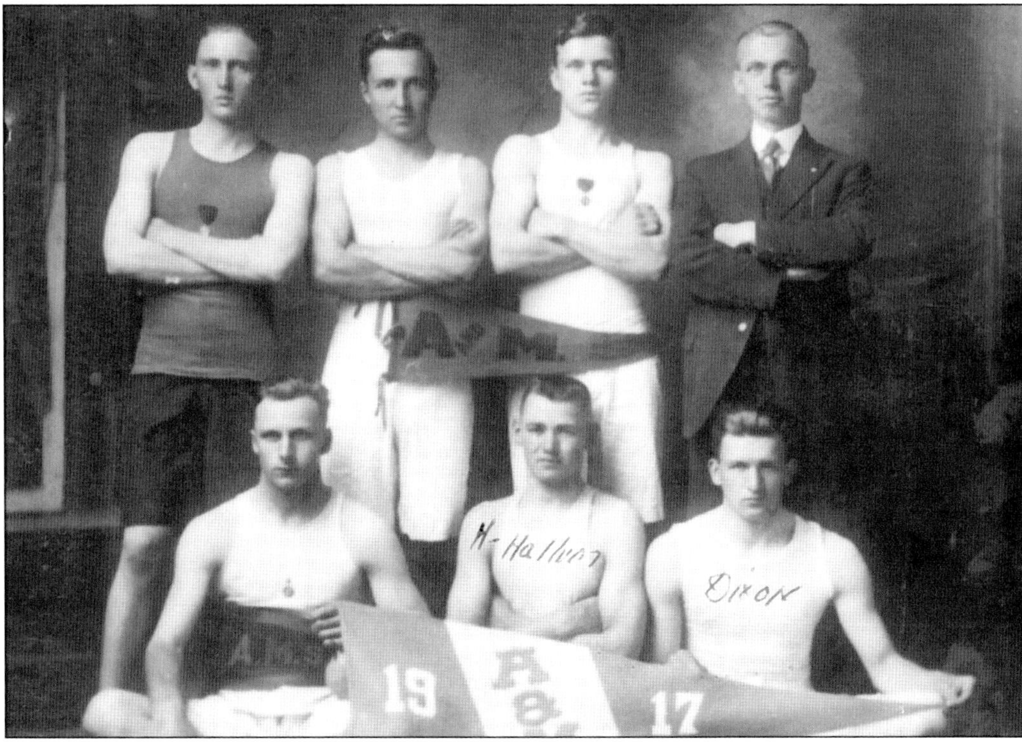

TRACK AND FIELD TEAM, 1917. A&M student Fred Hallum, seated in the middle, distinguished himself as the best all-around athlete in state competitions. In one meet, he won first place in four events and the one-mile relay. Hallum was featured in the 1913–1914 catalog for winning first place in eight track meets held among Fourth District schools. (Courtesy of UWG Special Collections.)

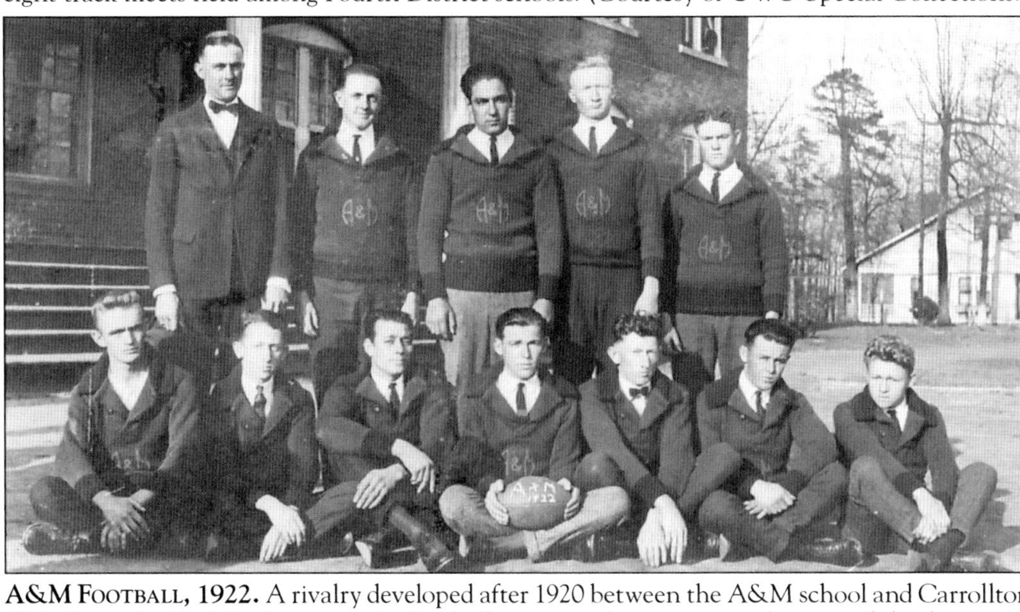

A&M FOOTBALL, 1922. A rivalry developed after 1920 between the A&M school and Carrollton High School, which had organized a football program that year. An observer of the first game remembered that the A&M coach, Ed Simms, had to referee and explain the rules to the high school team. (Courtesy of UWG Special Collections.)

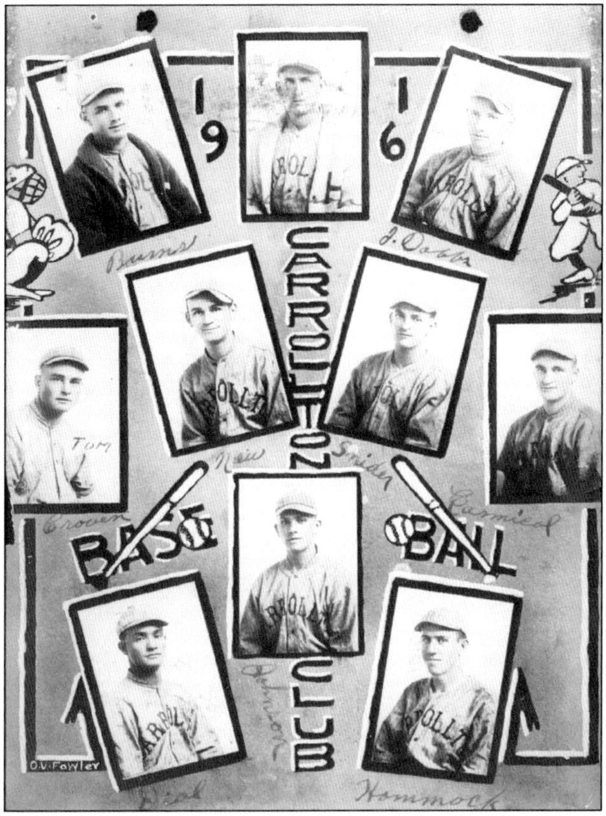

Carrollton Baseball Club, 1916. Before 1920, teams representing Carrollton were of the semipro variety. Carrollton's first team formed in the summer of 1914 and played teams from other cities, such as Griffin, LaGrange, and Cedartown. Carrollton's winning streak earned its team the nickname "Champs." Woodfin "Hall" Carmical, far right, was third baseman and an A&M graduate-turned-teacher. (Courtesy of UWG Special Collections.)

Pre-World War I Team. When the United States declared war on Germany in 1917, baseball was not a top priority, especially since many young players were called for service. Woodfin "Hall" Carmical, fifth from right, was one of those players who was drafted to serve stateside at Camp Gordon in Georgia. (Courtesy of UWG Special Collections.)

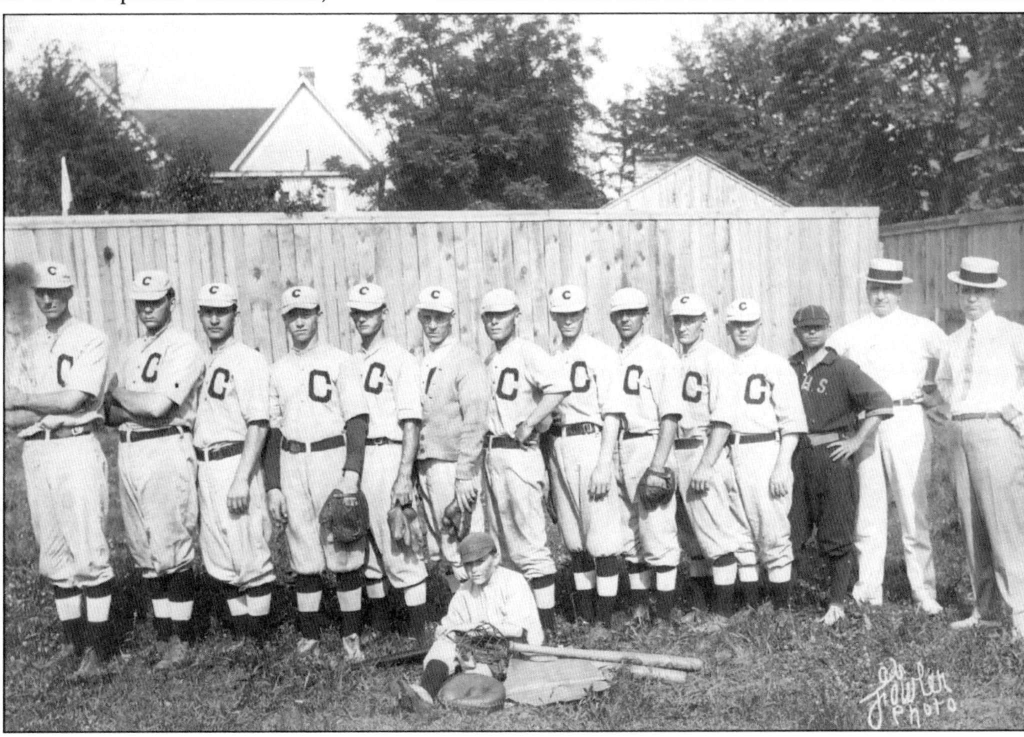

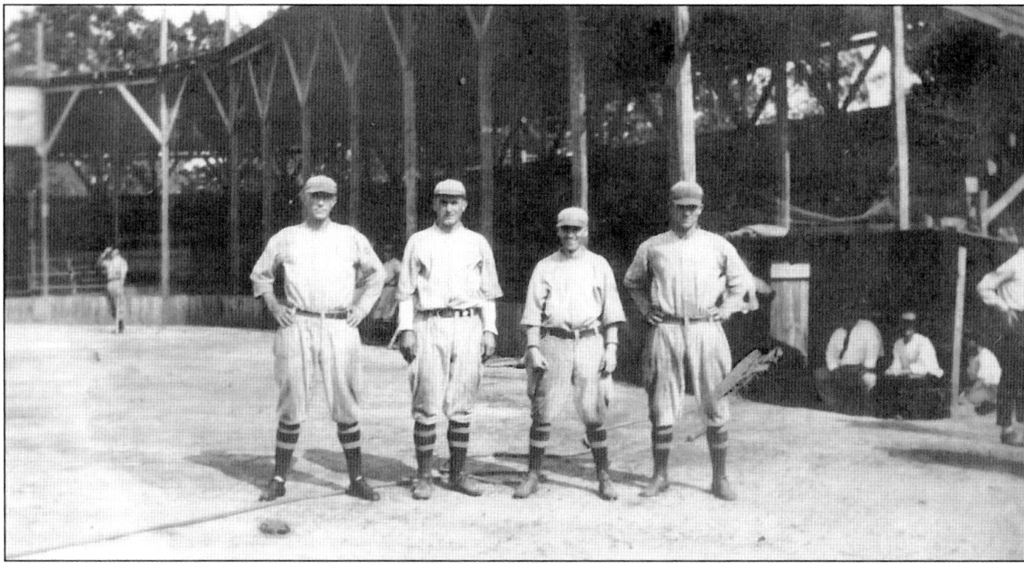

Georgia State League Team, 1920. The Carrollton team played its first game in 1920 as an official Class D minor league team. A new ballpark on South Street at Aycock Street was opened. The team owner was Benjamin "Mann" Long, a local photographer and insurance agent. This team photograph taken by him shows, from left to right, Jules Watson (second base), Jess Craven (first base), J.C. Pulliam (shortstop), and Charlie Bell (manager and pitcher). (Courtesy of Marion McNamara Dobbs.)

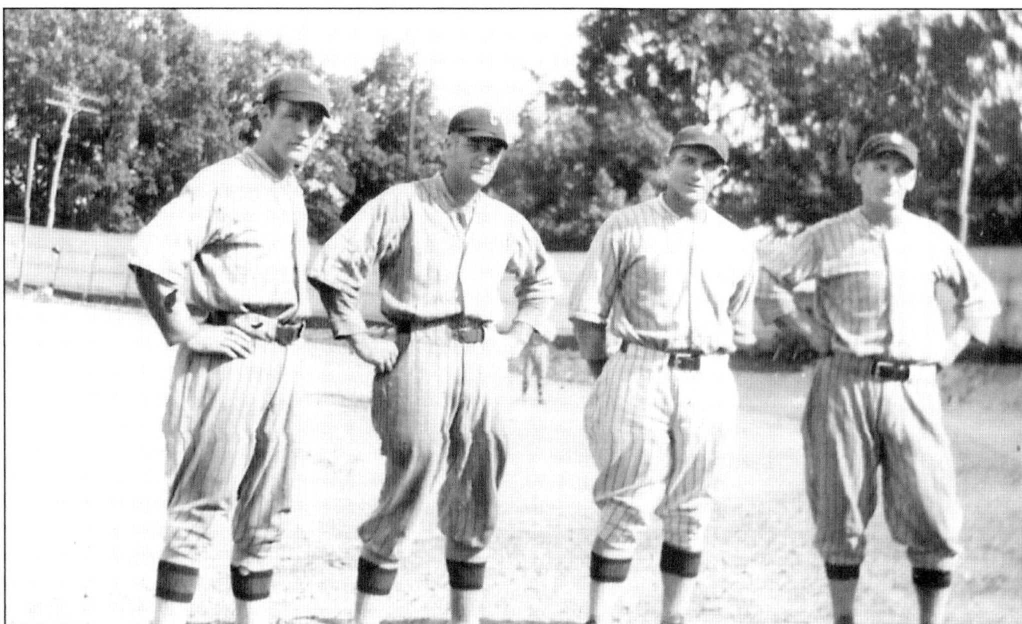

Georgia-Alabama League, 1928. After a six-year hiatus, Carrollton had a ball team again, called the Frogs. They played at the new City Athletic Field behind Carrollton High School on West Avenue. Pictured here are, from left to right, Miller Huggins (third base), Fob James (first base), Dick Taliaferro (shortstop), and Brant Boswell (second base). (Courtesy of Marion McNamara Dobbs.)

CARROLLTON HORNETS, 1948. The club during this time was part of the Georgia-Alabama League, which included the Alabama cities of Tallassee, Alexander City, Valley, and Opelika. Major league baseball commissioner Happy Chandler was on hand for the opening game at the City Athletic Field along with Ellis Arnall, Georgia's governor. The Hornets stung Newnan 13-5. Nearly 3,000 fans crowded the stands, a record opening day attendance for the circuit. Manager Charlie "Red" Roberts was sidelined during the season with complications from a war injury, which required hospitalization. Many fans thought Roberts's absence caused the team to lose the season. (Both, courtesy of UWG Special Collections.)

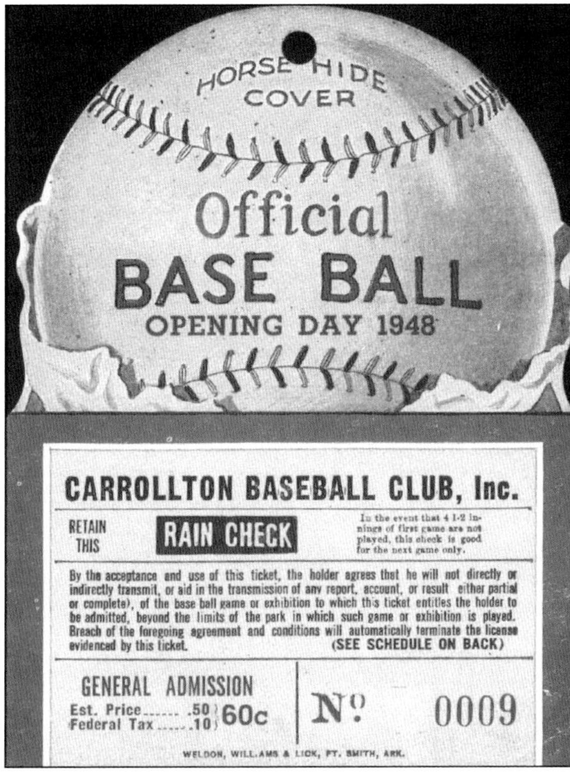

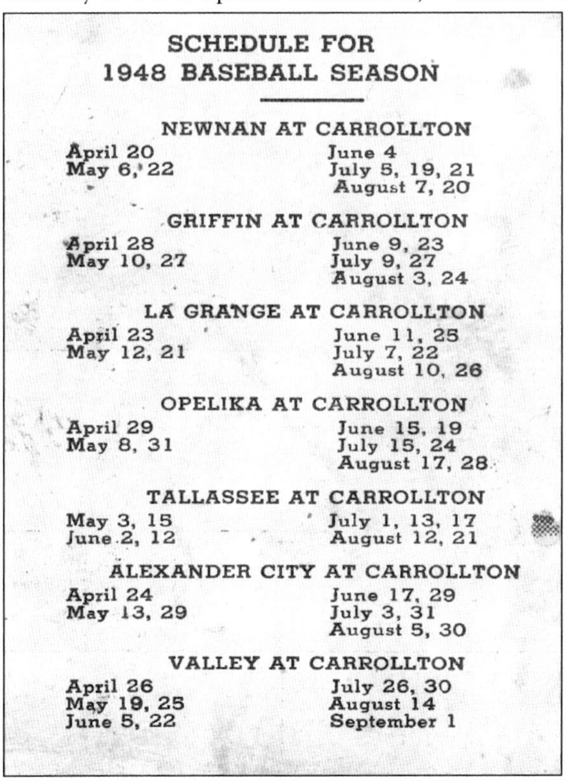

SCHEDULE FOR
1948 BASEBALL SEASON

NEWNAN AT CARROLLTON
April 20 — June 4
May 6, 22 — July 5, 19, 21
August 7, 20

GRIFFIN AT CARROLLTON
April 28 — June 9, 23
May 10, 27 — July 9, 27
August 3, 24

LA GRANGE AT CARROLLTON
April 23 — June 11, 25
May 12, 21 — July 7, 22
August 10, 26

OPELIKA AT CARROLLTON
April 29 — June 15, 19
May 8, 31 — July 15, 24
August 17, 28

TALLASSEE AT CARROLLTON
May 3, 15 — July 1, 13, 17
June 2, 12 — August 12, 21

ALEXANDER CITY AT CARROLLTON
April 24 — June 17, 29
May 13, 29 — July 3, 31
August 5, 30

VALLEY AT CARROLLTON
April 26 — July 26, 30
May 19, 25 — August 14
June 5, 22 — September 1

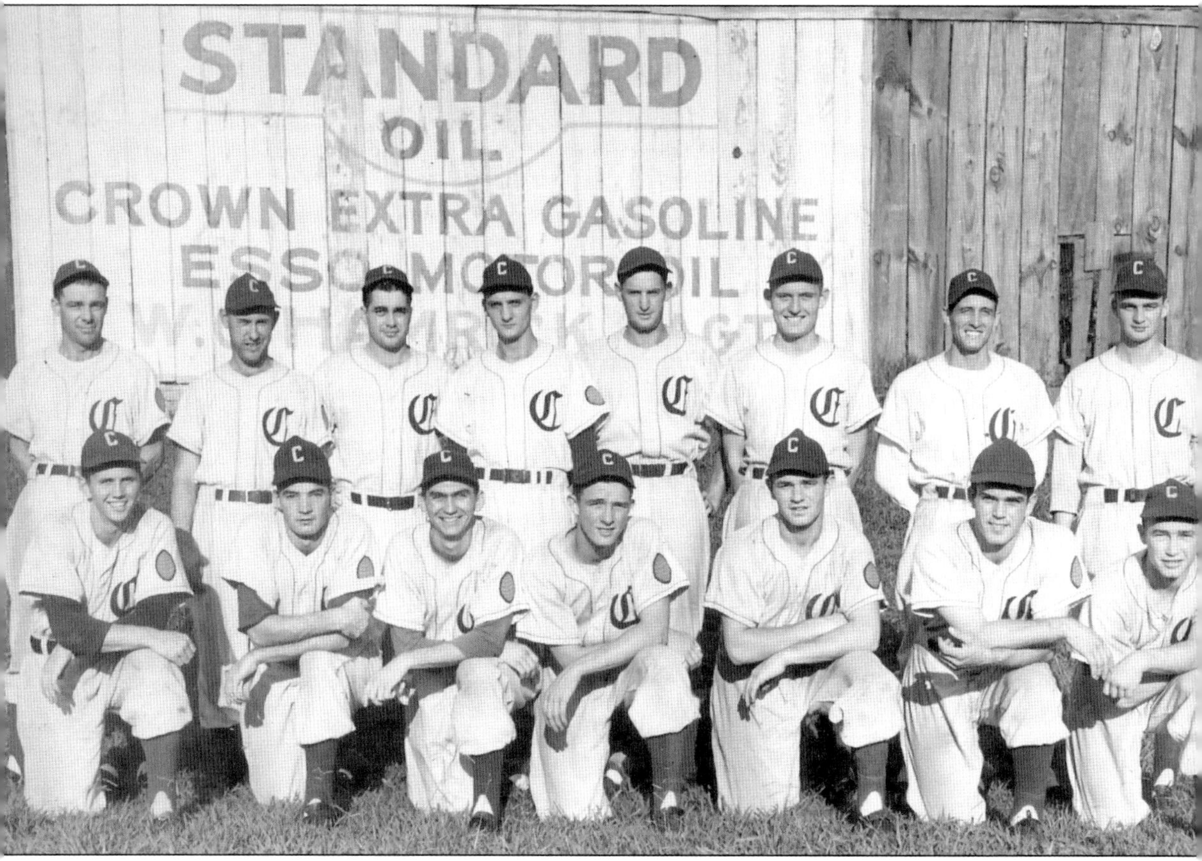

Carrollton Hornets, 1949. During this year, the club became affiliated with the Class B Southeastern League's Vicksburg Billies. It was a mixed blessing in that the team could have a good supply of talent to pull from but also had to face its best players being recruited to teams in higher classifications. Team presidents were William Cobb and P.L. Shaefer. From left to right are (first row) Jim Conhenney (second base), Luke Nasworthy (shortstop), Buddy Berman (second base), Jim Shirley (first base), Ricardo Cobellis (a Cuban), Virgil Jefts (catcher), and Jim Morelli (outfield); (second row) Walter Little (pitcher), Buck Matthews (pitcher), Richard Nelson (pitcher), Eddy Bobowski (pitcher), Bill Rucker (manager), John Tidwell (outfield), Casey Jones (pitcher), and Ozzie Wadewitz (pitcher). The Georgia-Alabama League that year was made up of the Newnan Brownies, Alexander City Millers, Tallassee Cardinals, LaGrange Troupers, Valley Rebels, Opelika Owls, Griffin Pimientos, and the Hornets. (Courtesy of Marion McNamara Dobbs.)

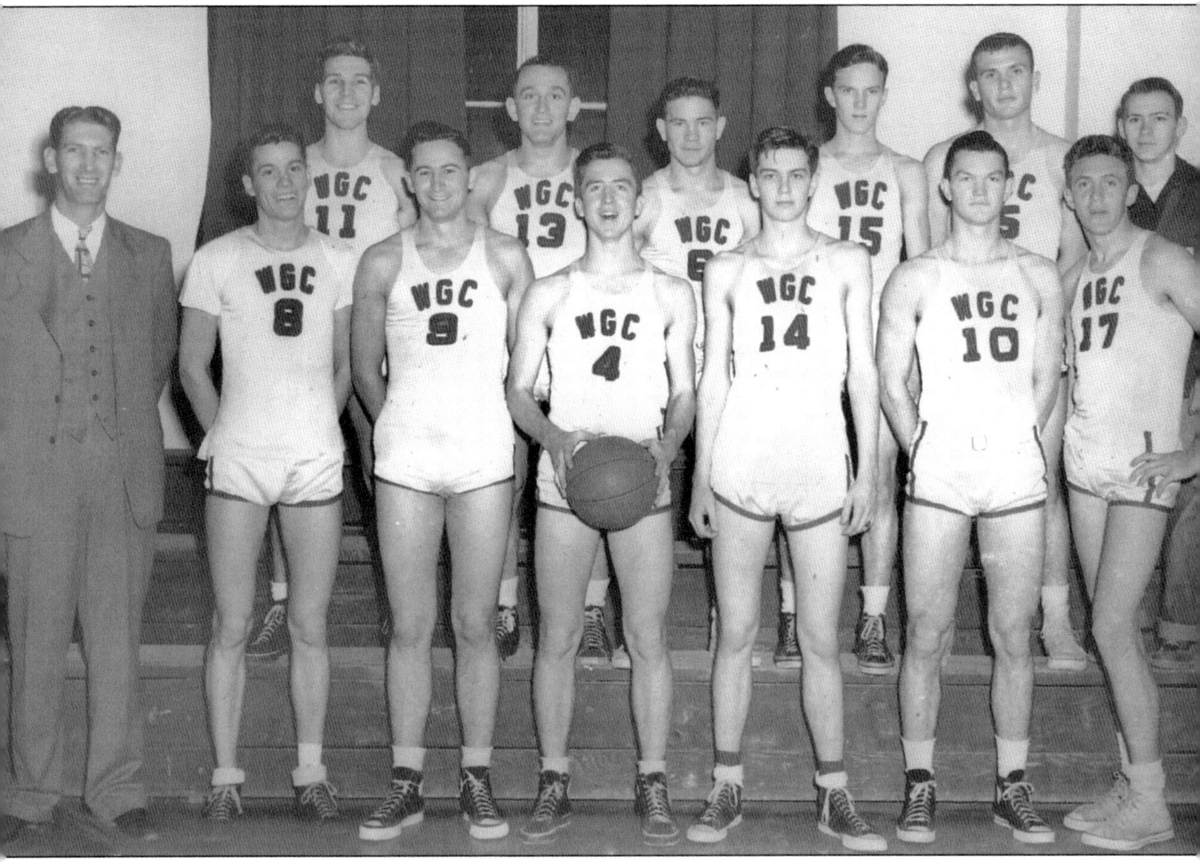

BASKETBALL BRAVES, 1949–1950. It was a losing season for the West Georgia College team with six wins and nine losses. The Braves played teams such as those from Georgia Military Academy, Berry College, Oglethorpe University, and Tech Institute. Named for the Creek Indian heritage of the region, the Braves team name was changed in 2006 to the Wolves. From left to right are (first row) coach Henry "Shag" Welch, Victor Goebel, Herbert Thompson, Barry Ricketson, Harry Alford, William Hall, and Wales Goebel; (second row) Bruce Williams, Charles Perry, James Massey, Charles Graham, Gerald Dailey, and Bill Allison. During the war, travel restrictions limited the teams WGC could play. Often, the Braves played varsity teams from local high schools or teams organized at local factories. When intercollegiate competition resumed, the Braves still did not produce any championship seasons. (Courtesy of UWG Special Collections.)

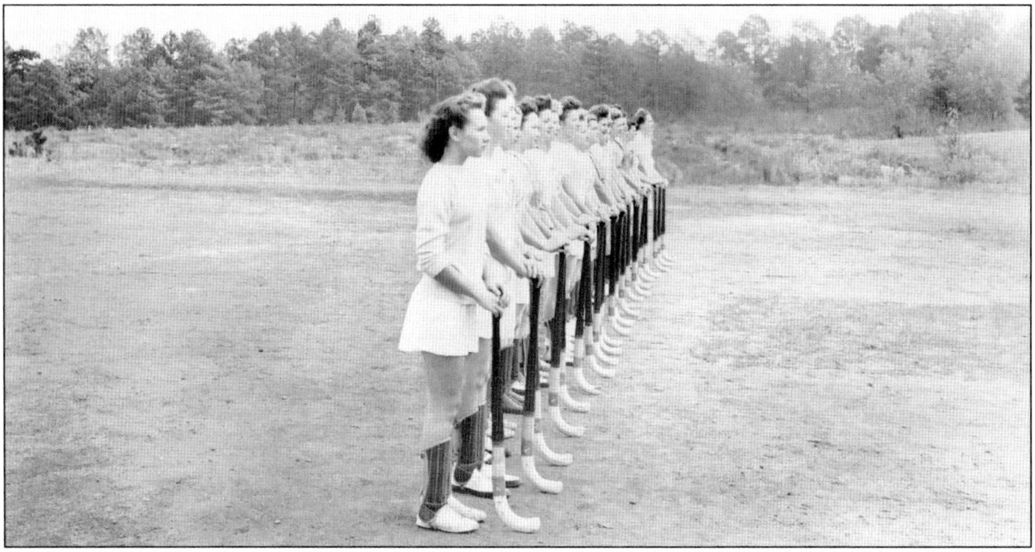

Women's Athletic Association, 1945. The WAA was formed in 1944 at West Georgia College in response to the perceived demands of the country's military involvement in World War II. In its charter statement, the WAA asserted, "War has demanded health and vigor on the home front as well as the battle front." These students are preparing to play field hockey. (Courtesy of UWG Special Collections.)

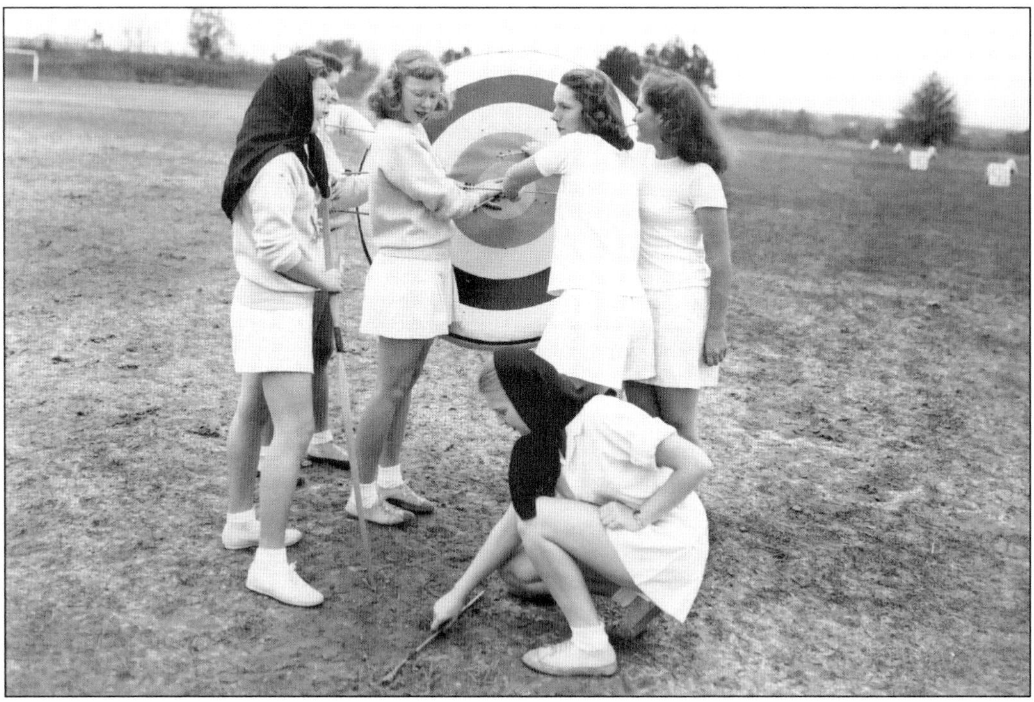

College Archery, 1948. The Women's Athletic Association required that all West Georgia students take physical education, which included hiking, soccer, touch football, and modern dance. The equivalent association for male students was called the "W" Club. All students were required to have tennis shoes and two pairs of white shorts and cotton shirts. (Courtesy of UWG Special Collections.)

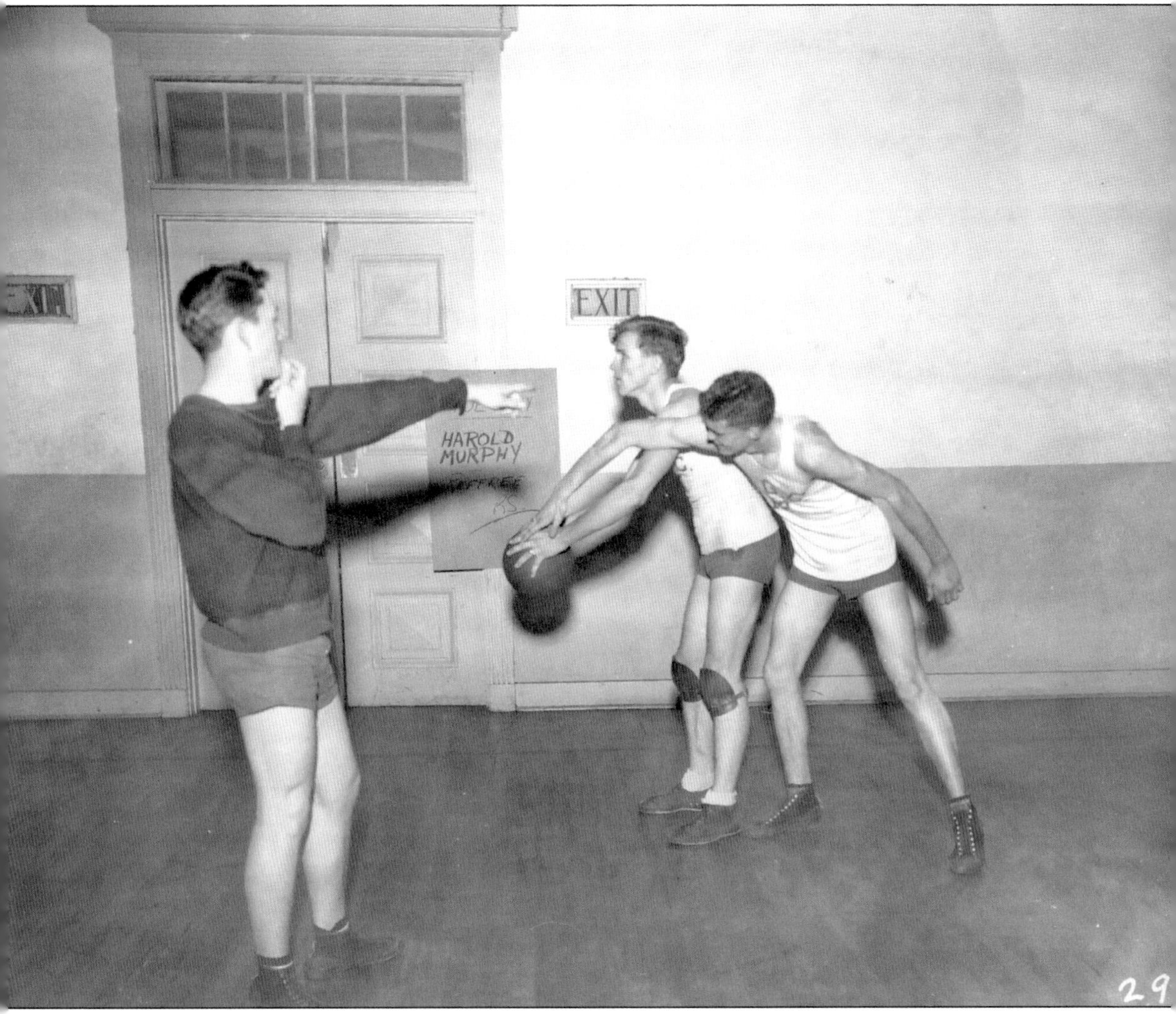

BASKETBALL PRACTICE, C. 1940. West Georgia College struggled in athletic competition, in part because its coaches were drawn from faculty members who had full-time jobs teaching and did not have the time to devote to coaching. In addition, many of the competing teams were senior colleges whose players were much bigger and more developed than players at West Georgia. Students pictured here are practicing in the Auditorium, a building constructed in 1939 that also housed a dining hall. It was one of several buildings designed to meet the needs of a growing college. In 1936, Mandeville Hall on the front campus drive was built as a women's dorm, and the Sanford Library at the end of the drive was dedicated. The Rural Arts Building, later renamed the Martha Munro Building (in honor of college president Ingram's wife), was completed in 1938. Prior to the Auditorium, college athletes used an old barn, which dated to the earliest A&M days, for a gym. (Courtesy of UWG Special Collections.)

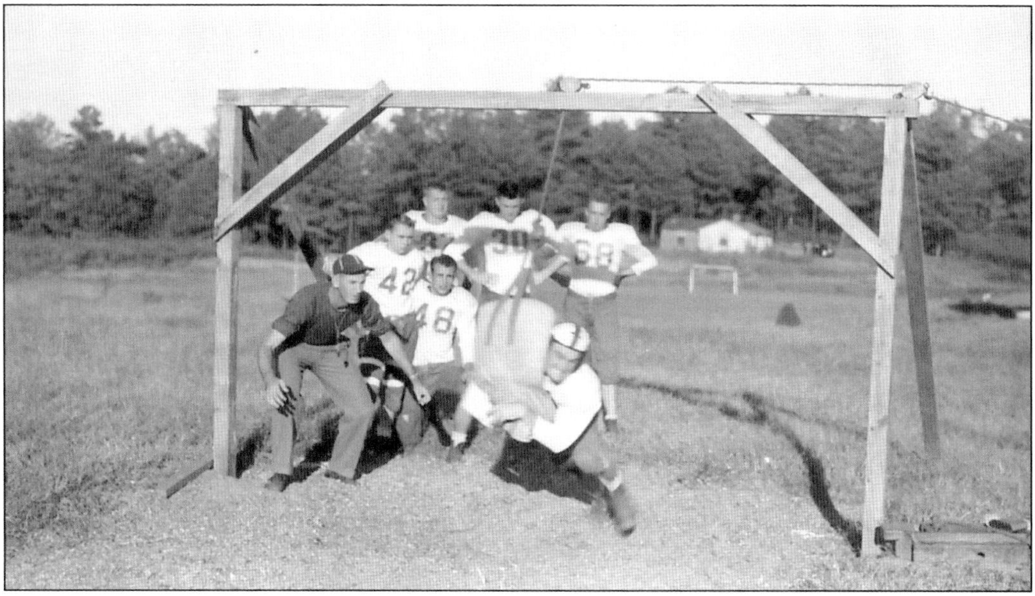

Football Practice Tackle, 1949–1950. A Braves football player is pictured practicing a tackle, but the team had a losing season anyway. West Georgia College started the season in a tie game with Brevard Junior College from North Carolina. The score was 0-0; however, West Georgia did beat Middle Georgia 13-7 that year. (Courtesy of UWG Special Collections.)

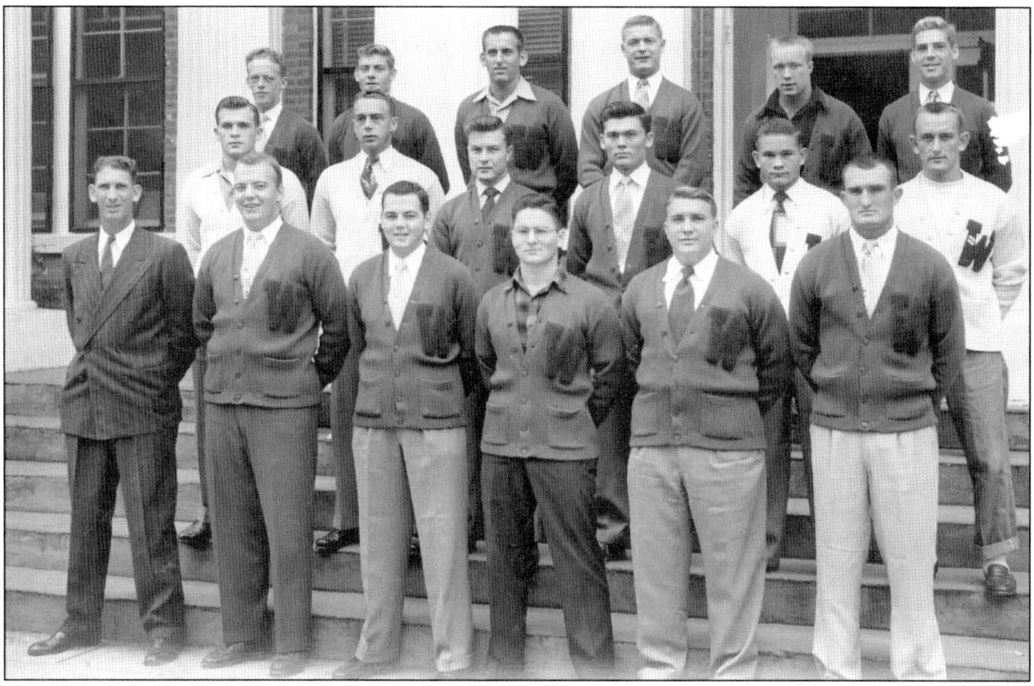

"W" Club, 1949–1950. By this time, the wartime influence promoting physical fitness on the home front had reverted to a school spirit and good sportsmanship theme. Lettermen in the main sports of football and basketball were eligible for membership in the "W" Club. Coach Henry Welch, far left, was director of physical education. His wife worked in the college library. (Courtesy of UWG Special Collections.)

Six

Mount Zion Seminary

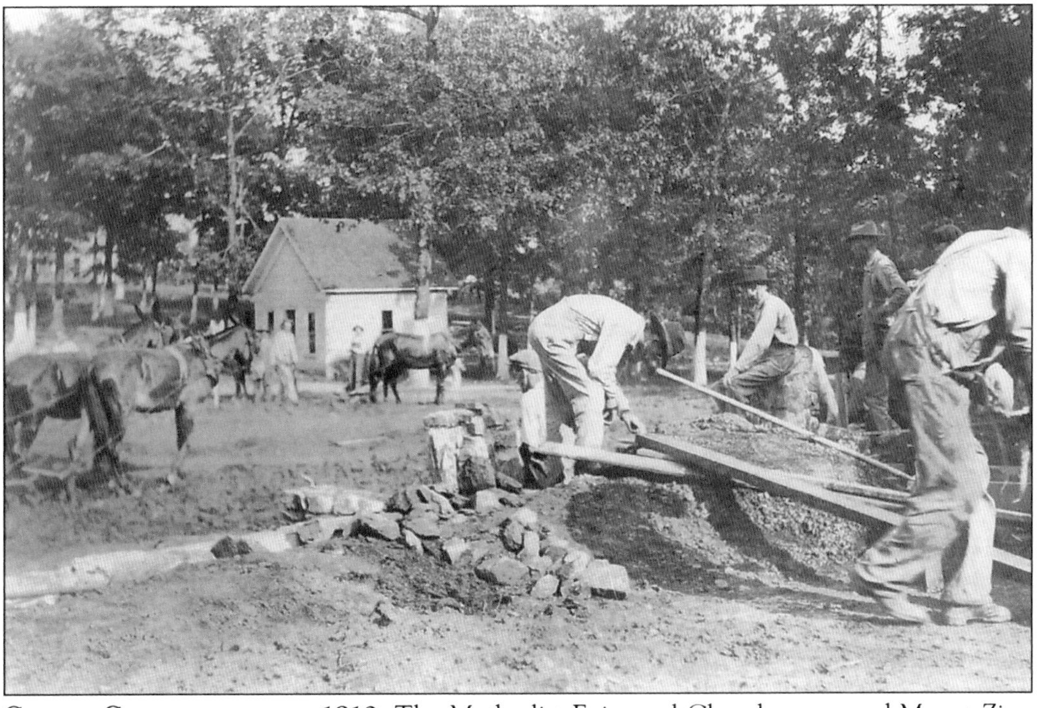

Campus Construction, c. 1910. The Methodist Episcopal Church sponsored Mount Zion Seminary, a high school for girls and boys in northwest Carroll County. It was the pet project of Dr. James Mitchell (1818–1903). Mitchell, an Irish immigrant and Methodist minister who served in Abraham Lincoln's cabinet, formed a corporation in 1880 with local citizens to pay for the school. The small building shown here still stands. (Courtesy of Jack Dorsey.)

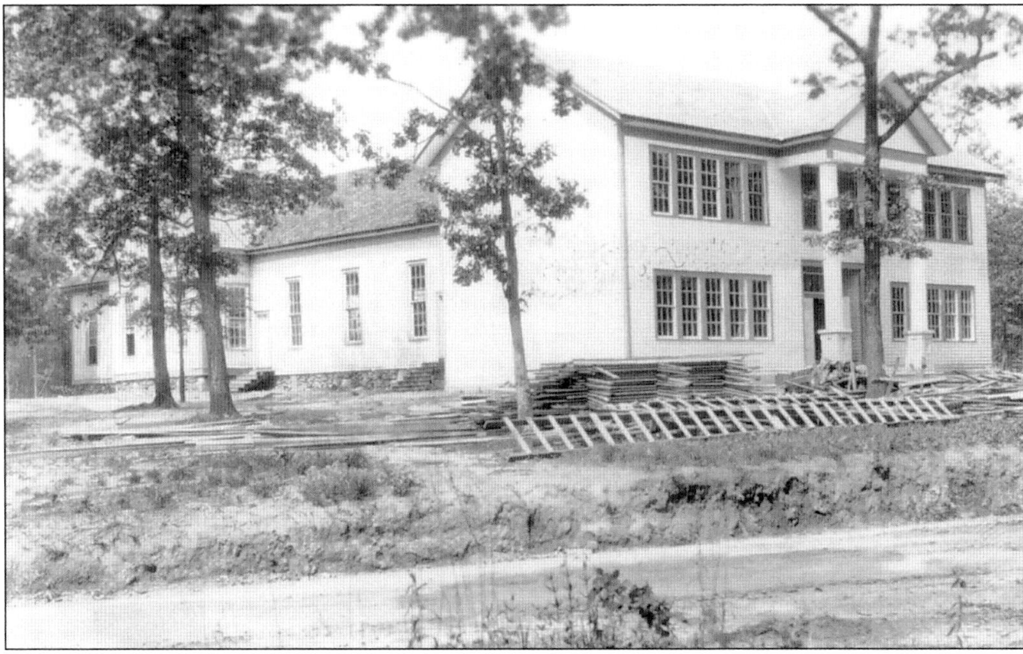

Academic Building, 1923. The Academic Building came to be constructed in four parts over about 40 years. The first section, at the rear of this photograph, was constructed in 1881. Two later additions were put up in 1885 and again around 1900. The last addition with the portico was finished in 1923. The building no longer stands. (Courtesy of Jack Dorsey.)

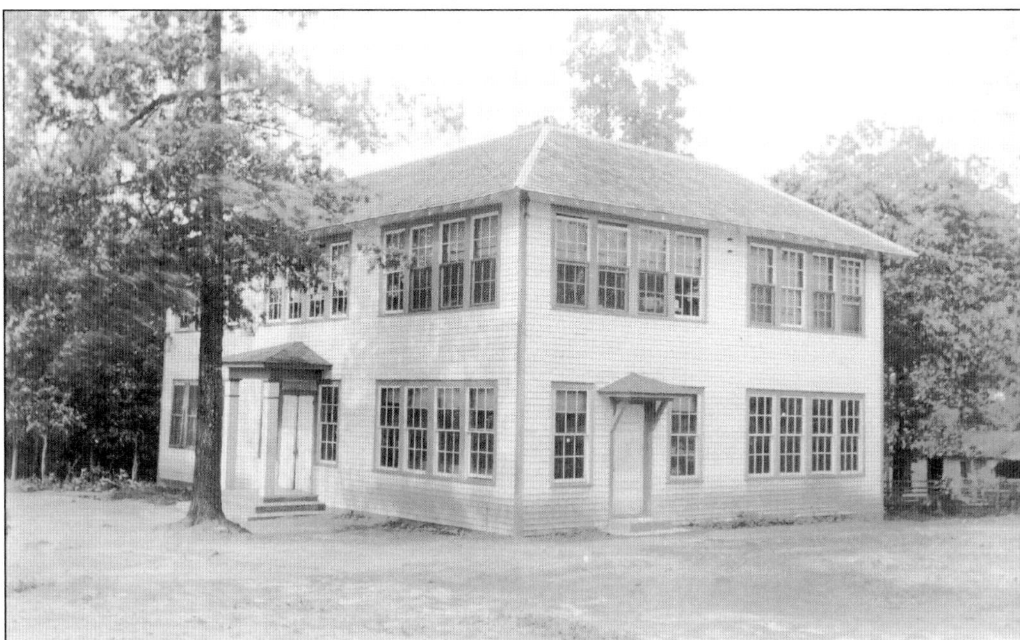

Vocational Building, c. 1927. The widow of the school's last president took over upon his death in 1926, and secured funds for a vocational training department to teach home economics for girls and furniture making for boys. This building burned in the 1940s, after Mount Zion Seminary was no longer operating. (Courtesy of Jack Dorsey.)

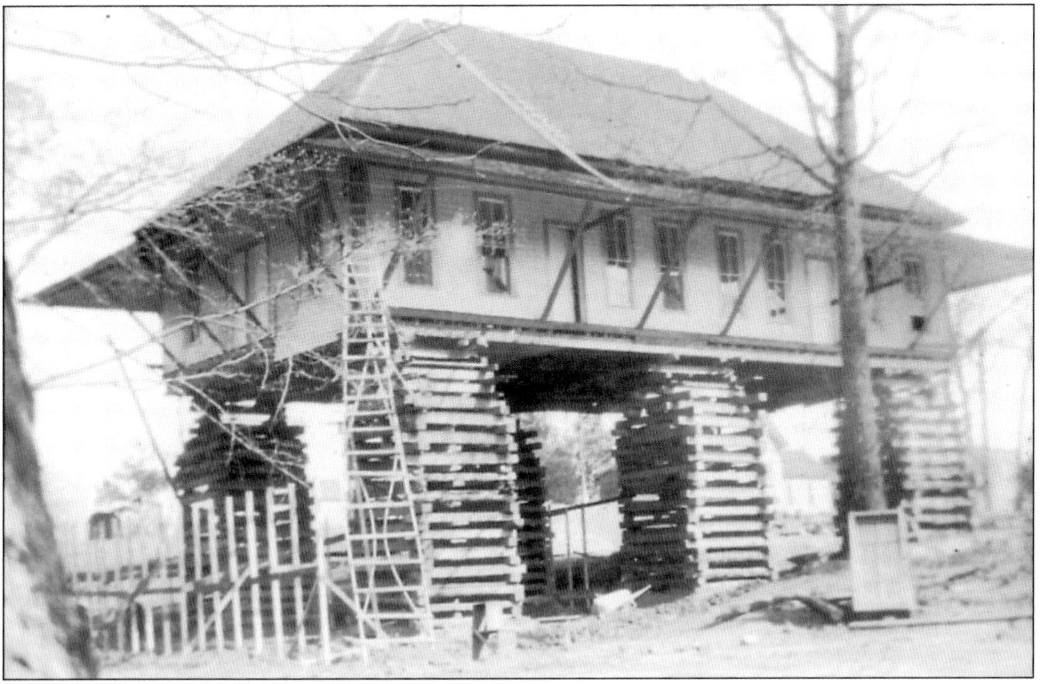

Raising Boys' Dormitory, c. 1920. Some time after the turn of the century, the 1885 boys' dormitory was enlarged by raising it from a one-story to a two-story building. In this photograph, taken mid-construction, the piers are shown that allowed a first story to be built under the original building. It was torn down in the late 1950s. (Courtesy of Jack Dorsey.)

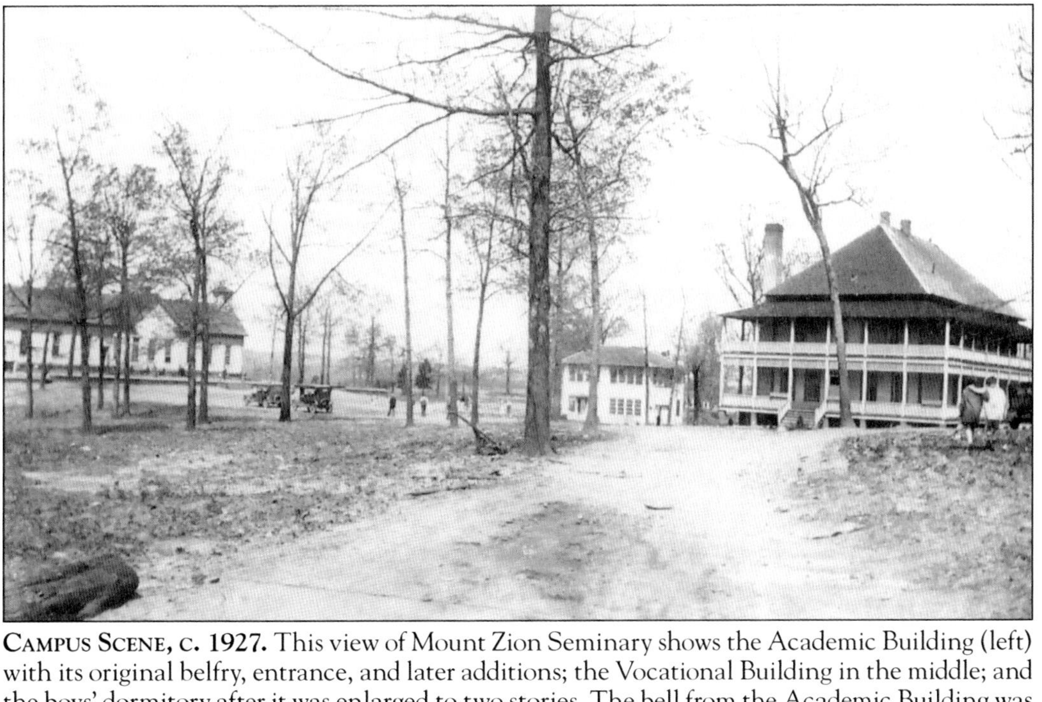

Campus Scene, c. 1927. This view of Mount Zion Seminary shows the Academic Building (left) with its original belfry, entrance, and later additions; the Vocational Building in the middle; and the boys' dormitory after it was enlarged to two stories. The bell from the Academic Building was salvaged and placed at the current Mount Zion Elementary School. (Courtesy of Jack Dorsey.)

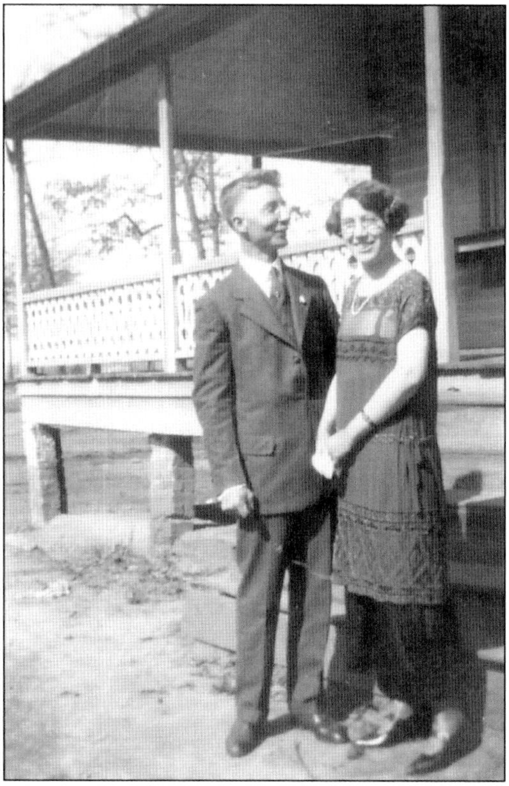

STUDENT AND TEACHER, C. 1915. J. Roy Martin enjoys a humorous moment with Carrie Hudson, who, at the time of this photograph, was Martin's teacher at Mount Zion Seminary. Considerably older than Martin, she married him several years later. Martin was a Carroll County poultry farmer who distinguished himself by joining the Peace Corps when he was 65. (Courtesy of Jack Dorsey.)

***SPINSTER'S RETURN* CAST, C. 1900.** Students are pictured in their costumes for a play. It was not unusual for boys to play female roles, as a close look at some of the faces will show. By the turn of the century, enrollment in the school was around 200. Students came from Carroll and adjoining counties, and even from Alabama. (Courtesy of Jack Dorsey.)

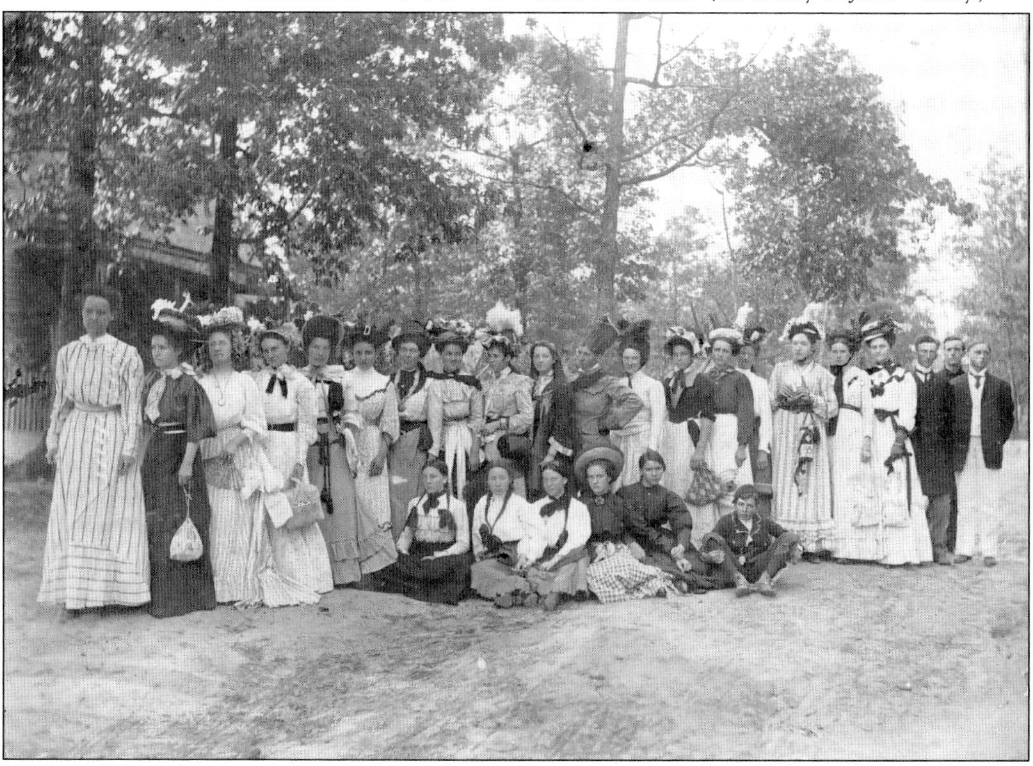

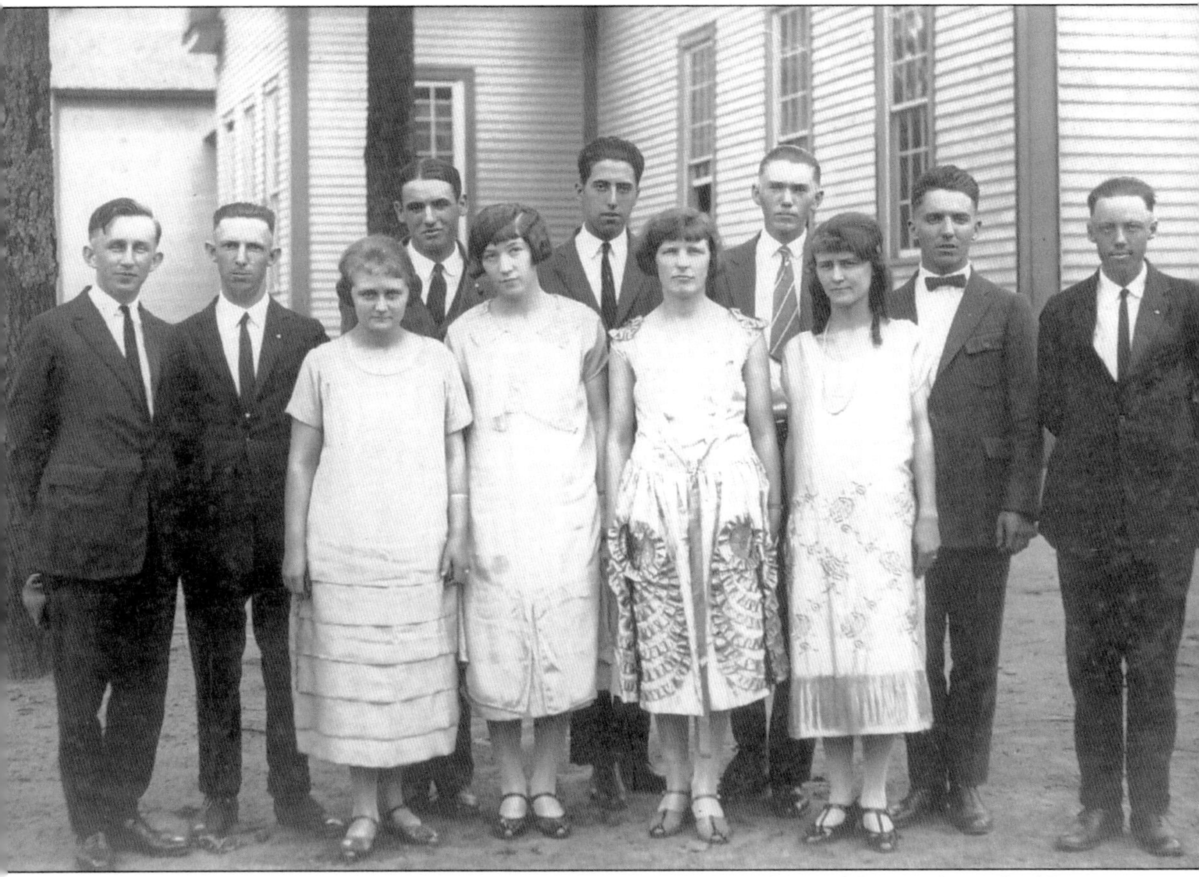

SENIOR CLASS, 1925. Members of the 1925 graduating class pose in front of the Academic Building. At the time, Dr. Herbert Howard was president of the seminary. In 1921, failing health had forced him to return to the United States from a church mission in Africa. His wife, Estella, took over as president when he died in 1926. During the 1870s, Dr. James Mitchell preached at a log church in this community, which was then called Turkey Creek. Based on the enthusiasm and interest of the local citizens, along with a lack of publicly supported schools, Mitchell pursued the idea of a church-affiliated seminary. In the process, the community name changed to Mount Zion to reflect the biblical site in Jerusalem. While James Mitchell originally envisioned a collegiate education at Mount Zion, that department faded within a decade of the seminary opening. (Courtesy of Jack Dorsey.)

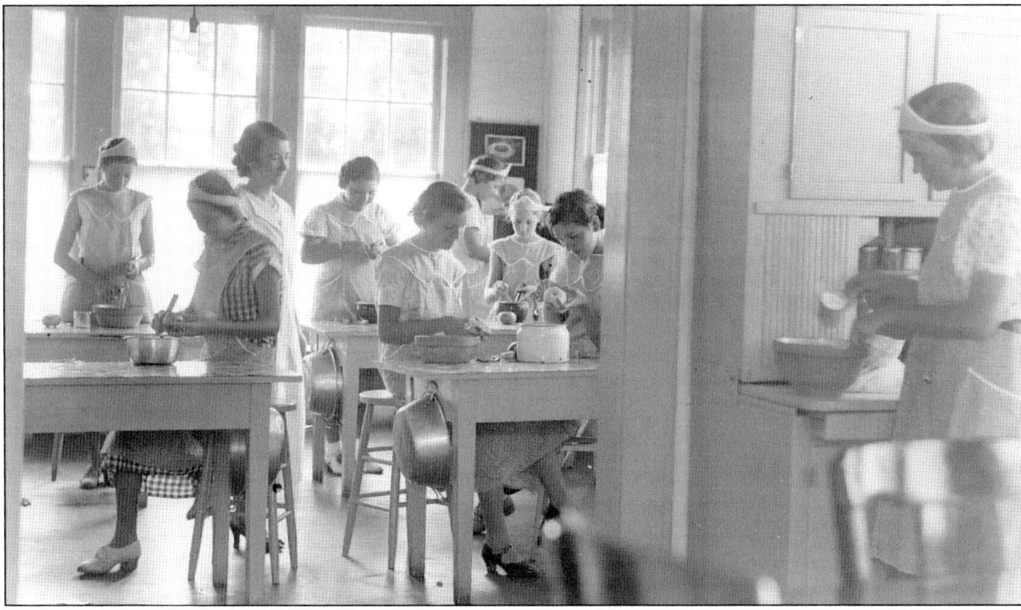

VOCATIONAL TRAINING, C. 1930. Mount Zion Seminary's last president, Estella Howard, was known as an ambitious fundraiser among church philanthropies in the East. Her efforts resulted in construction of a building for the Department of Home Economics, including a shop for furniture making. The girls appear to be coring and peeling apples, perhaps for baking pies. The photograph below shows furniture made by students in shop class. Estella Howard was able to get state money to support the elementary school program, while church money supported the high school during the economically depressed 1930s. She left the seminary in 1937 to work at a mission school in Puerto Rico. (Both, courtesy of Jack Dorsey.)

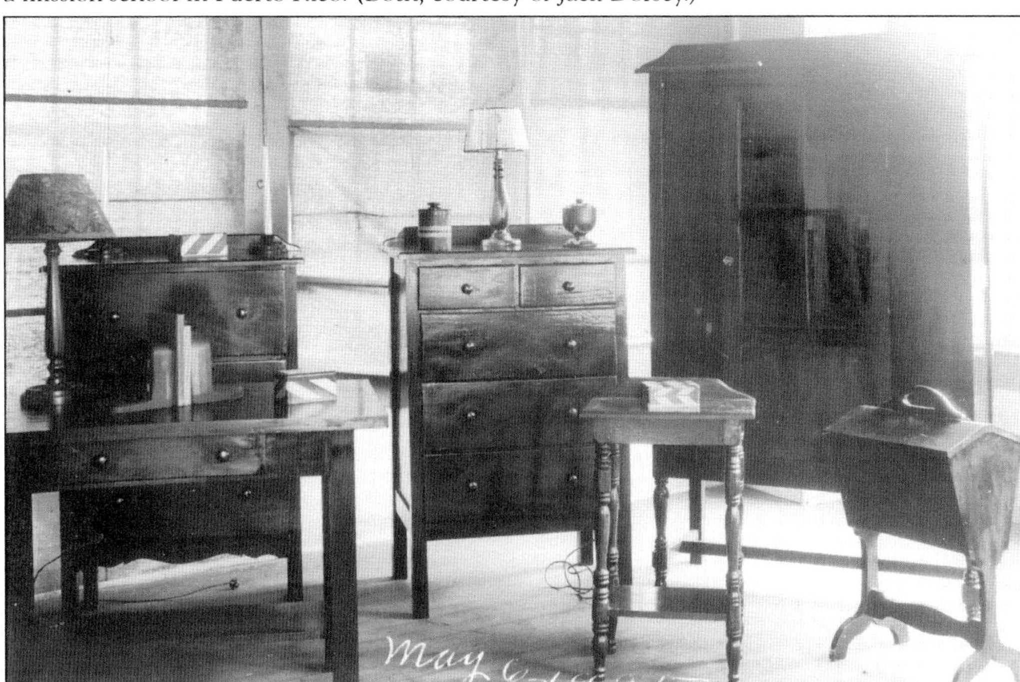

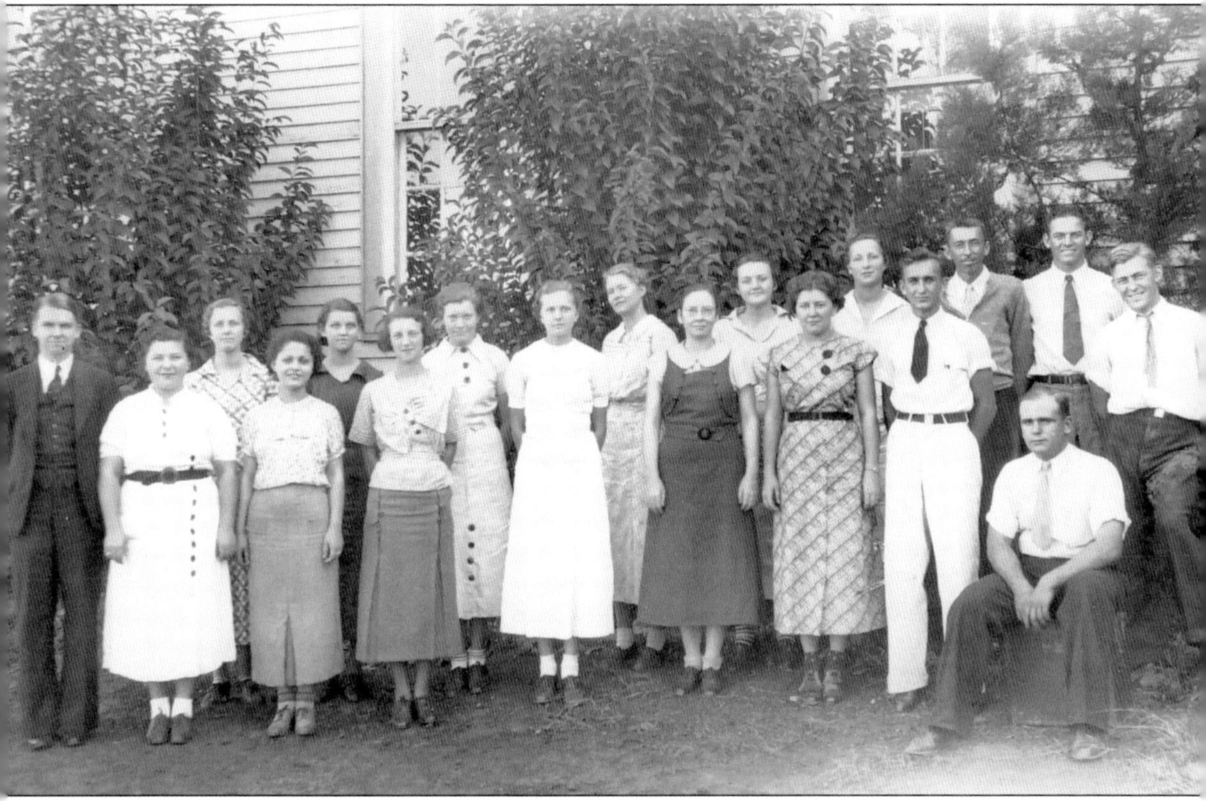

Glee Club, c. 1930. Members of the Glee Club are pictured on the seminary campus. The 1930s saw much discussion in the Methodist Church for reuniting the factions that formed over the issue of secession during the mid-19th century. The small church schools, such as Mount Zion's, were vulnerable to closure if the northern and southern Methodists came together. As church support for the Mount Zion Seminary dwindled, a local board was formed to represent the school in negotiations with the state and county school departments for relinquishing the campus. Representing the seminary were E.C. Dewey, N.N. Johnson, P.L. Shaefer, T.H. Shaw, C.W. Flint, C.A. Martin, H.F. Martin, W.C. McGarrity, W.R. Perkins, and Estella Howard, the last president of the school, who signed off on the deed that was dated September 1, 1939. (Courtesy of Jack Dorsey.)

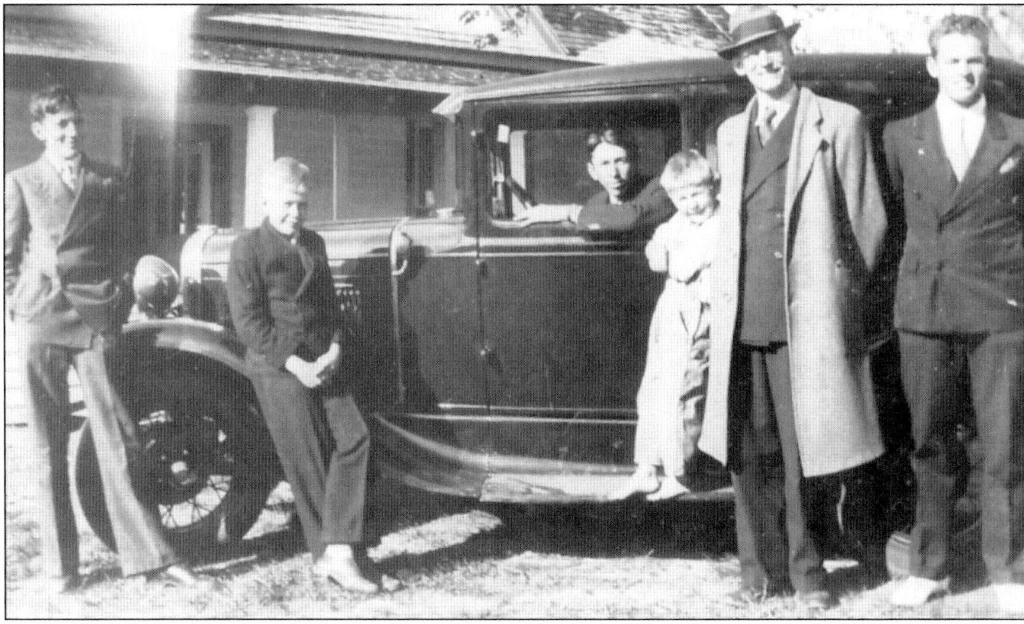

Dean Argelander, c. 1930. The dean poses with students during a decade that ended with the transfer of Mount Zion Seminary to the Carroll County school system. Dr. James Mitchell's dream of bringing education to all young people had come true with the seminary serving the region's youth for more than 60 years, until the state and county could provide them with public education. (Courtesy of Jack Dorsey.)

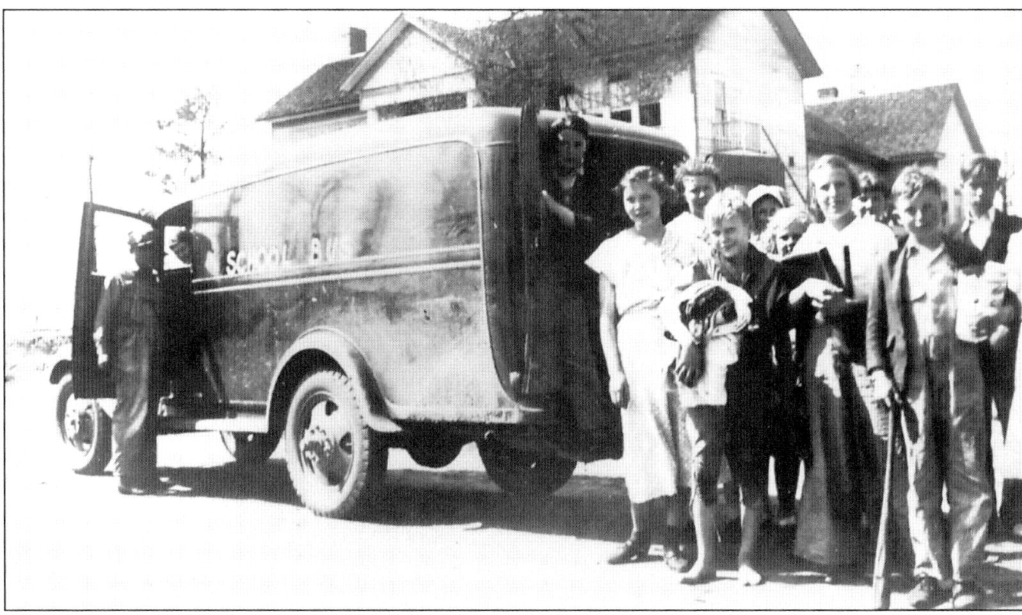

School Bus, c. 1930. Judging from the baseball bat and bundle of clothing, these students appear to be posing with picnic paraphernalia next to the Mount Zion school bus. The school's earliest school buses were actually covered wagons, which began transporting students in 1906 when most roads were still dirt. (Courtesy of Jack Dorsey.)

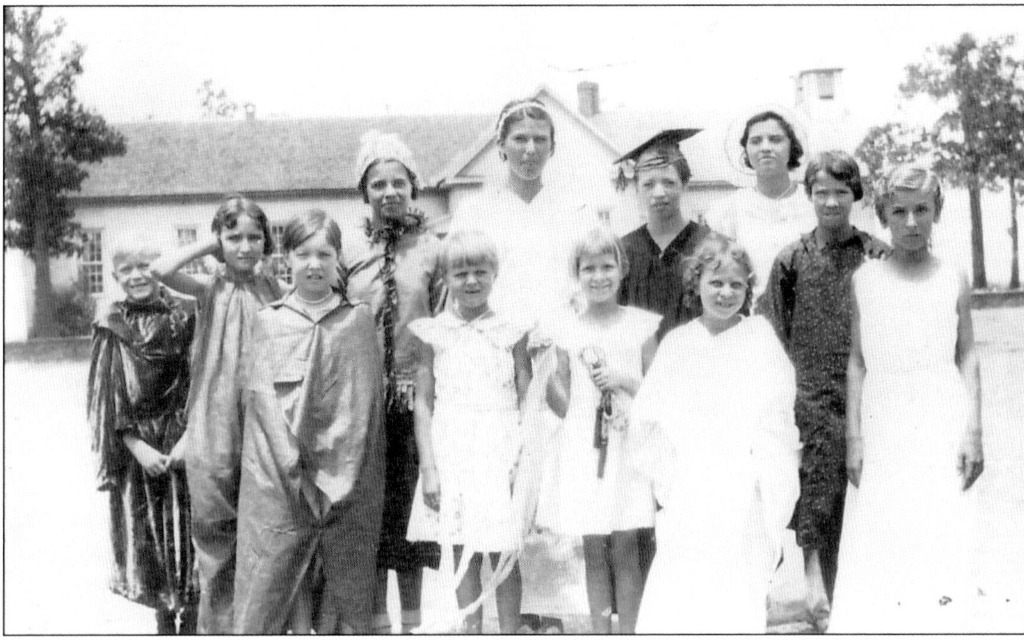

COSTUMED STUDENTS, C. 1930. These children pose in various costumes outside the Academic Building of the school. The seminary served children from Carroll and surrounding counties, as well as children from Alabama. The state line is only a few miles from Mount Zion. (Courtesy of Jack Dorsey.)

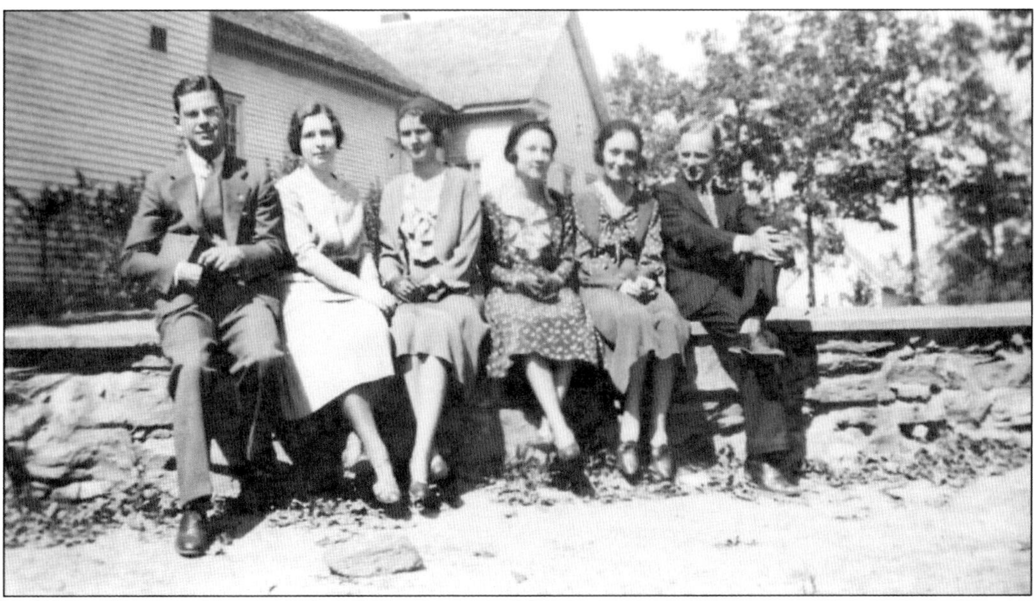

FACULTY, C. 1935. The Mount Zion Seminary faculty pose on a wall outside the Academic Building. From left to right are Joel Johnson, Sara Wilhelm, Marie Thrash, Gladys Shaw, Sara Kate Strickland, and Maynor Entrekin. By the 1930s, the state education department was recommending consolidation of county high schools. Small church schools such as Mount Zion were becoming obsolete. (Courtesy of Jack Dorsey.)

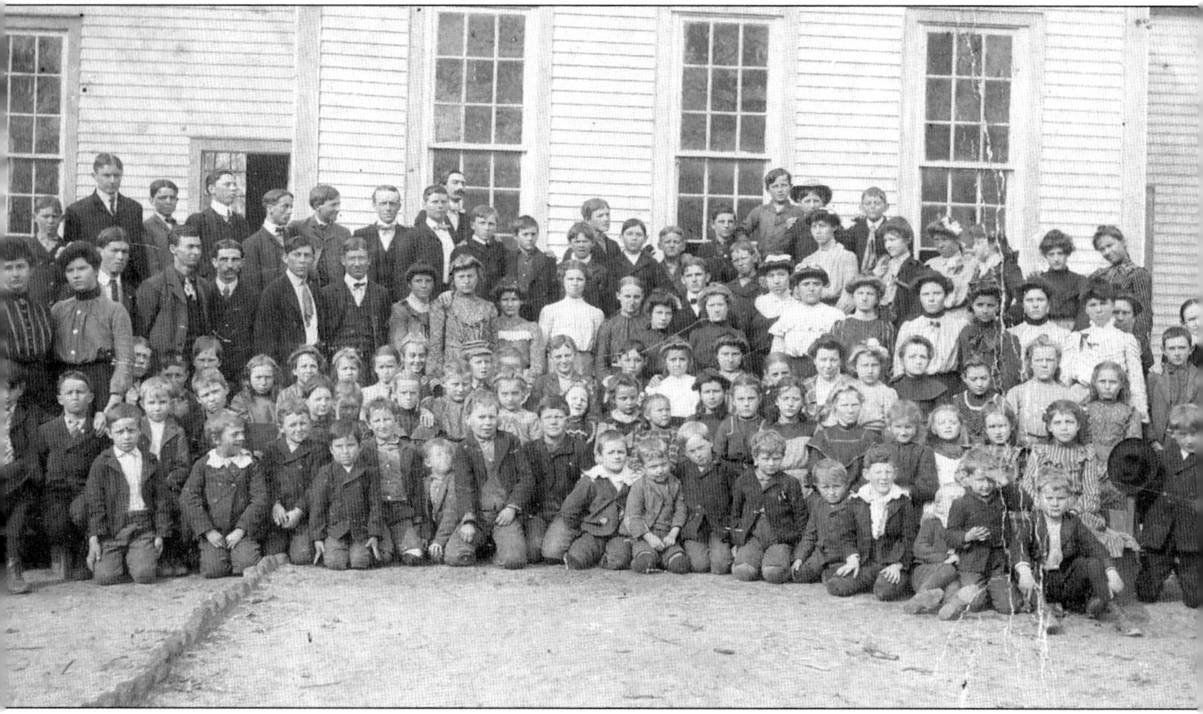

CLASS PHOTOGRAPH, 1900. The students of Mount Zion Seminary pose at the Academic Building about 20 years after the school opened. The ages of these children reflect the primary, normal, and college preparatory classes offered. At this time, brothers Perry and Mose Weston were coprincipals of the school, and had recruited a number of students from Alabama, whose state line was only a few miles from Mount Zion. Many students boarded in private homes at a cost of $6 per month. Founder Dr. James Mitchell died in 1903, not long after this photograph was taken. Over the years, he had bought up lots around the original campus; these were deeded to the school after his death. He also purchased a house adjacent to campus and had it refurbished into a president's home. It still stands today next to the community center, though it is not inhabited. (Courtesy of Jack Dorsey.)

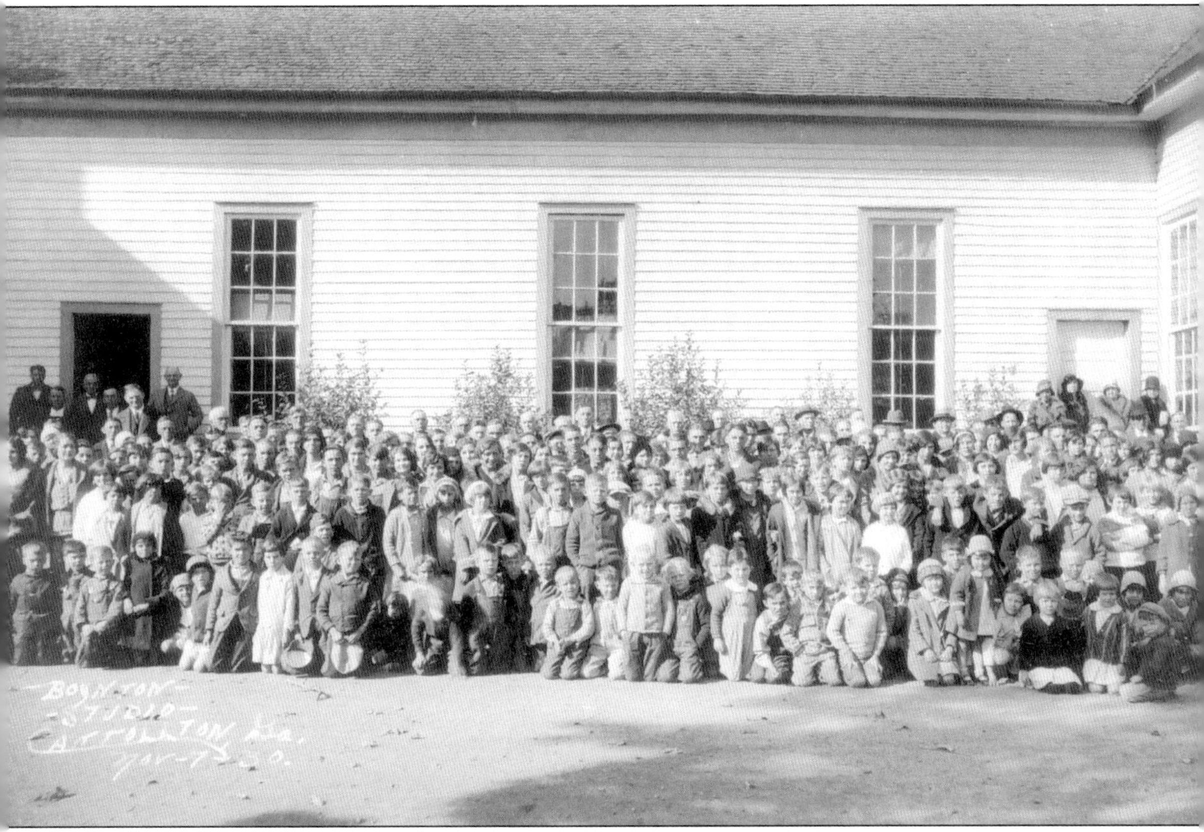

CLASS PHOTOGRAPH, 1930. In about the same setting, this class photograph was taken by the well-known Boynton Studio from Carrollton. Lee Trimble, a former student who would later become president of the school from 1917 until 1921, and then a well-known lawyer and banker, paid tribute to the school by saying, "I can testify as to how much the experience meant to me, the love of books, the ability to write, to read and the inculcation of a deep appreciation for the finer things of life." Under Dr. James Mitchell's presence, the school maintained a distinct religious atmosphere. Many of the older students at Mount Zion were already teachers needing the short course that would help them pass the state teachers exam. When Mount Zion was deeded to the public school system, county high schools were consolidated. Improved roads, shifting population centers, and better transportation allowed students to travel farther for high school education. (Courtesy of Jack Dorsey.)

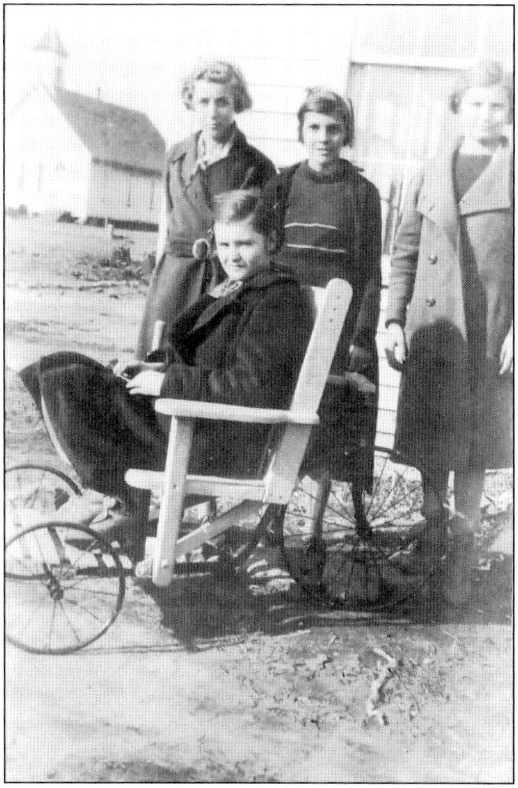

WHEELCHAIR MADE IN SHOP, 1935. Faith Murphy is shown seated in a crude wheelchair made by the shop class. Standing are, from left to right, Sarah Shaw, Ruth Phillips, and an unidentified girl. In the background is the Mount Zion Methodist Church, which includes the cemetery where Dr. Mitchell is buried. The church was a log cabin when Dr. Mitchell first came to preach. (Courtesy of Jack Dorsey.)

STUDENT AND TEACHER, C. 1925. Pictured is a student being taught how to curtsy by one of her seminary teachers. A widower, James Mitchell lived out his life in Mount Zion, bringing his nephew's family and other relatives from Illinois to live there. Their influence was said to have changed the students' speech patterns, so a Mount Zion graduate could be recognized by his Midwestern accent. (Courtesy of Jack Dorsey.)

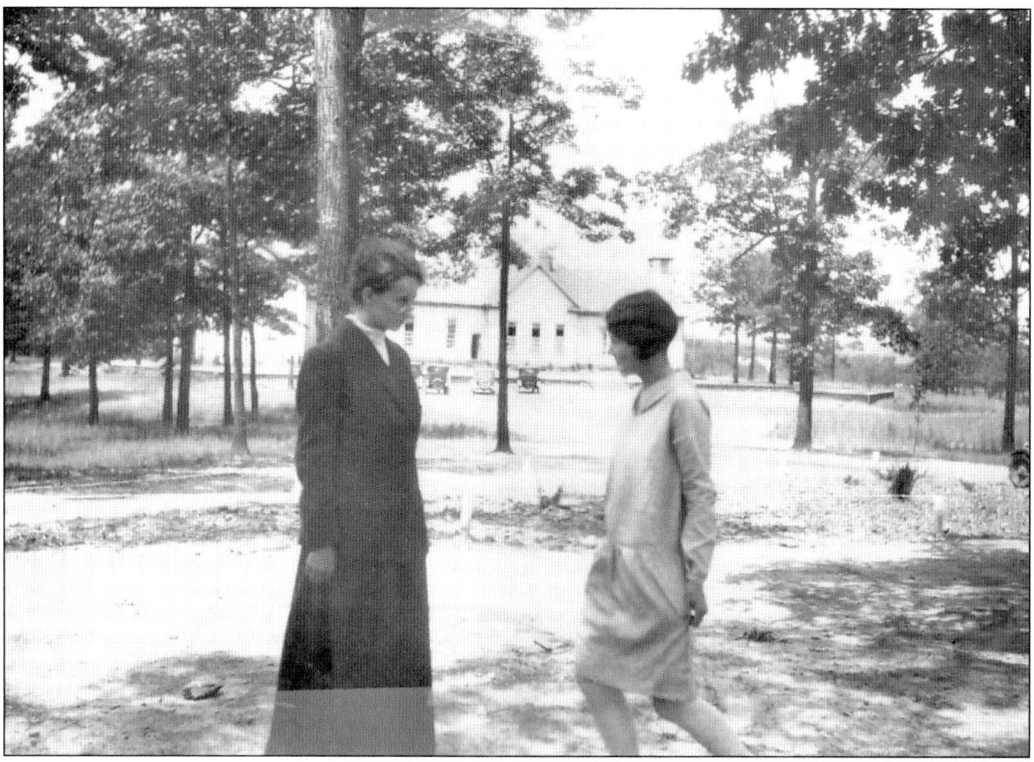

Seven

THE A&M SCHOOL

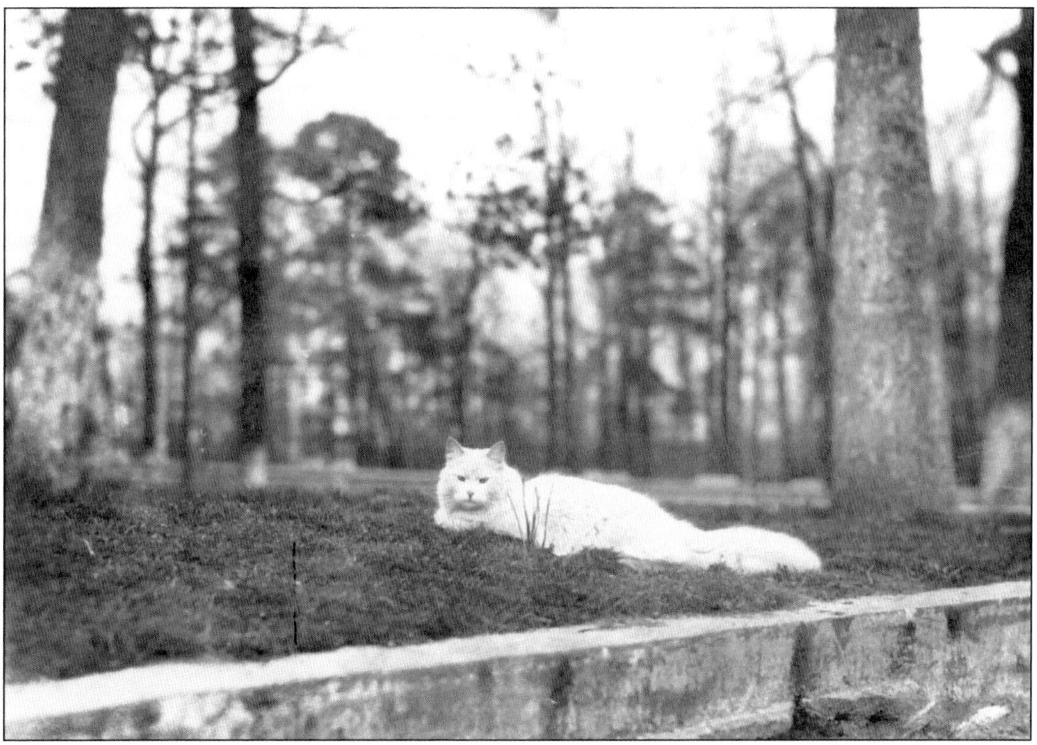

GEORGY PORGY, 1928. The original campus cat belonged to Irvine S. Ingram, the second principal of the Fourth District A&M School. Ingram, who was later named the first president of West Georgia College, was a cat lover all his life. Today, the campus has an active trap-neuter-release program for its wild felines. (Courtesy of UWG Special Collections.)

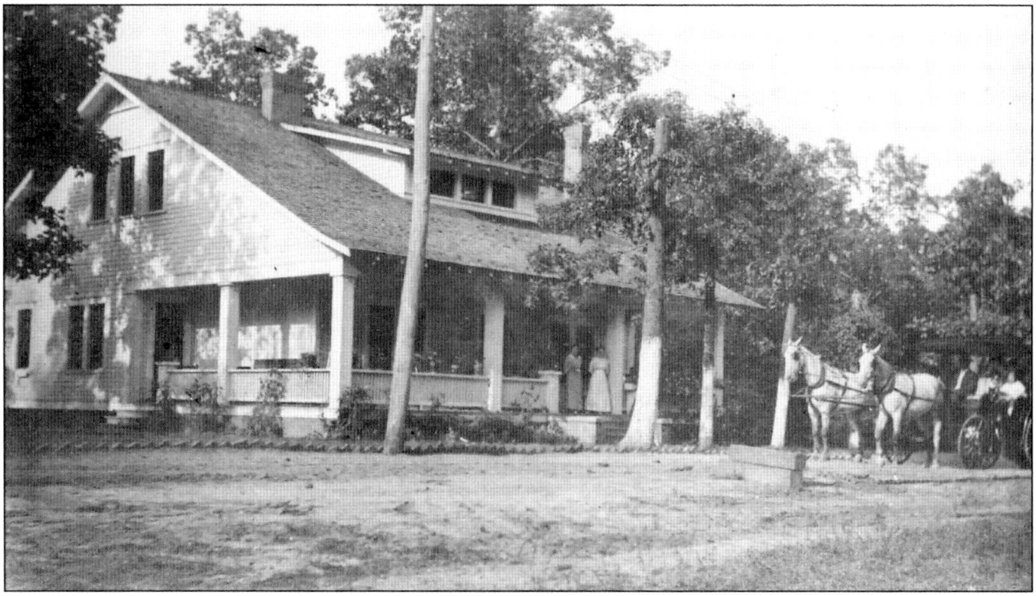

PRESIDENT'S HOME, 1912. This house was constructed for the first principal of the A&M school, John H. Melson. Its original location was in the vicinity of Cobb Hall. It was moved to its current site on the corner of Maple Street and West Georgia Drive in the 1950s, and today, it is the Honors House. (Courtesy of UWG Special Collections.)

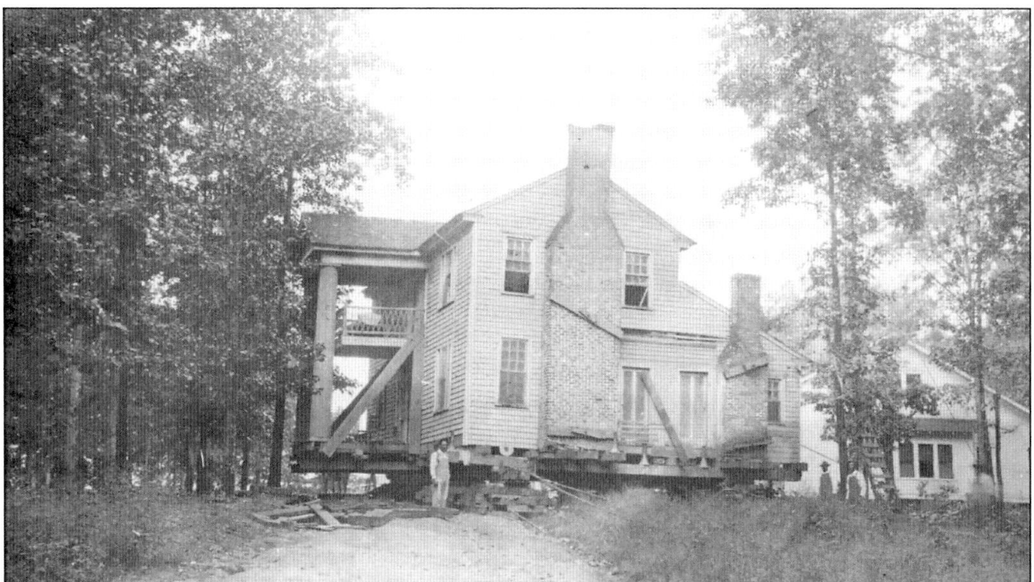

MOVING THE BONNER HOUSE, 1913. This was the 1840s home of cotton planter Thomas Bonner. It originally stood on the knoll between Maple Street and Adamson Hall, but was moved to its current location after the A&M school was organized. It has served many functions over the years. Today, it houses the student services offices. (Courtesy of UWG Special Collections.)

CHILDREN OF THE FACULTY, c. 1915. These youngsters' fathers were teachers at the A&M school. Pictured are, from left to right, Frank Melson, whose father was the principal; Evelyn Causey, whose father taught vocational agriculture; and John Amos Stephens, whose father, Amos Stephens, also taught farming. (Courtesy of UWG Special Collections.)

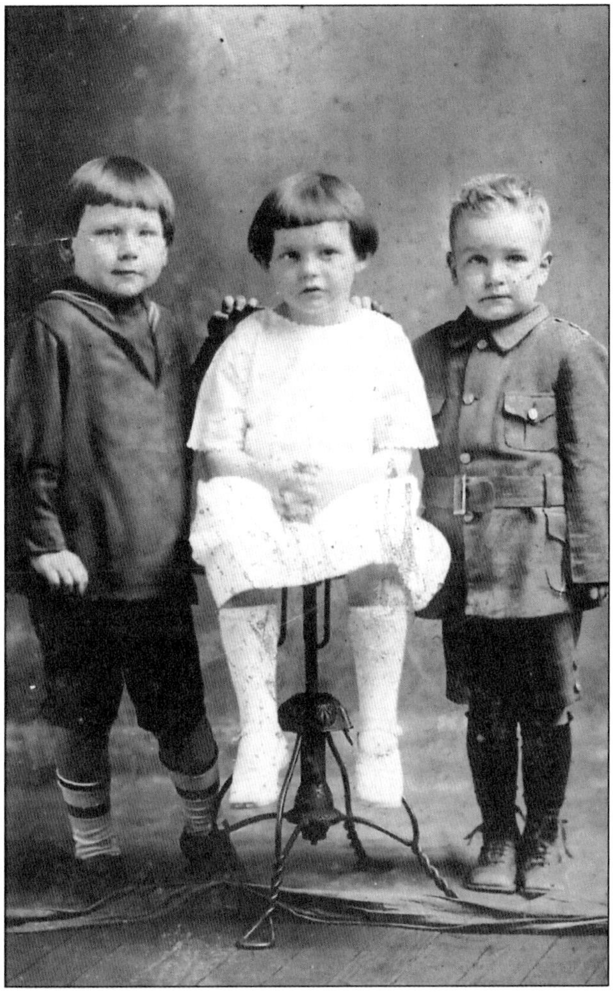

COMMENCEMENT, 1914. The Administration Building can be seen along the front campus drive. In 1907, it was the first building erected for the A&M school along with a boys' dormitory, now called Melson Hall. A shop building with dining hall and kitchen was built in 1908 behind the Administration Building. (Courtesy of UWG Special Collections.)

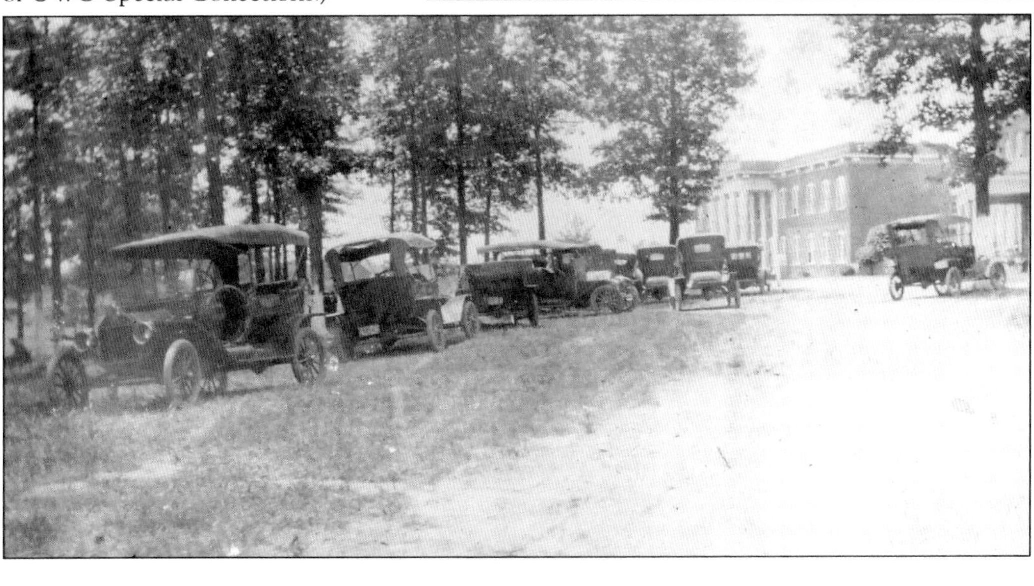

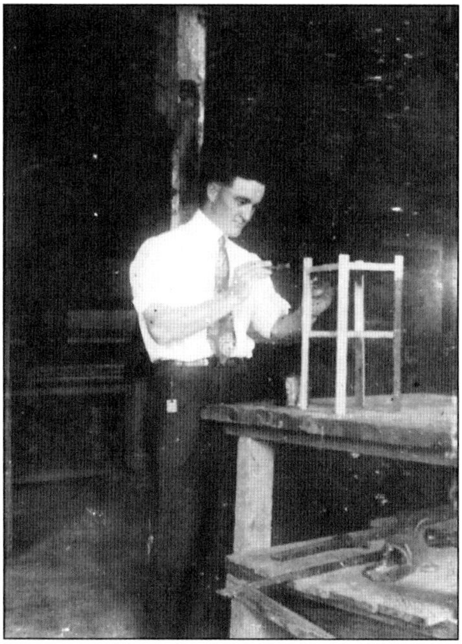

Shop Class, c. 1912. Woodfin "Hall" Carmical is shown working on a piece of furniture in shop class. The A&M schools in Georgia were created along congressional district lines to offer a secondary education with farming, mechanical, and domestic science training. Carroll and Muscogee Counties competed for the location of the Fourth District school, but Carroll offered the most in terms of modern amenities and a large rural population needing the agricultural and vocational coursework. (Courtesy of UWG Special Collections.)

Coeds, c. 1914. Five young women are posing during a rare snow in front of the Administration Building. They are, from left to right, M. Bolus, M. Robison, R. Remeaux, E. Crewes, and A. Jenkins. Vocational training for women included sewing and cooking under the subject of Domestic Science. (Courtesy of UWG Special Collections.)

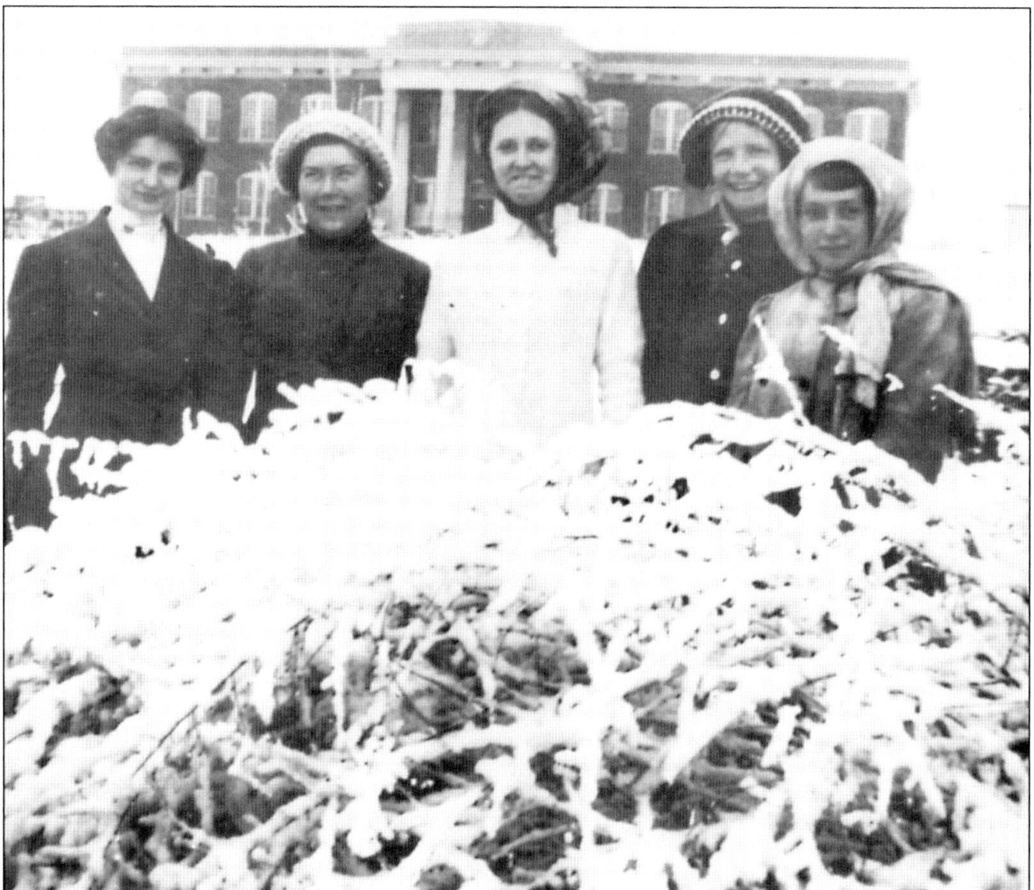

Painting the Boys' Dorm, 1911. All students had to contribute to the maintenance and upkeep of the A&M campus. While academic subjects were taught, students got a heavy dose of vocational training. Painting what is now Melson Hall are students Henry Cleveland (left) and Woodfin "Hall" Carmical. (Courtesy of UWG Special Collections.)

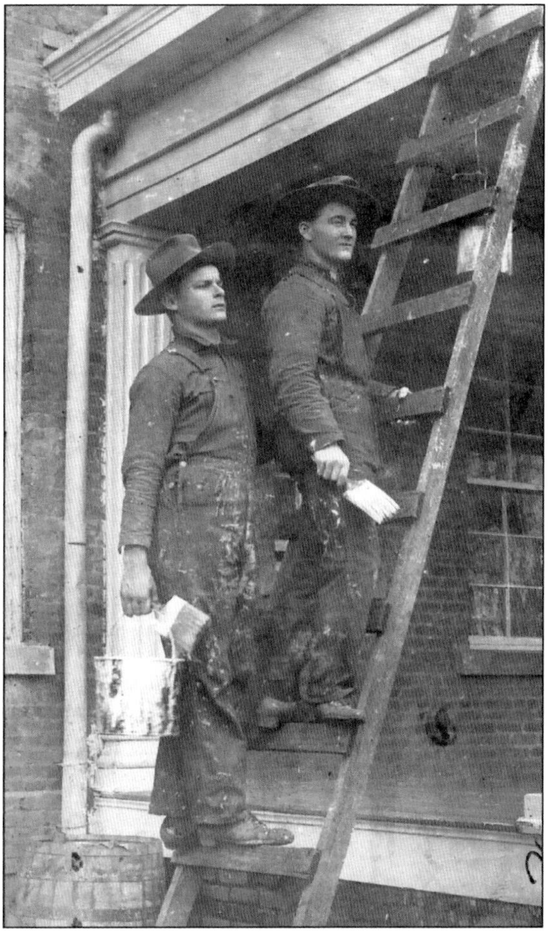

A&M Fair, 1914. Begun in 1909, the annual A&M Fair was originally meant to showcase the work of the students. Over the next 10 years, it took on more of a carnival atmosphere until it was relocated and operated as a county event. The girl in the black hat is Gertrude Hamrick, and Woodfin "Hall" Carmical is second from right. (Courtesy of UWG Special Collections.)

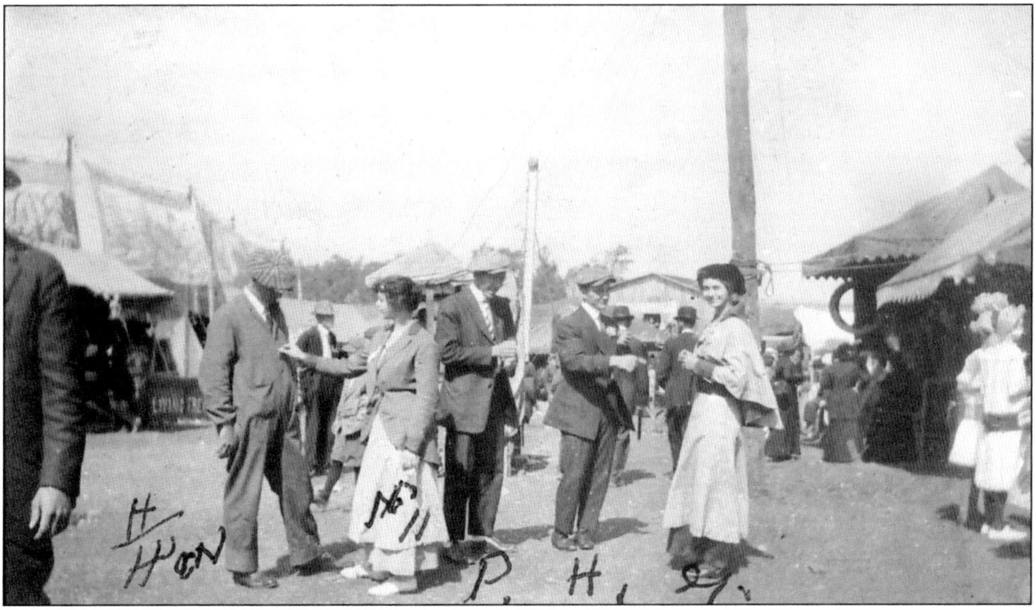

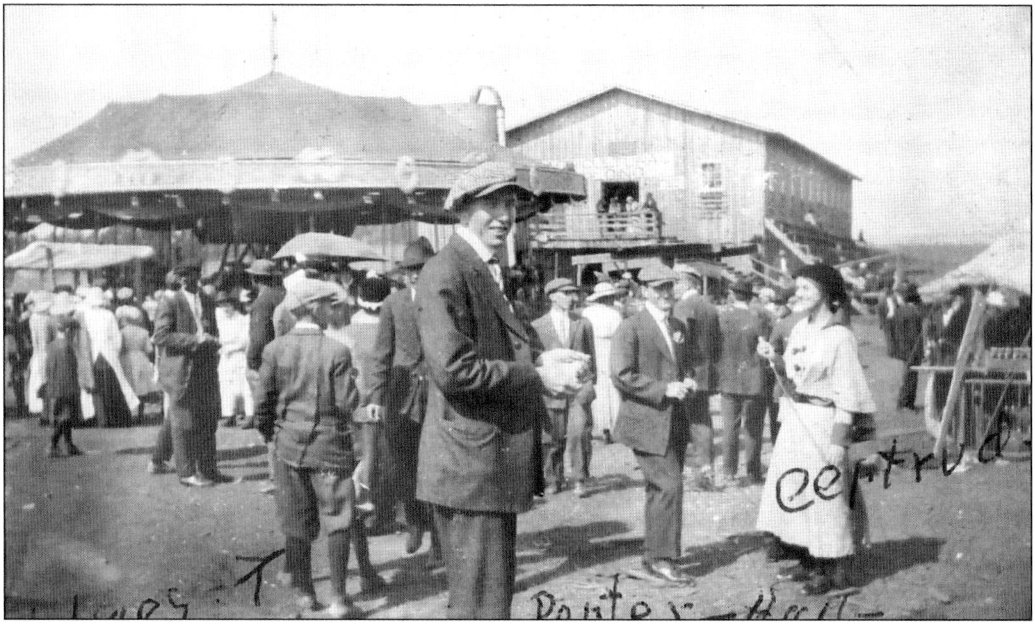

MIDWAY AT A&M FAIR, 1914. The fair was held at the back of campus near the cow barn, which stood about where the library is today. It included a track, with grandstands, which hosted horse races. It was a community event and featured Governors Day, drawing thousands of visitors from around the county. (Courtesy of UWG Special Collections.)

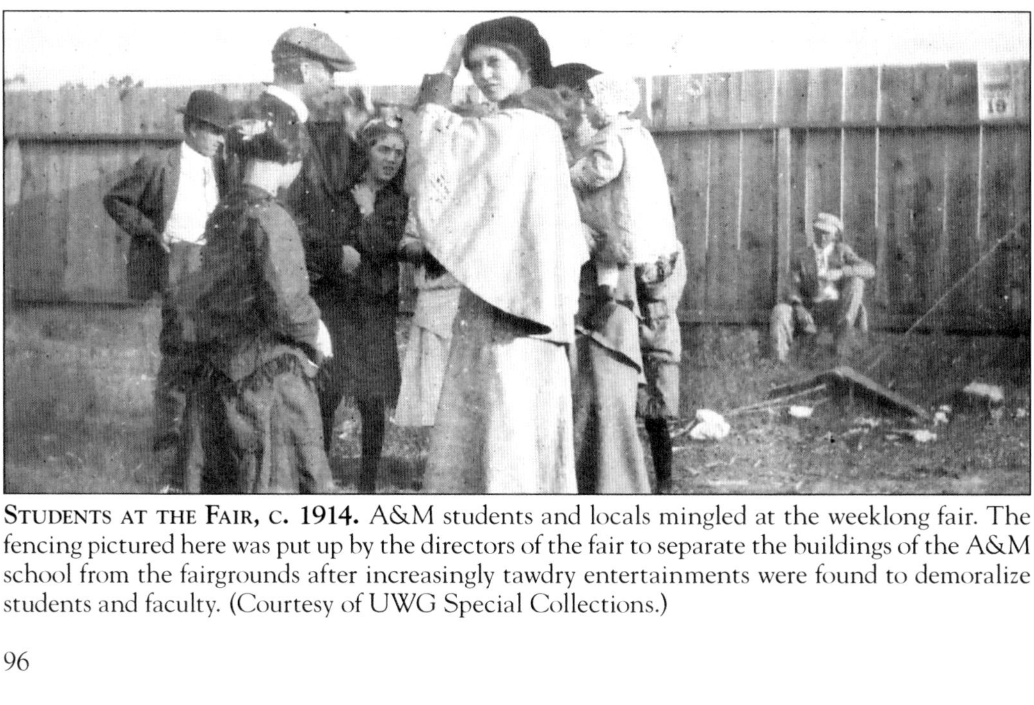

STUDENTS AT THE FAIR, C. 1914. A&M students and locals mingled at the weeklong fair. The fencing pictured here was put up by the directors of the fair to separate the buildings of the A&M school from the fairgrounds after increasingly tawdry entertainments were found to demoralize students and faculty. (Courtesy of UWG Special Collections.)

SHOP TEACHER, 1915. Woodfin "Hall" Carmical of Newnan, Georgia, was first a student and then a teacher at the Fourth District A&M School. He graduated in 1914 and was hired as a shop teacher the next year. He served in World War I and returned to Carrollton to teach for two more years. (Courtesy of UWG Special Collections.)

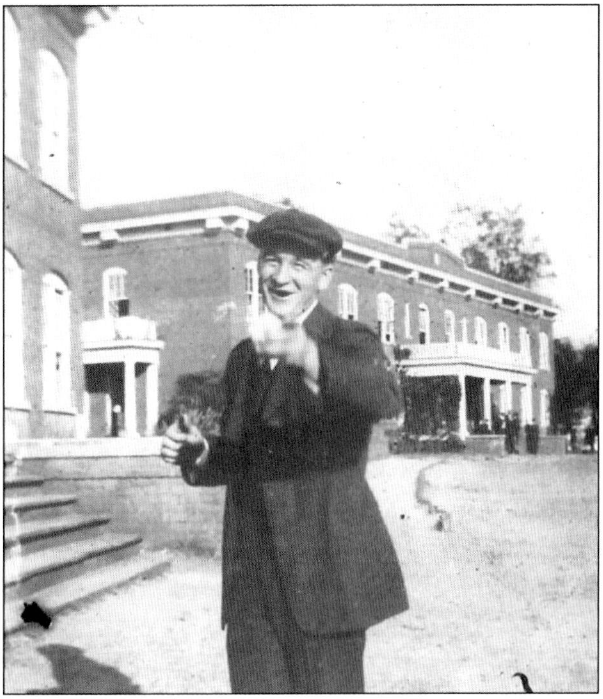

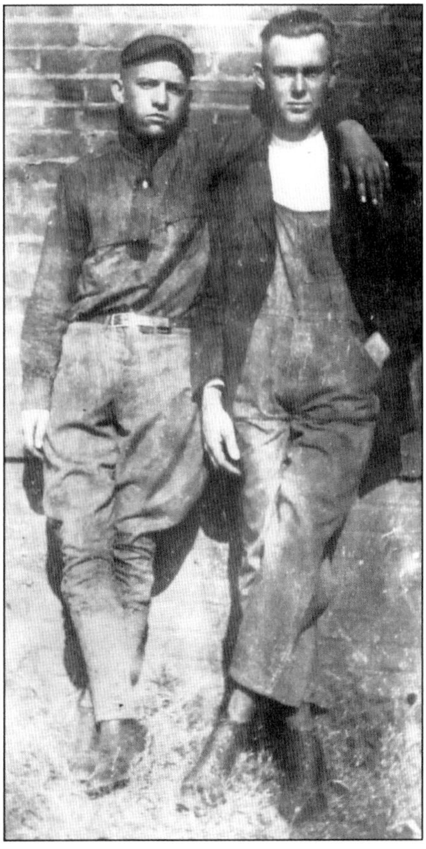

RURAL YOUTH TURNED STUDENTS, C. 1914. Early enrollees of the Fourth District A&M School were mostly boys and young men from outlying farms. They were taught scientific farming methods and performed manual labor as part of their education on the campus, which was as much a cotton, hog, and chicken farm as it was an academy. (Courtesy of UWG Special Collections.)

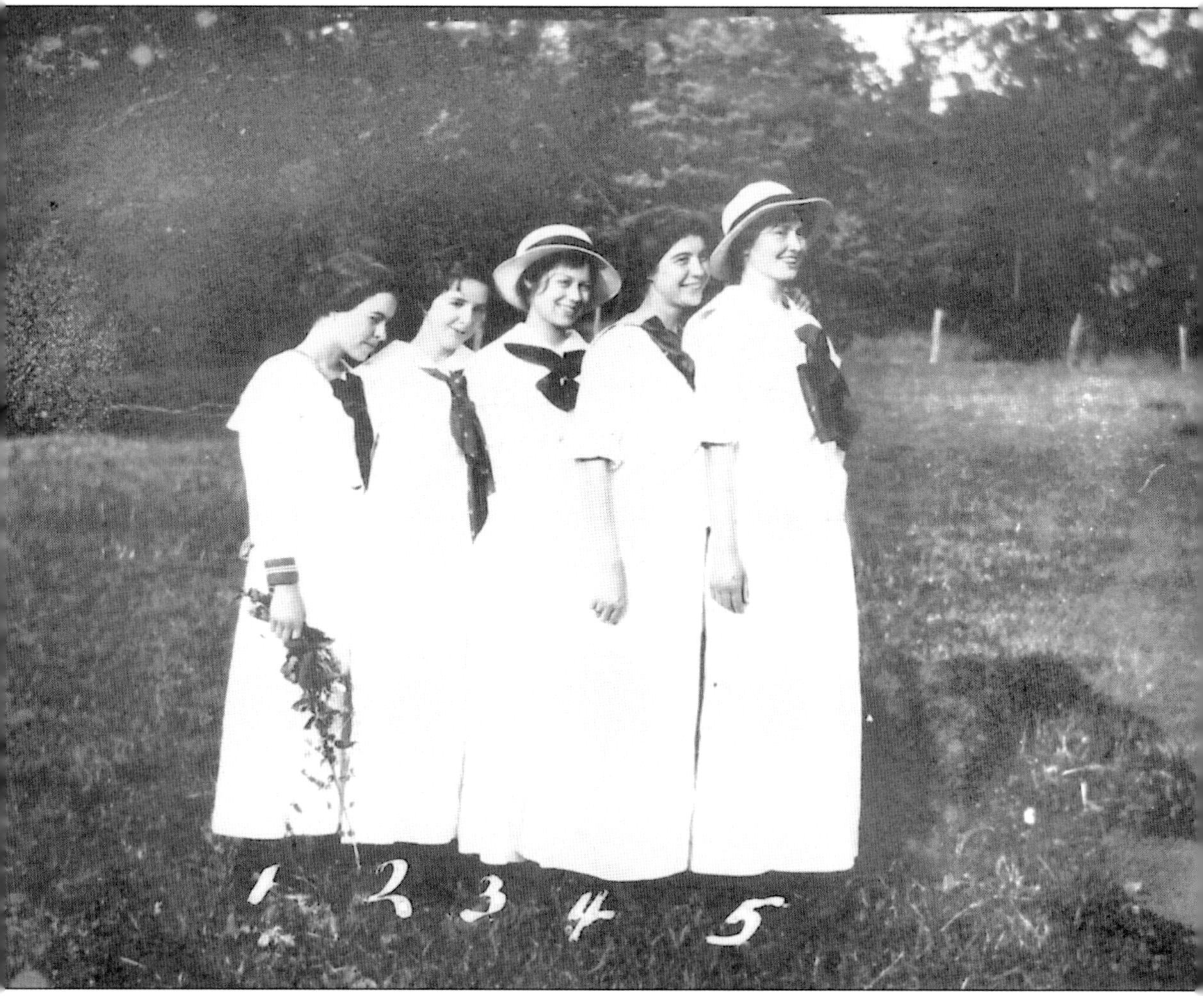

Senior Girls, 1915. Pictured from left to right are Ethel Nixon, Dora Lou Foster, Laura Turner, Jessie Henry, and Ruth Crain. According to the 1916 bulletin, Nixon and Henry became farm superintendents, Turner was a florist, and Crain was a teacher in Hogansville, Georgia. The original school principal, John H. Melson, wanted to limit the number of girls enrolled until a dorm could be constructed, but the A&M school did not get a girls' dormitory until 1916. Adamson Hall was that building, and it still stands on the front campus. It is named for Carrollton lawyer and US congressman W.C. Adamson, who contributed $1,500 towards its construction. The square in downtown Carrollton was also named for him. Before Adamson Hall, female students either boarded locally, or the few who did not live nearby stayed in the Bonner House. (Courtesy of UWG Special Collections.)

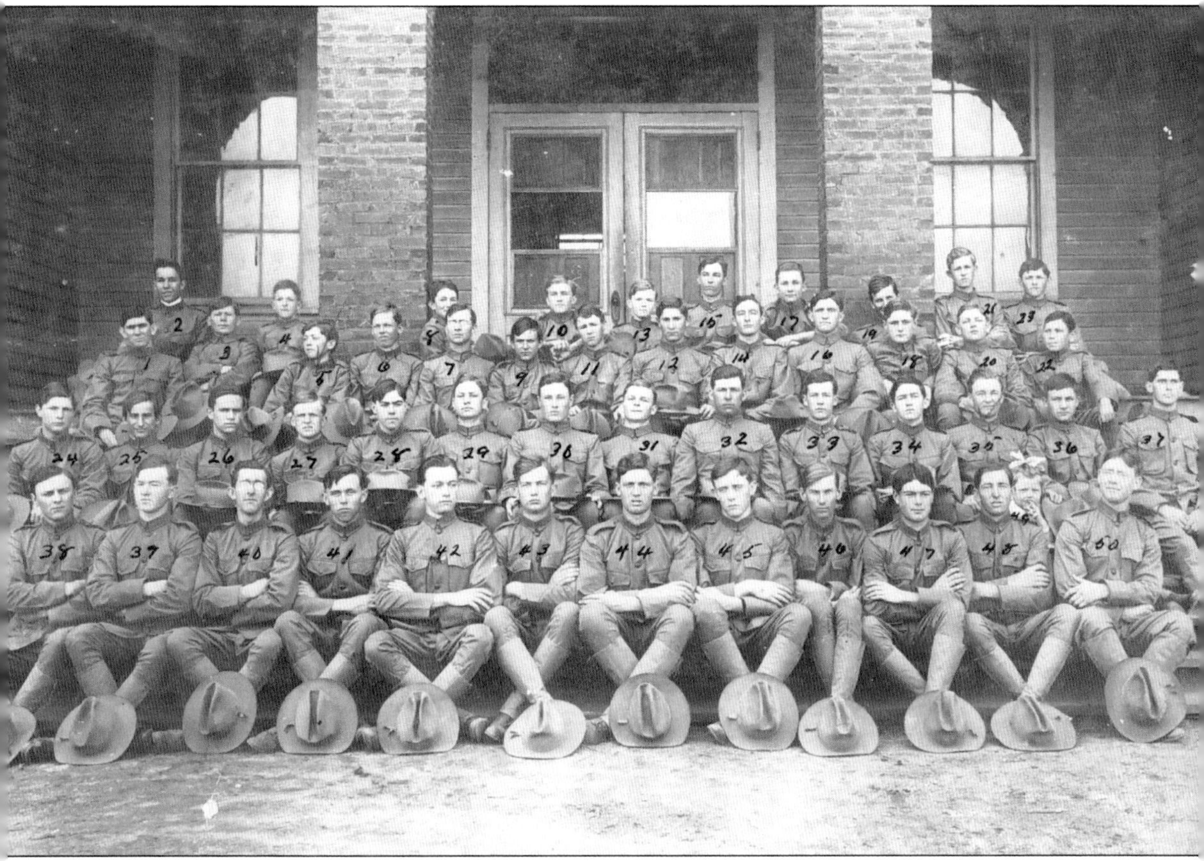

STUDENT UNIFORMS, C. 1911. For a short time, A&M boys adopted a military-style uniform with felt hats and canvas leggings, as shown in this photograph. It was intended to give the students a distinctiveness not unlike a private military school; however, the uniforms proved impractical for the farm and manual labor activities in which students engaged. The A&M school produced a number of accomplished professionals. Charles Fitts would become a Carrollton physician, Reese Adamson would be an executive of the Ford Motor Company in Birmingham, and Lee Wyatt was later a presiding justice of the Georgia Supreme Court. James C. Bonner was an early student who later taught history when the school became West Georgia College. He went on to teach at Randolph-Macon College, in Virginia, and at Georgia College in Milledgeville. (Courtesy of UWG Special Collections.)

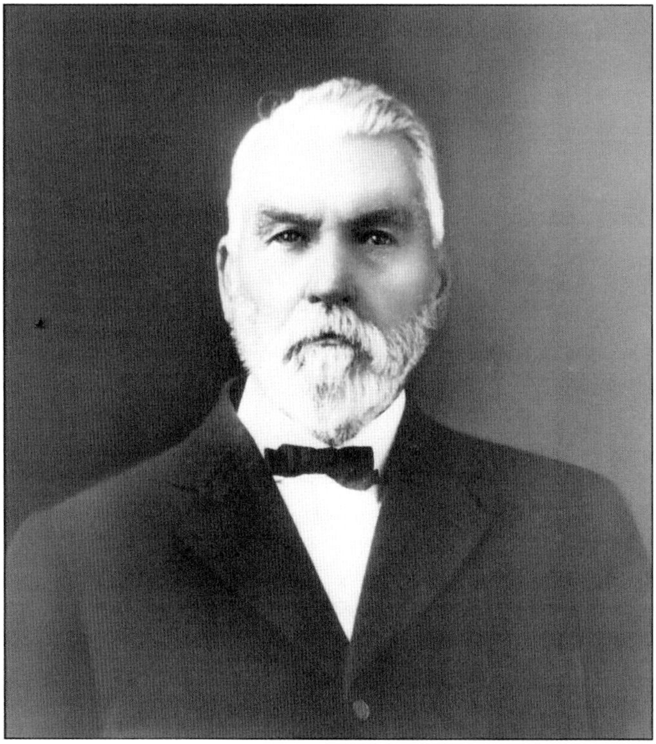

Bluford A. Sharp. The last owner of the farm property before it was sold to the A&M school in 1907, Sharp farmed there for about 20 years. A literary club was formed at Sharp's residence in 1891, giving rise to a community dubbed the West End, which at the time was outside the Carrollton city limits. (Courtesy of UWG Special Collections.)

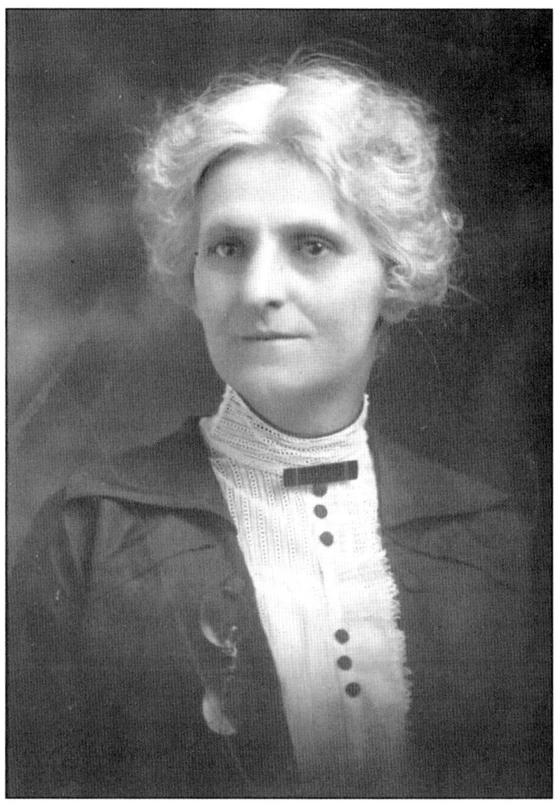

Laura Josephine Rozar, c. 1914. Teaching history and English for nine years, Laura Josephine Rozar was one of the first faculty members at the A&M school. She had taught Latin earlier, at the Temple Model School in Carroll County. A&M student Woodfin "Hall" Carmical called her an "anchor of my life." (Courtesy of UWG Special Collections.)

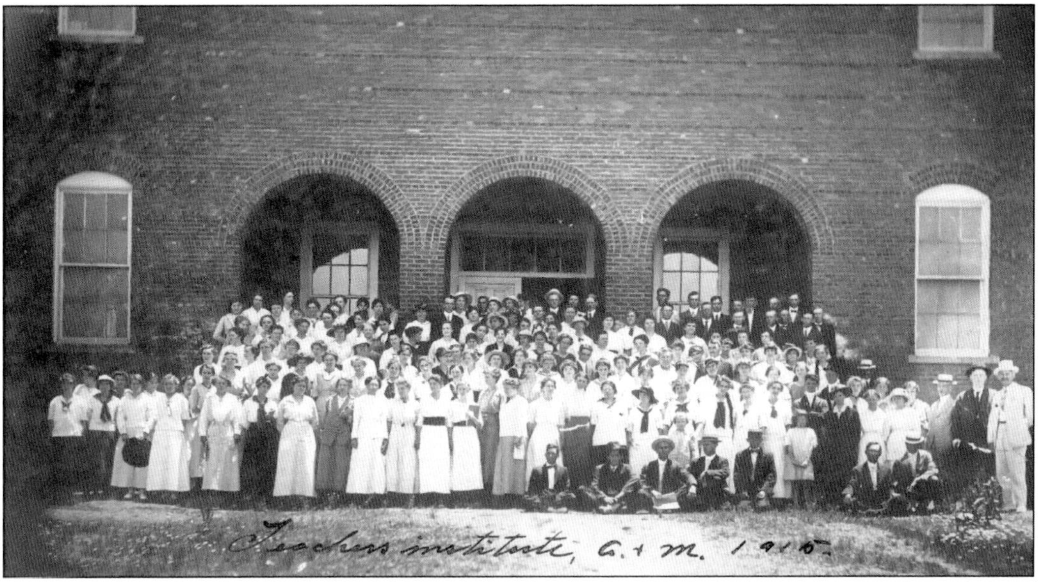

FIRST TEACHERS' INSTITUTE, 1915. The state's department of education sponsored the first of many annual teacher institutes at the A&M school. The two-week training drew 200 teachers who wanted to upgrade their teaching licenses. Later, it would develop into a six-week summer school so teachers could get their certification without interrupting the school year. (Courtesy of UWG Special Collections.)

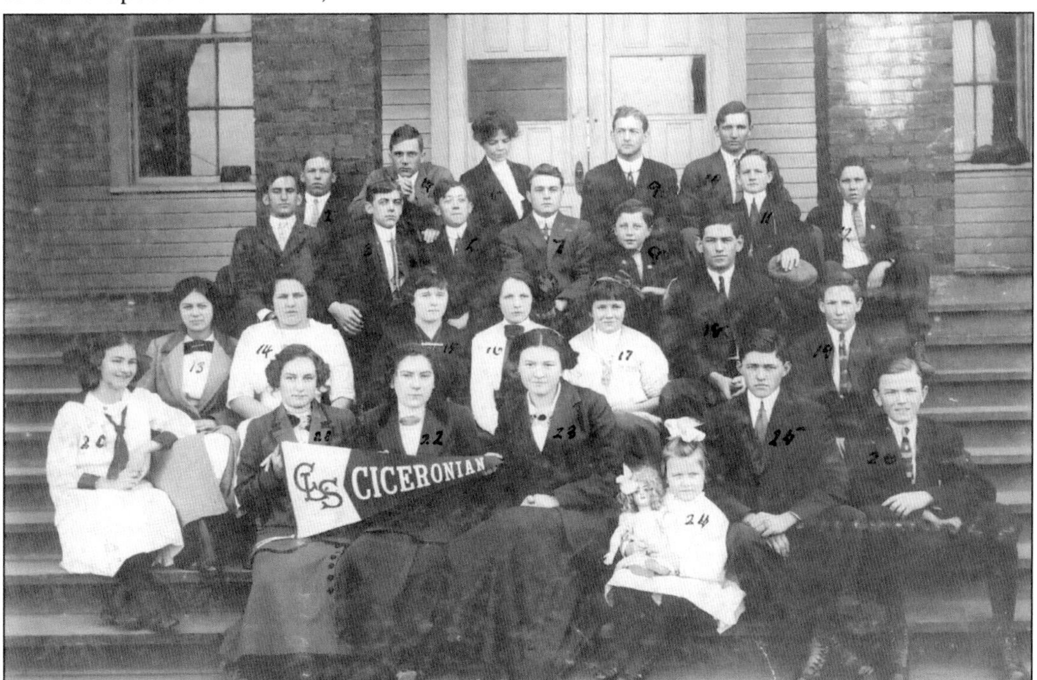

CICERONIAN LITERARY SOCIETY, C. 1910. The school sponsored two literary societies, and every student was required to join one. They met on Saturdays for debates, readings, and songs. Martha Melson, daughter of principal J.H. Melson, is holding her doll in the first row of this photograph. (Courtesy of UWG Special Collections.)

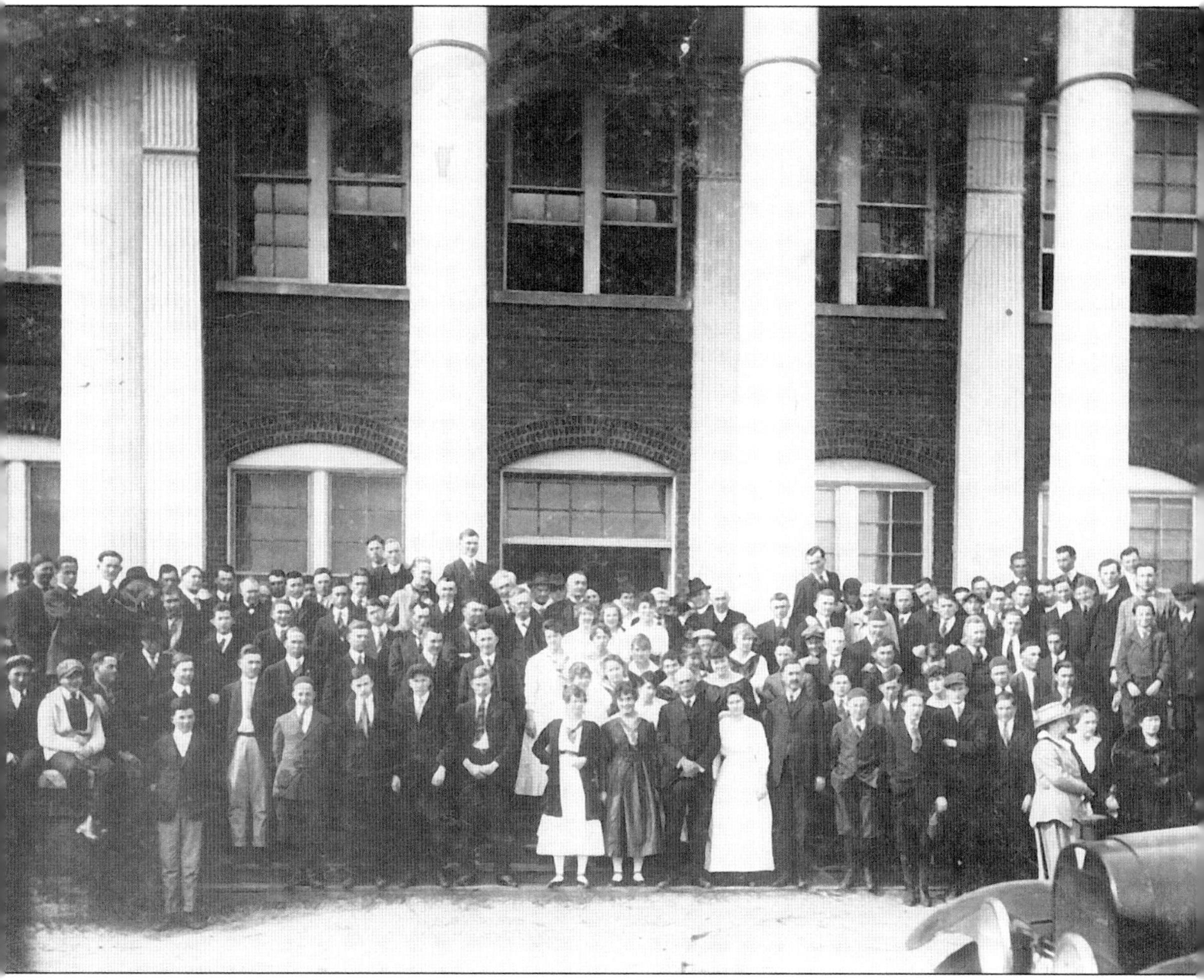

STUDENTS, FACULTY, AND TRUSTEES, 1917. This photograph was taken on the steps of the Administration Building. During that year, the girls' dormitory was dedicated, perhaps the occasion for this photograph. The dorm was named Adamson Hall, for US congressman W.C. Adamson, and stands at the site of the entrance to the old A&M fairgrounds. In 1917, the A&M school graduated 15 students. Many more students attended the school than actually graduated. Due to the looming war in Europe, military training was made part of the curriculum in 1917 and 1918, and both students and faculty enlisted. The war department supplied Springfield rifles from the Spanish-American War, and a firing range near Hay's Mill was used for rifle practice. The school's service flag contained 160 stars by the end of World War I. (Courtesy of UWG Special Collections.)

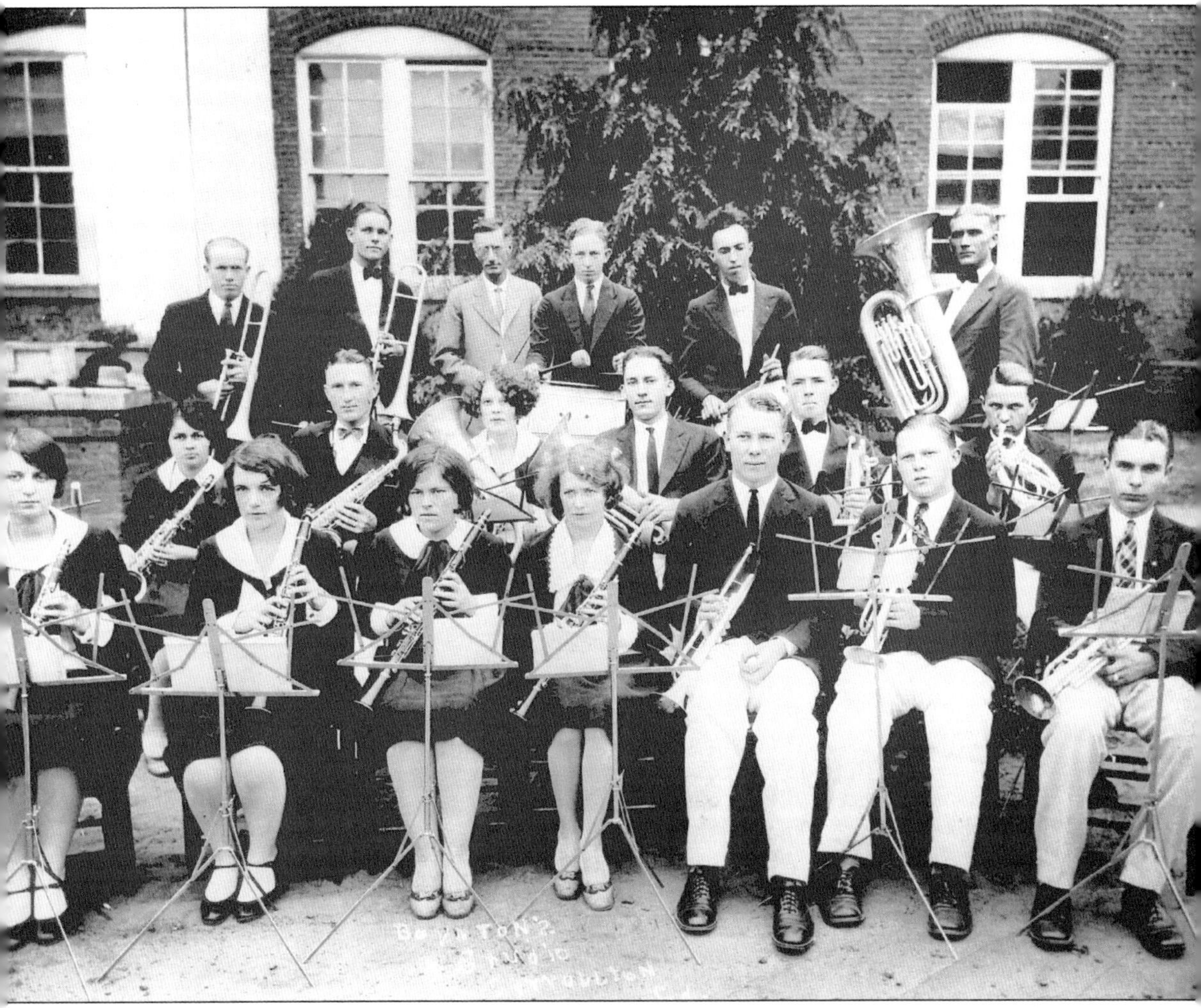

A&M Band, c. 1927. The school organized a band in the mid-1920s, with instruments being furnished to the students. They were required to pay $2 per month and were expected to complete a full year of playing. During the 1920s, the A&M school adjusted its programs to counteract the economic devastation of the destructive boll weevil on cotton. It operated a successful poultry hatchery and developed purebred livestock to upgrade herds in the local area. The school instituted adult education programs and offered secretarial training to students. By 1930, the A&M school was taking in students from several Carroll County communities, with the county paying their transportation costs. The increase in enrollments in accredited Georgia high schools was drastic between 1905 and 1915: from 420 students to nearly 13,000. By 1930, the number of students attending accredited high schools was close to 60,000. This was due in large part to the creation of the A&M schools. (Courtesy of UWG Special Collections.)

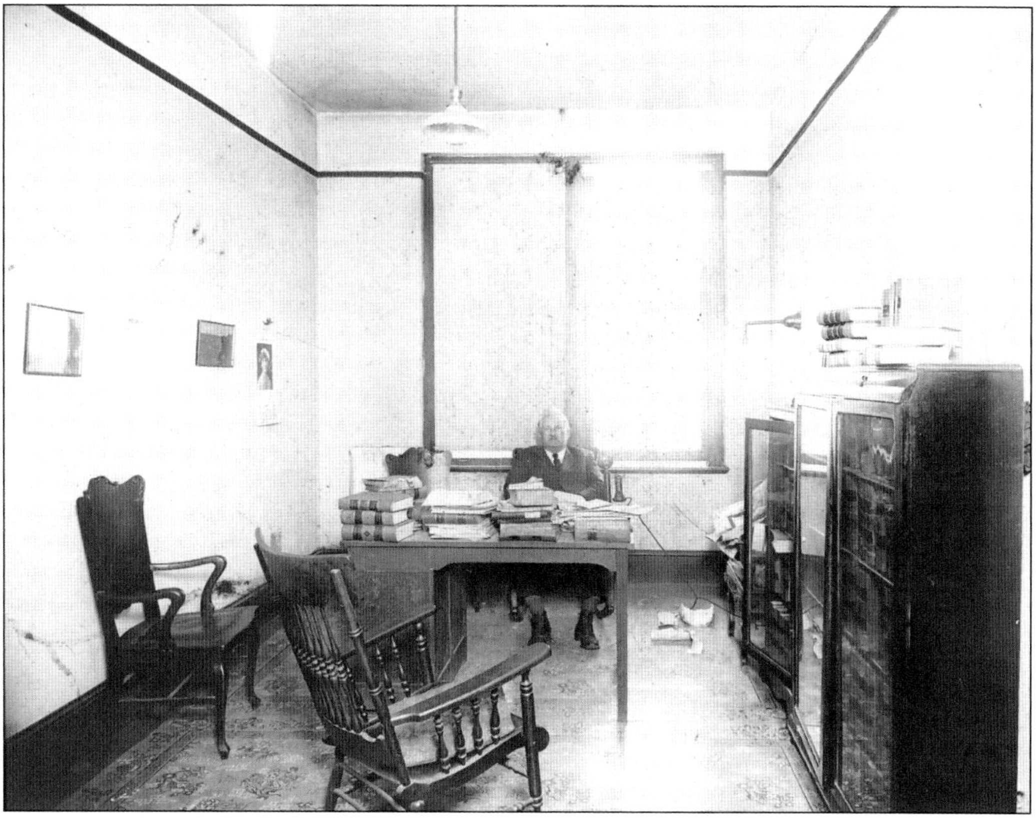

TRUSTEE GEORGE P. MUNRO, C. 1925. Munro was a judge and chairman of the A&M school's board of trustees. He is pictured in his Columbus, Georgia, law office. His daughter Martha came to teach at the A&M school in 1919, where she would meet and marry Irvine S. Ingram. She died of cancer in 1954, and the Rural Arts Building was renamed in her memory. (Courtesy of UWG Special Collections.)

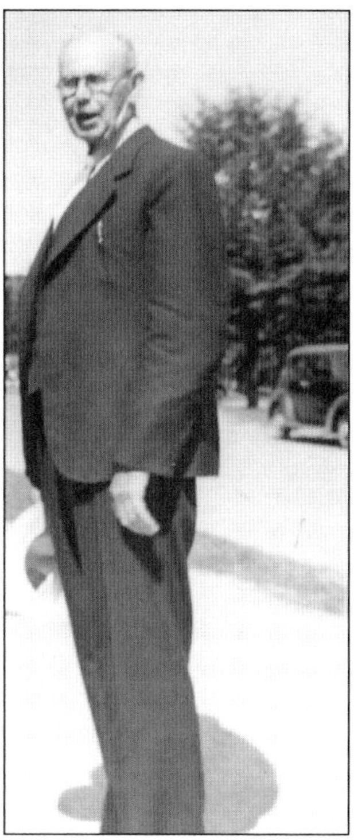

PRINCIPAL JOHN H. MELSON, C. 1940. The first principal of the Fourth District A&M School is pictured here at a school reunion. He served from 1907 until 1920, when he moved to Hogansville, Georgia. The original boys' dormitory, built in 1907, was named for Melson and still stands on front campus. (Courtesy of UWG Special Collections.)

Eight

A College and a County

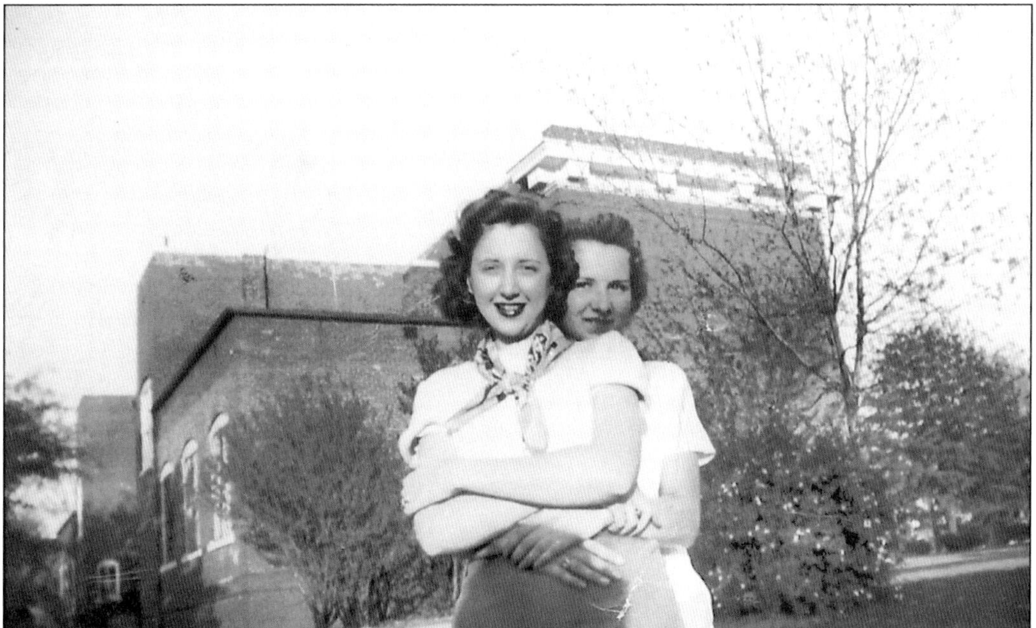

Coeds at West Georgia College, c. 1945. Posed behind the Administration Building on the West Georgia College campus, these young women are more than likely studying to be teachers. The college was originally charged with providing a junior college general education, and also with training badly needed elementary schoolteachers. (Courtesy of UWG Special Collections.)

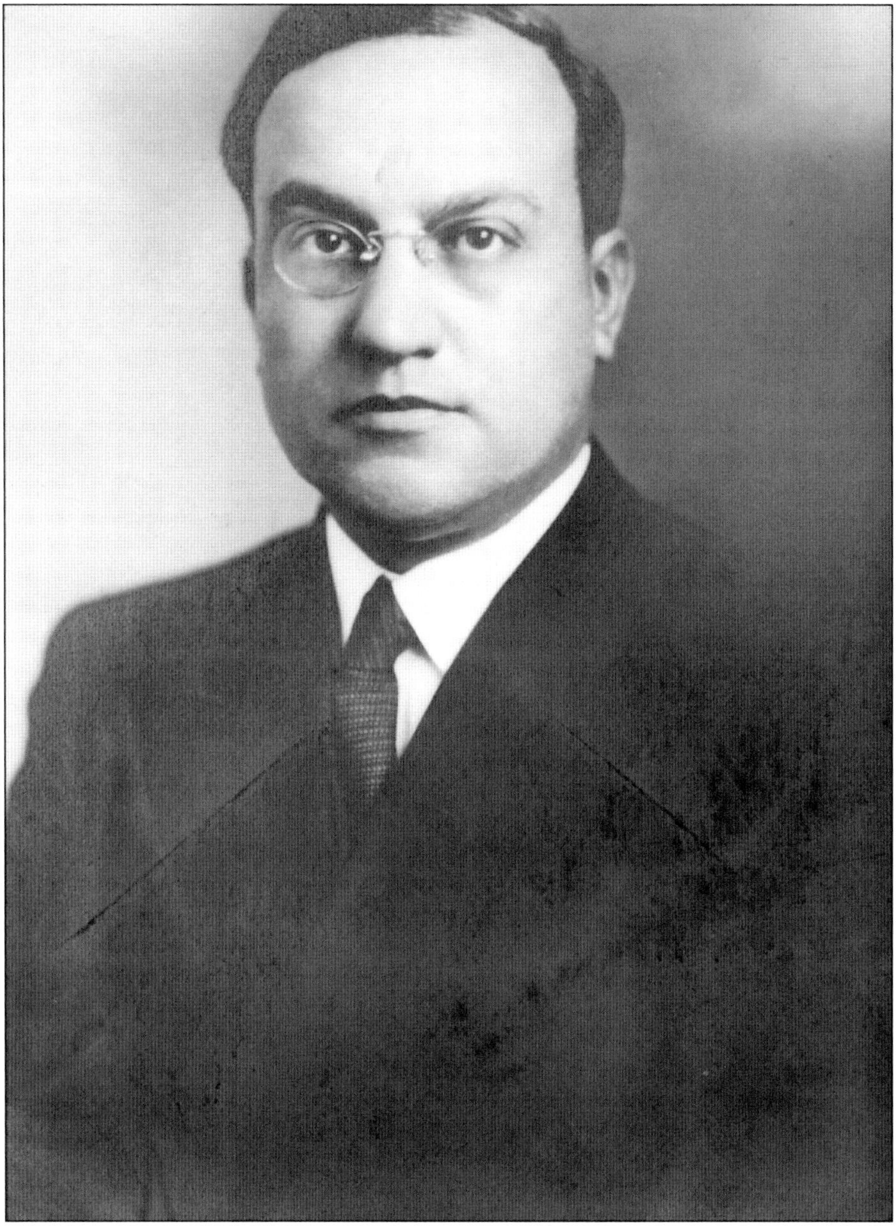

Irvine Sullivan Ingram (1892–1981). Ingram was principal of the Fourth District A&M School from 1920 until its dissolution in 1933. In that year, the Georgia Board of Regents chartered the two-year West Georgia College, which was established on the grounds of the A&M school. It was intended to provide associate's degrees to students who would later transfer to a four-year school, and would train grade school teachers who were in short supply in rural school districts, such as Carroll County. Ingram would lead the school for the next nearly 30 years, retiring in 1960. His years of dedication and lobbying with the Georgia Board of Regents paid off in 1957, when the college was granted four-year status. Ingram married Martha Munro, daughter of the A&M school's board chairman. In a departure from BOR policy, which usually restricts buildings from being named for persons still living, the library was named for Ingram in 1980. (Courtesy of UWG Special Collections.)

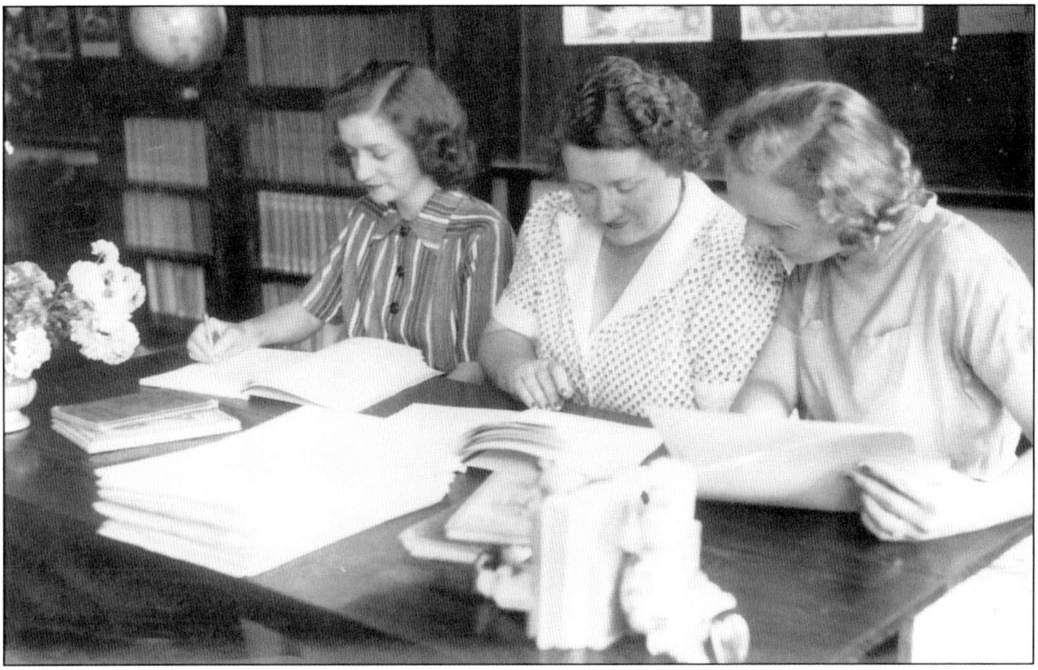

RURAL STUDENT TEACHERS. The Georgia Board of Regents initially charged West Georgia College with exploring new directions in education. As early as 1938, West Georgia College, with assistance from the Rosenwald Fund over a 10-year period, began building a Rural Life program that eventually drew attention from educators in other countries, such as China and England. (Courtesy of UWG Special Collections.)

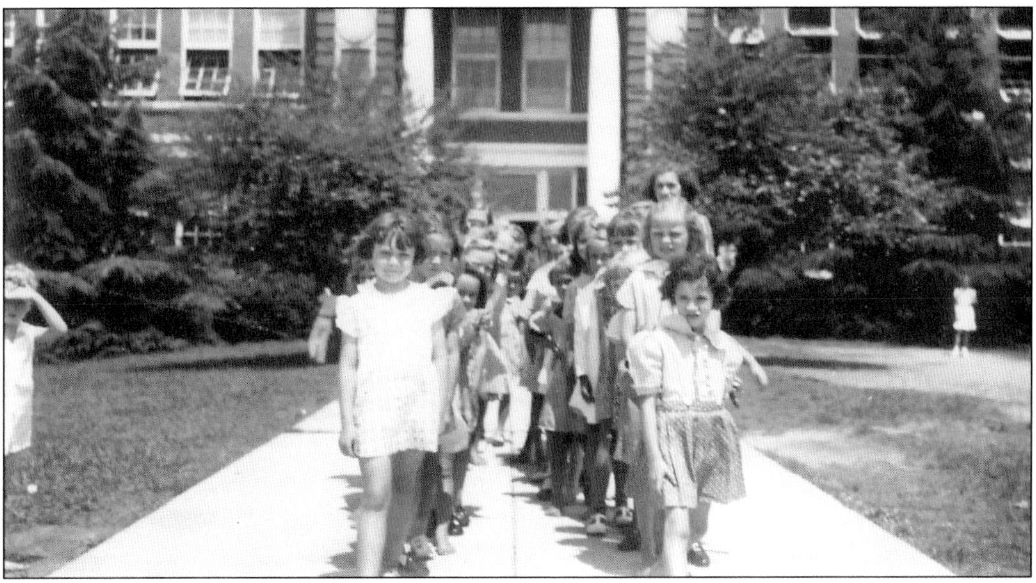

PRACTICE TEACHING IN TOWN. The college's second-year students did practice teaching at Carrollton's Maple Street School, pictured here. The college had a director of teacher training who worked closely with the city school superintendent and observed the student teachers. Field work shifted from city to county as the rural school teaching program developed. (Courtesy of UWG Special Collections.)

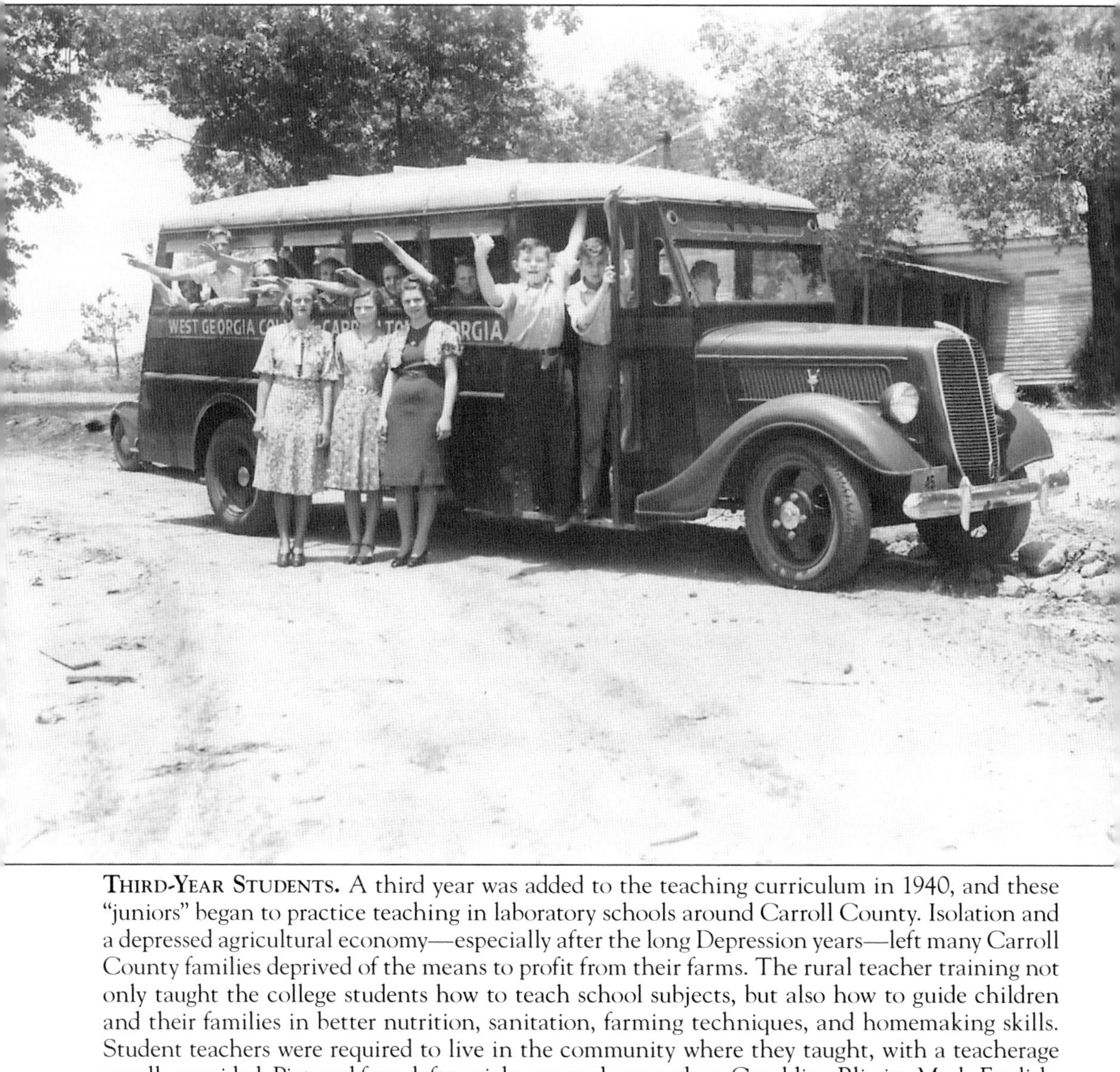

Third-Year Students. A third year was added to the teaching curriculum in 1940, and these "juniors" began to practice teaching in laboratory schools around Carroll County. Isolation and a depressed agricultural economy—especially after the long Depression years—left many Carroll County families deprived of the means to profit from their farms. The rural teacher training not only taught the college students how to teach school subjects, but also how to guide children and their families in better nutrition, sanitation, farming techniques, and homemaking skills. Student teachers were required to live in the community where they taught, with a teacherage usually provided. Pictured from left to right are student teachers Geraldine Blissitt, Merle English, and Patria Robinson. They are taking these rural children on a trip to see points of interest in Atlanta. (Courtesy of UWG Special Collections.)

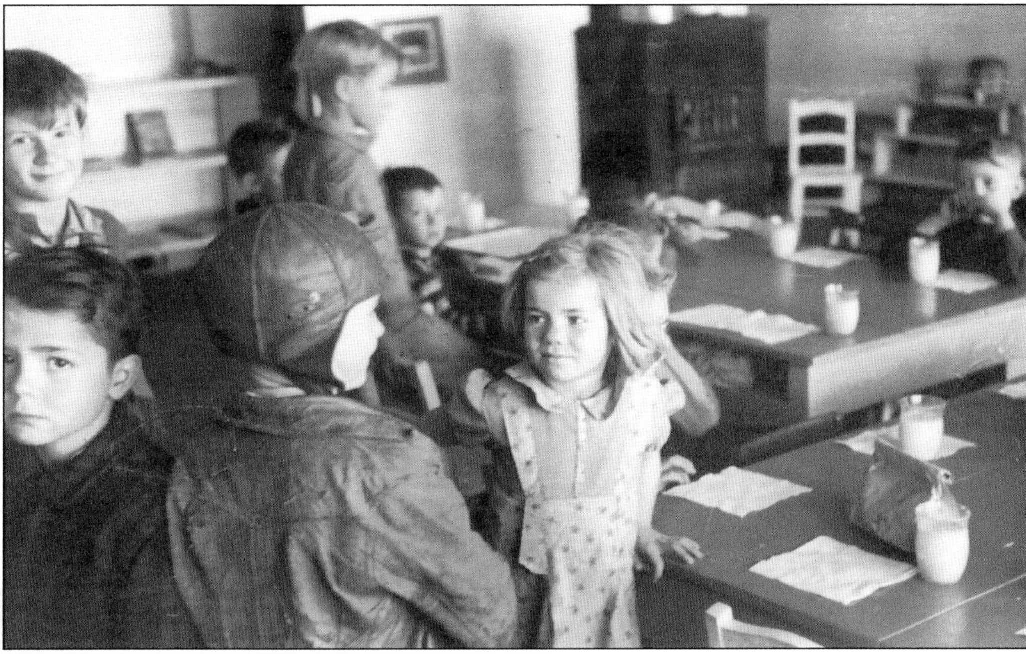

LUNCHROOM AT SCHOOL. Part of the rural school program included health and nutrition support for children. A *Primer on Food* was one of four children's books written for the college's rural education program to instruct schoolchildren on good eating habits. Notice a glass of milk sits at each child's place. (Courtesy of UWG Special Collections.)

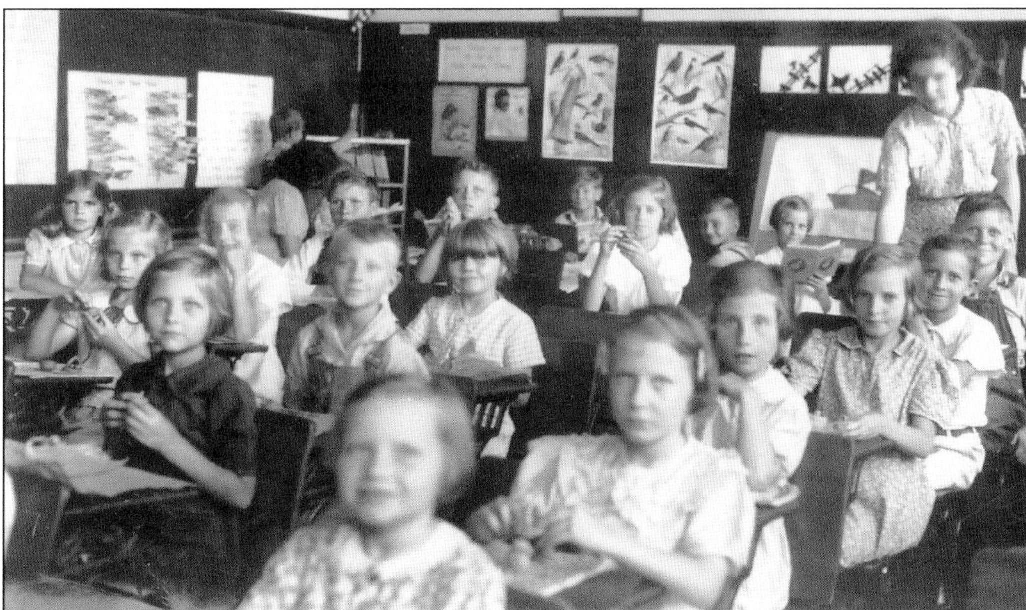

CLASSROOM AT ATTENTION. During World War II, teachers were in short supply because of high-paying factory jobs available for women in the military industry. The teacher training program served to increase the number of qualified women in the profession, helped to staff the struggling rural county schools, and brought community resources and services to the children. (Courtesy of UWG Special Collections.)

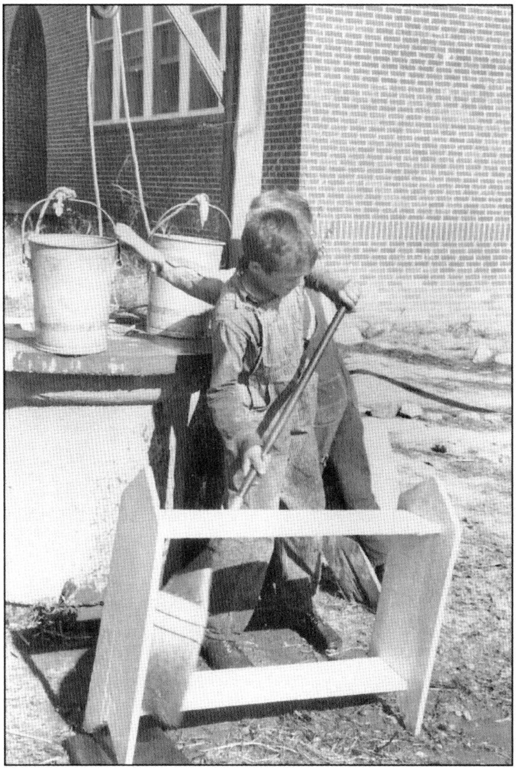

"Healthy Schoolhouses." Part of the rural teacher training included instructing children how to make their schools more attractive, clean, and healthy. Children were given tasks, such as planting trees and flowers, painting, or cleaning furniture used in classrooms. Because state and county tax support was so nominal, the work of the student teachers benefitted the schools in ways the taxpayers could not have afforded otherwise. In the agreement between the college and one school community, the college took on all responsibility for the maintenance of the school building. (Both, courtesy of UWG Special Collections.)

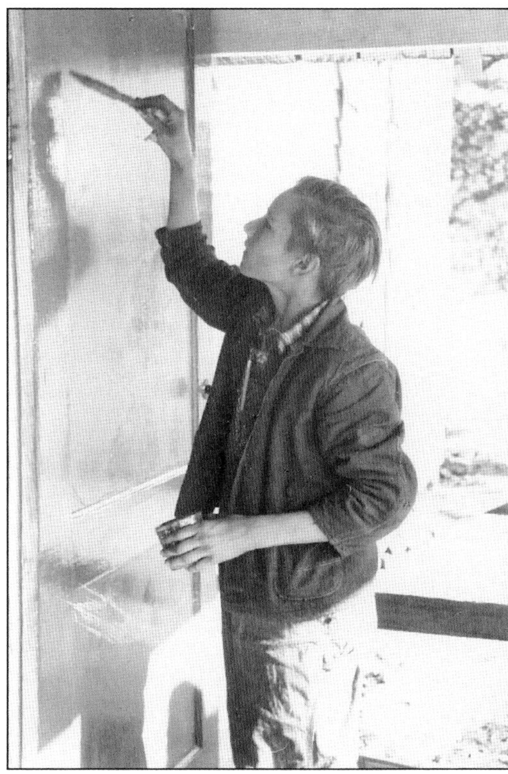

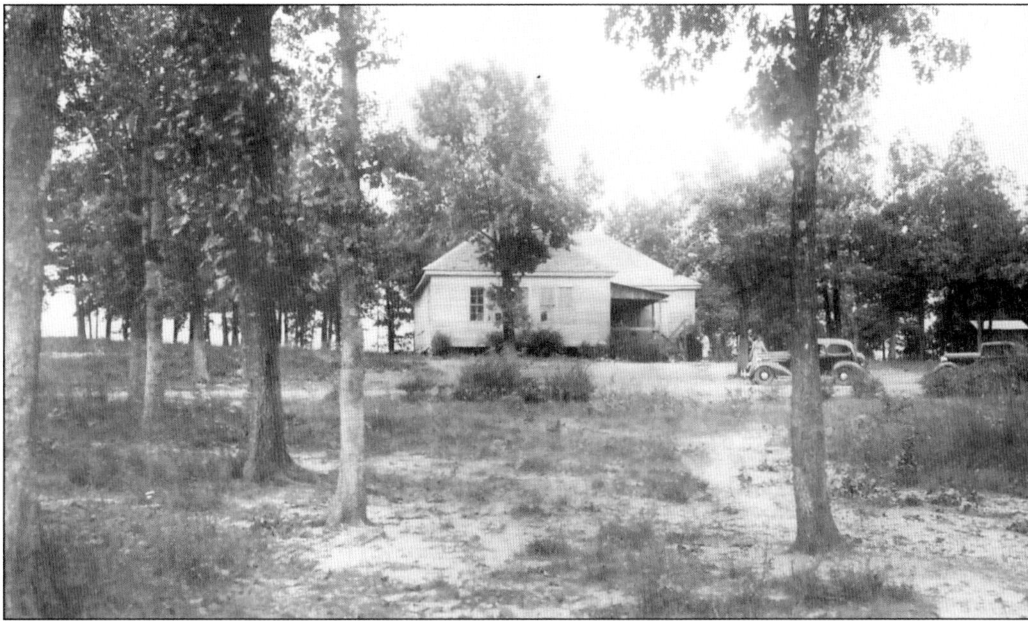

Tallapoosa School, 1941. This schoolhouse community was located a couple of miles southwest of West Georgia College. It was a community built around the schoolhouse, not to be confused with the city of Tallapoosa in Haralson County. The building still stands on Tyus Road, serving as the Tallapoosa Center for Inner Arts today. (Courtesy of UWG Special Collections.)

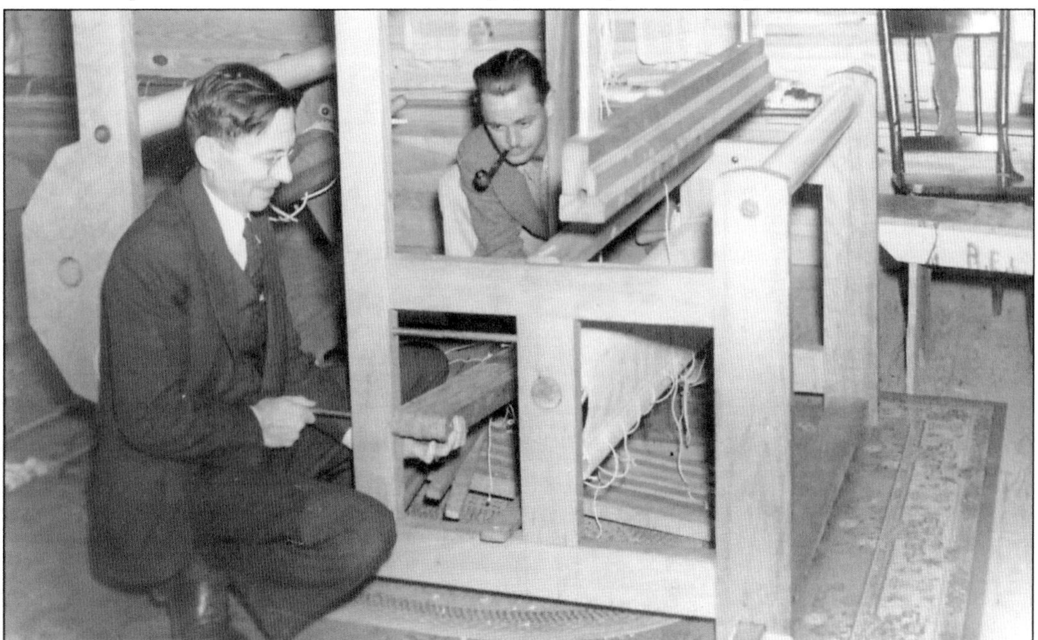

Faculty at Tallapoosa School, 1942. The dean of students, Fred Gunn, is pictured on the left with Lamar Barfoot, the principal of the Burwell Junior High School. They are shown helping to set up a loom, funded in part by grants from the Farm Security Administration. It would be used by people in the Tallapoosa community to create a small industry. (Courtesy of UWG Special Collections.)

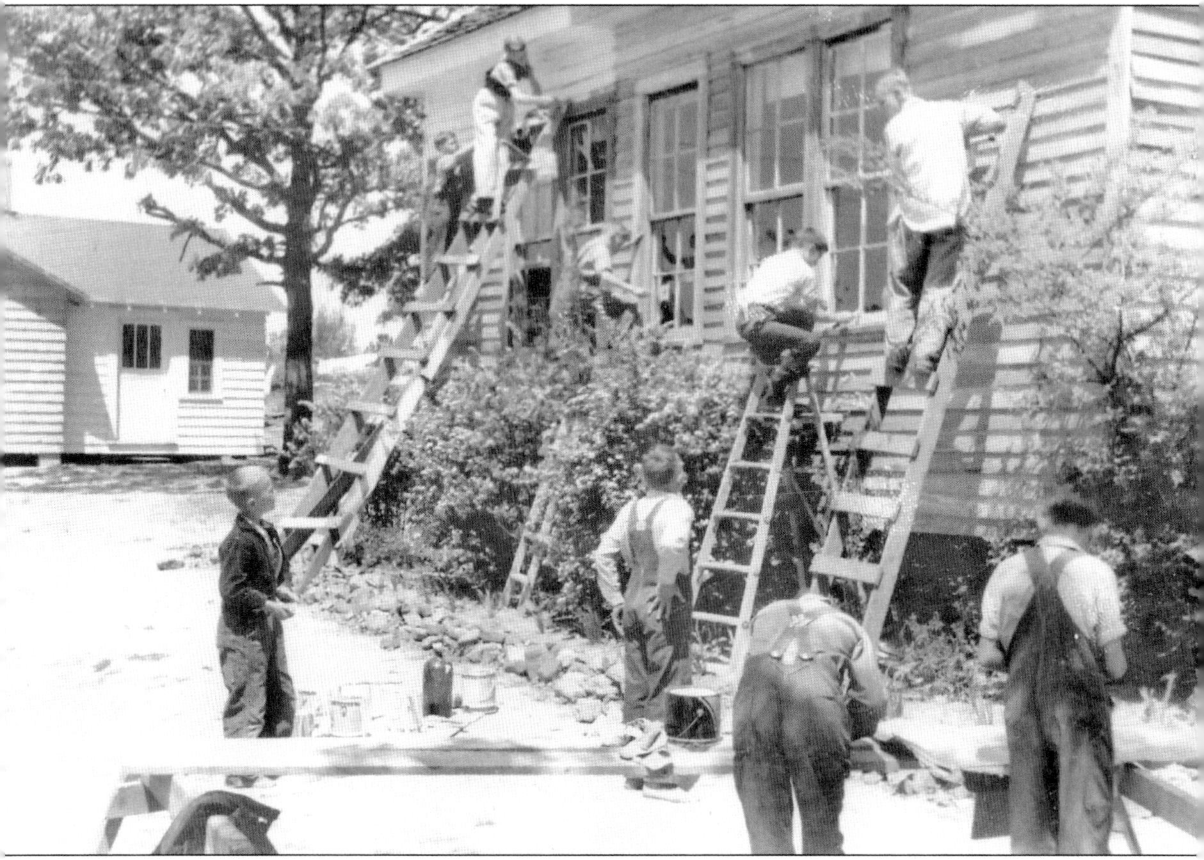

Painting Tallapoosa School, 1941. West Georgia College hired a Rural Life Arts director, C. Porter Claxton, to teach college courses in rural life so that student teachers would be better prepared to work in a rural setting. He was the son of P.P. Claxton, the US commissioner of education. The younger Claxton introduced home gardening, fruit growing, and landscaping to the curriculum. He also provided training in soil studies and household science to accompany shop classes and the college farm as areas of study. The Tallapoosa School was the first site for the college's rural teacher training. With help from the Rosenwald Fund, the college provided a principal and nine student teachers every year beginning in 1938. Carroll County schools gave the college control of the school, allowing it to flourish. The college's mission was simple—to improve rural living via the rural elementary school. (Courtesy of UWG Special Collections.)

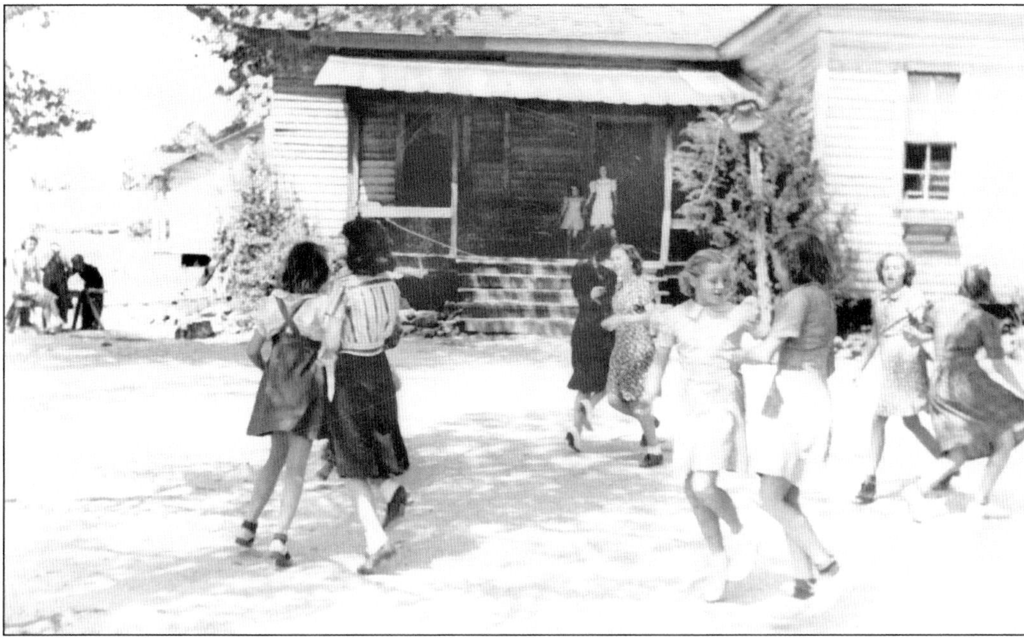

School Recreation. Outdoor exercise was taught as a healthy and necessary activity during the school day. With little money to work with, the teachers, parents, and community pitched in with simple bars and benches to create crude playgrounds, such as this one at the Tallapoosa School. The girls are pictured practicing square dancing at the school. One aspect of teacher training was to learn good record keeping. Photography was one element of that documentation, resulting in a wealth of photographs for future generations to look back on and to display in books such as this one. (Both, courtesy of UWG Special Collections.)

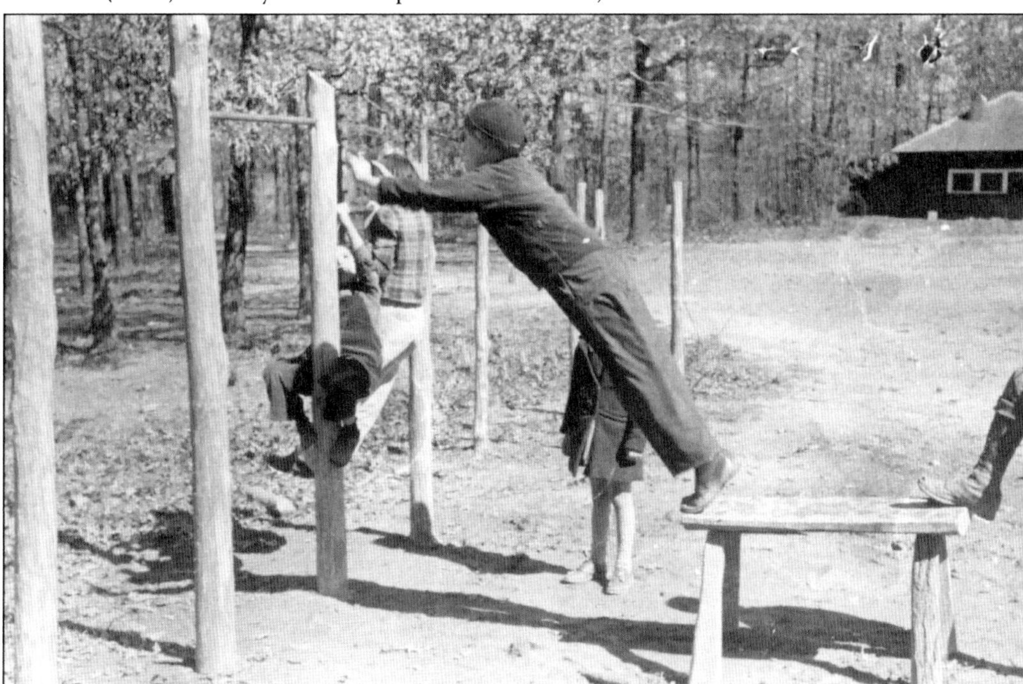

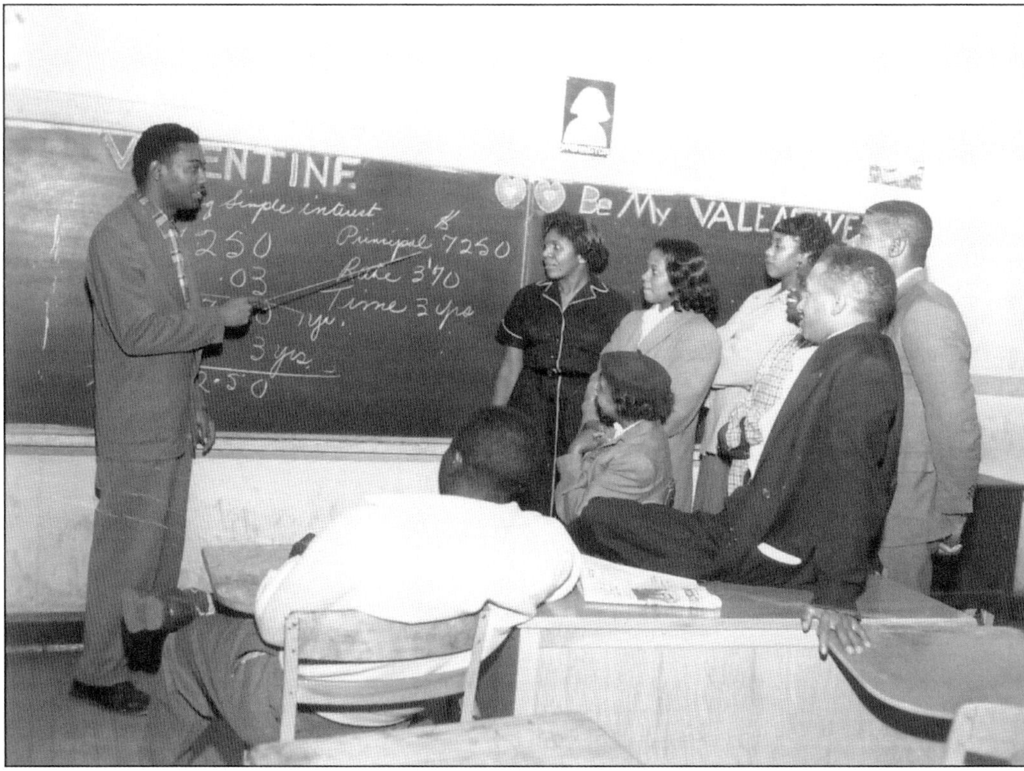

STUDY NIGHTS, C. 1951. Education for blacks in the South was the original focus of the Rosenwald Fund, a Chicago-based philanthropy that donated a quarter of a million dollars over 10 years to West Georgia College. Most of this money supported the rural teacher training programs. As part of its community education mission, the college hired a supervisor for the black schools in Carroll County. Later, the college offered "diplomas" to blacks who completed a course of study in nutrition and home economics. By the early 1950s, study meetings were organized by the college in rural black schools and churches for these adults, whose average educational level was about the fourth grade. (Both, courtesy of UWG Special Collections.)

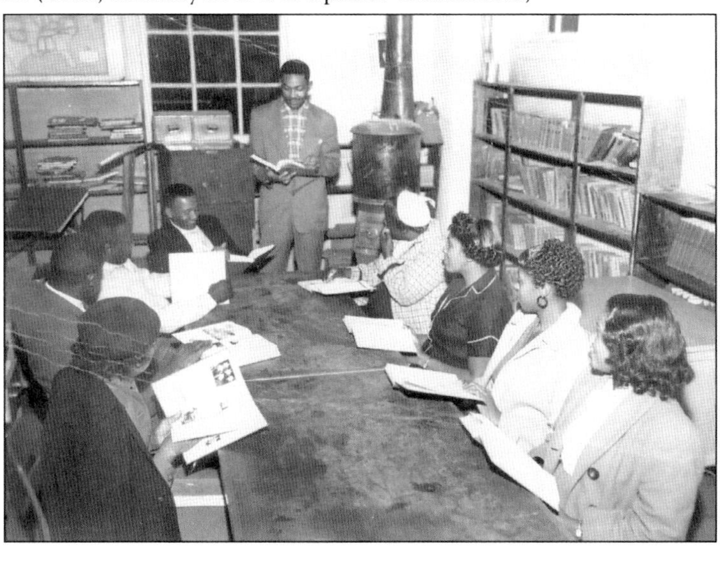

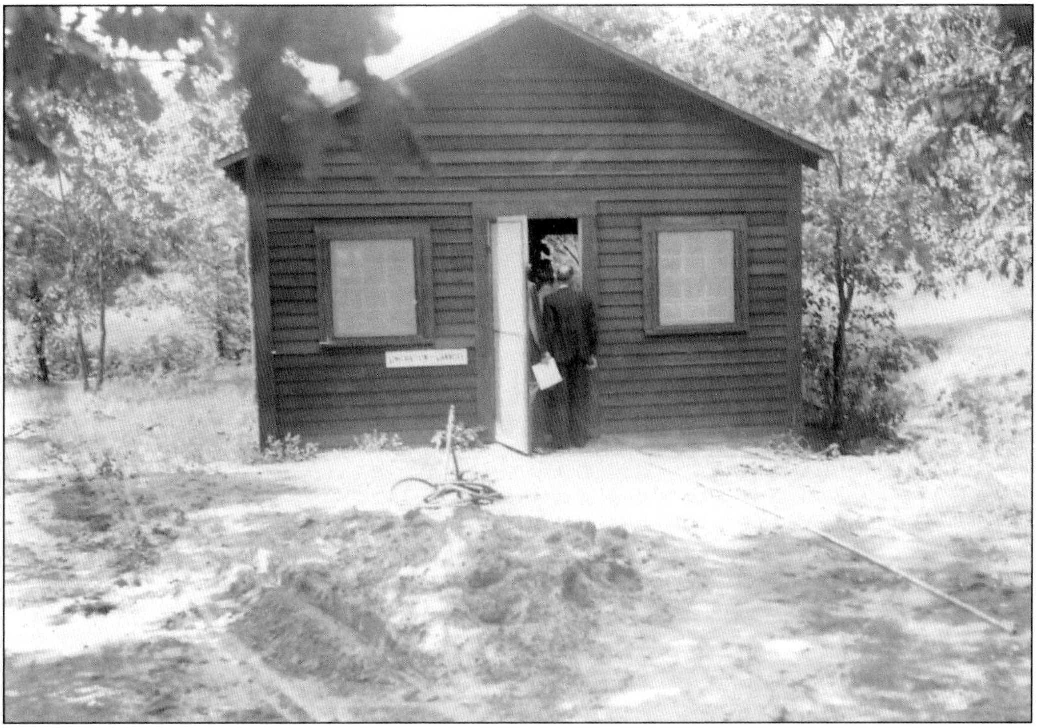

McGiboney School, 1939. This two-room schoolhouse, named for county school superintendent J.H. McGiboney, was built in the woods on the west edge of campus as a laboratory school for the children of mill workers. J.A. Mandeville, owner of the mill in Carrollton, proposed that the county, city, and college provide a new school for the children, who were not allowed to attend the nearby Maple Street School and whose old schoolhouse was in disrepair. Children are pictured helping to paint a bookcase at the school. This was the second laboratory school, after the Tallapoosa School for West Georgia students to engage in fieldwork. (Both, courtesy of UWG Special Collections.)

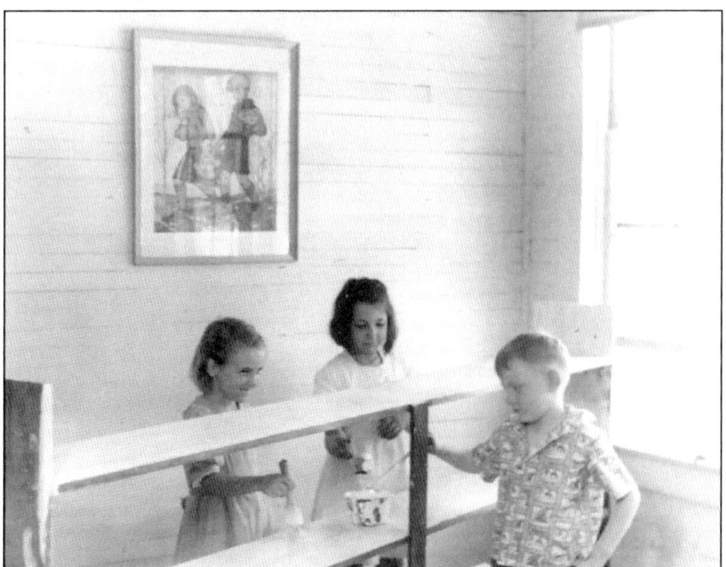

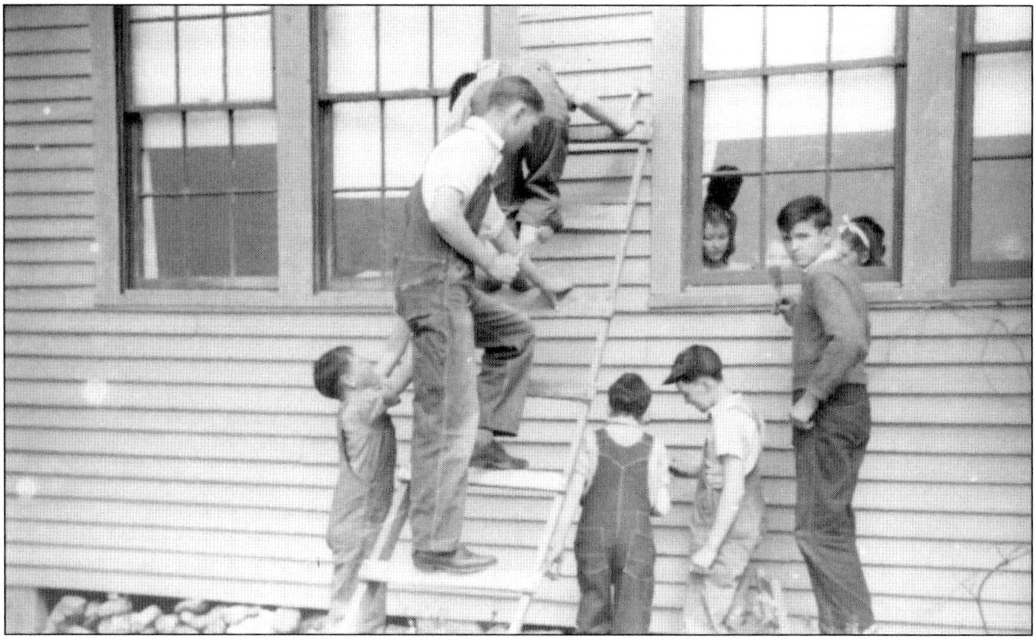

Smyrna School Colors. The schoolhouse at Smyrna still stands and is located on US 27, a few miles north of Carrollton. It was a "black house," as represented in pictures done by the local children. Like so many houses in the county, it had never been painted, so children used black when drawing it. When the rural teacher training program began there, an artist from West Georgia College painted the schoolhouse pink. This inspired children and teachers to paint the interior in shades of aqua, copper, and blue. (Courtesy of UWG Special Collections.)

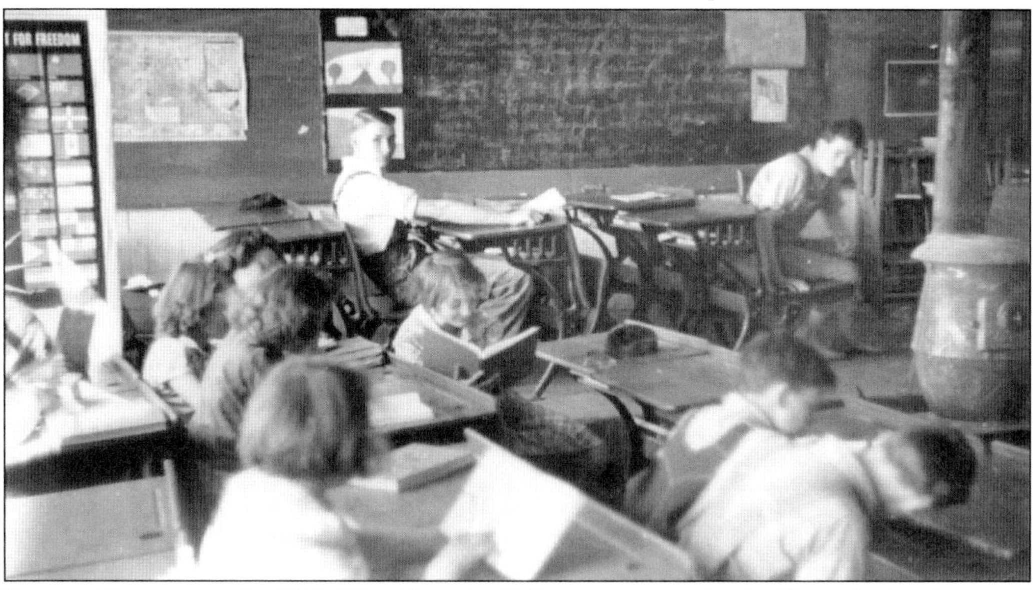

Smyrna Classroom. By 1944, West Georgia College was operating in 13 rural schools around the county. Rural teachers wrote of struggling with the question of whether to influence young people to stay on the farm or adapt to an urban, mechanized society. Carroll County remains an agricultural region today, though industry has established itself there. (Courtesy of UWG Special Collections.)

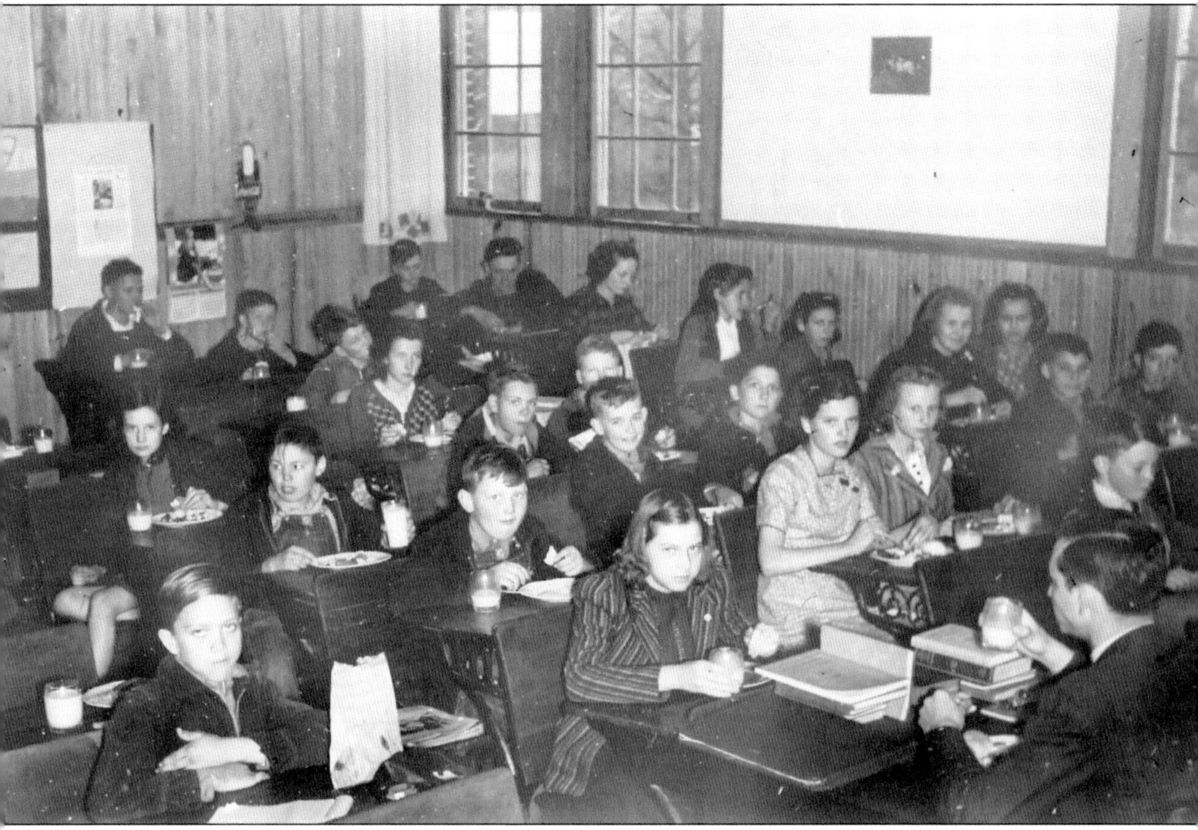

SAND HILL SCHOOL, 1941. Because many children did not have adequate food at home, the children were served lunch, including a glass of milk, at their desks. Instead of student teaching at the Maple Street School in Carrollton, the college students began going to the rural community of Sand Hill in northeast Carroll County in 1939. Sand Hill had a long history with the college that lasted well into the 1950s. When the college program began there, the community had an unfinished brick schoolhouse that was held up by controversy among the school trustees. Eventually, the building was completed for the upper grades, and an annex was built for the lower grades. Sand Hill School was featured in a *Look* magazine article in 1946, when it was named one of the country's top 100 schools. (Courtesy of UWG Special Collections.)

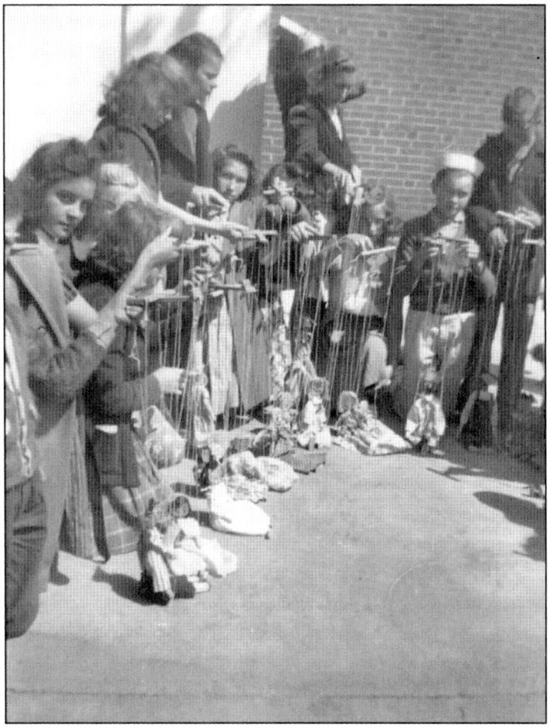

Sand Hill School Puppets, 1944. Rural children were exposed to new outlets for their imaginations with resources like these marionettes. Teachers worked to make the schools a happy place that children would look forward to attending. The college supplemented state expenditures at Sand Hill to pay for extra teachers, art and music materials, and even part of a janitor's salary. (Courtesy of UWG Special Collections.)

Sand Hill Co-Op Store. The cooperative movement in Carroll County was very active during the late Depression and World War II era, when cash-poor farmers needed assistance in obtaining equipment to make farming profitable. Rural children were taught the concept that many together could accomplish more with shared resources. (Courtesy of UWG Special Collections.)

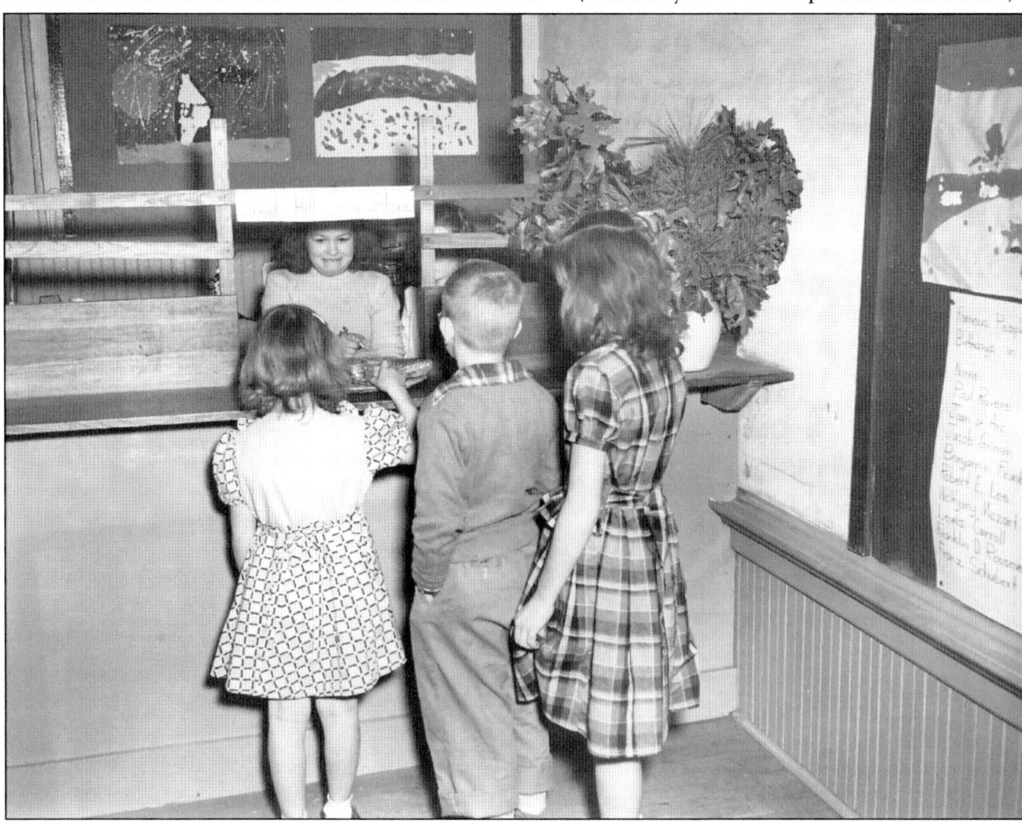

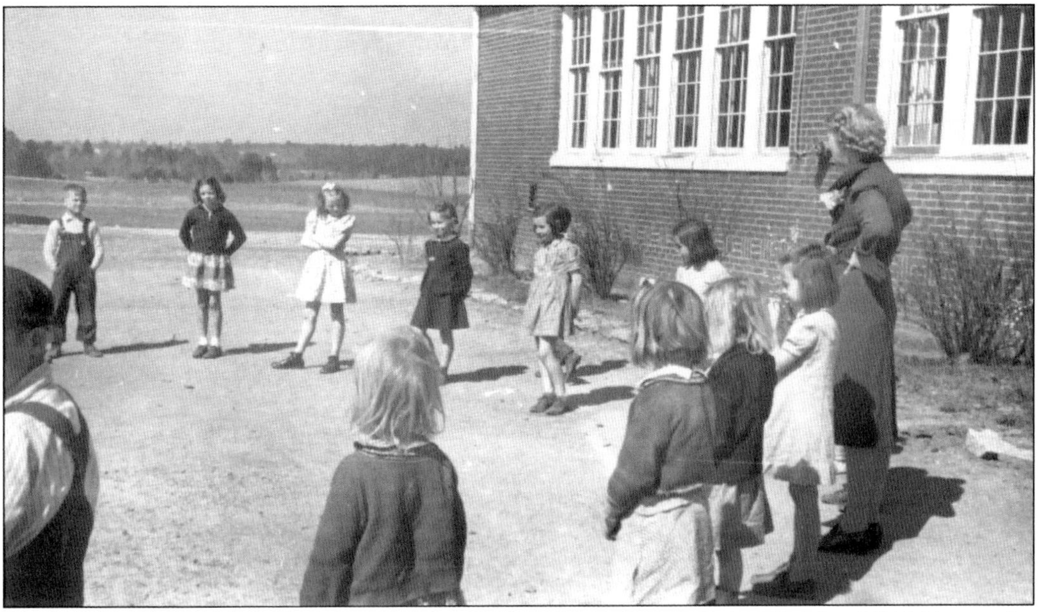

Recreation at Sand Hill. West Georgia College loaned the Sand Hill School $5,000 in order to install flooring in its unfinished school building. The community had to obtain a bond issue to pay that money back, but the college's investment paid off in years of service as a laboratory school. (Courtesy of UWG Special Collections.)

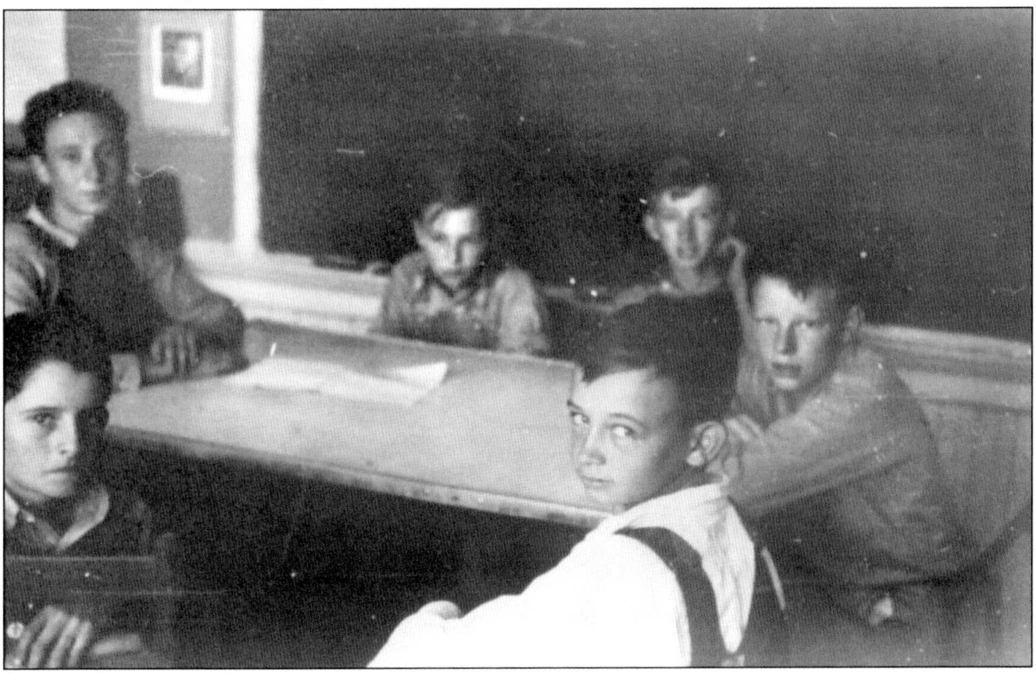

Farmers' Children. These Sand Hill school students were part of a school-age population of 6,000 in Carroll County. Farming was the chief occupation for the county's 36,000 citizens, but the majority were tenant farmers and would be considered low-income. The rural teaching program was one of several movements to bring the rural population out of isolation and into the democratic process. (Courtesy of UWG Special Collections.)

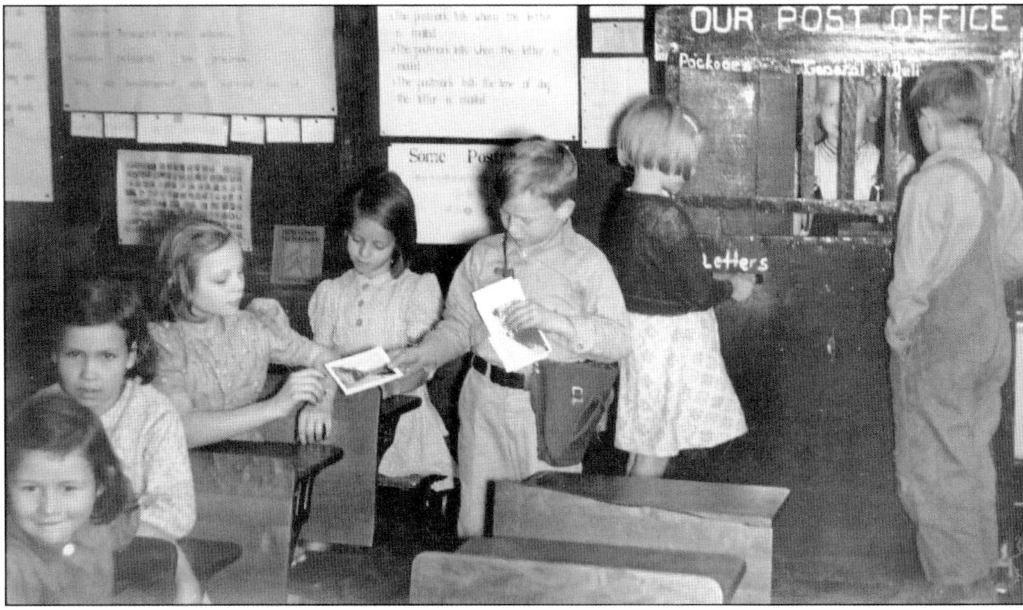

Playing Post Office. At the Sand Hill School, students learn how a post office works, an important civic lesson for rural youngsters. *Look* magazine featured the Sand Hill School in its October 1, 1946, issue as an example of the success of public education. The rural school program was listed as one of the country's 100 best school systems. (Courtesy of UWG Special Collections.)

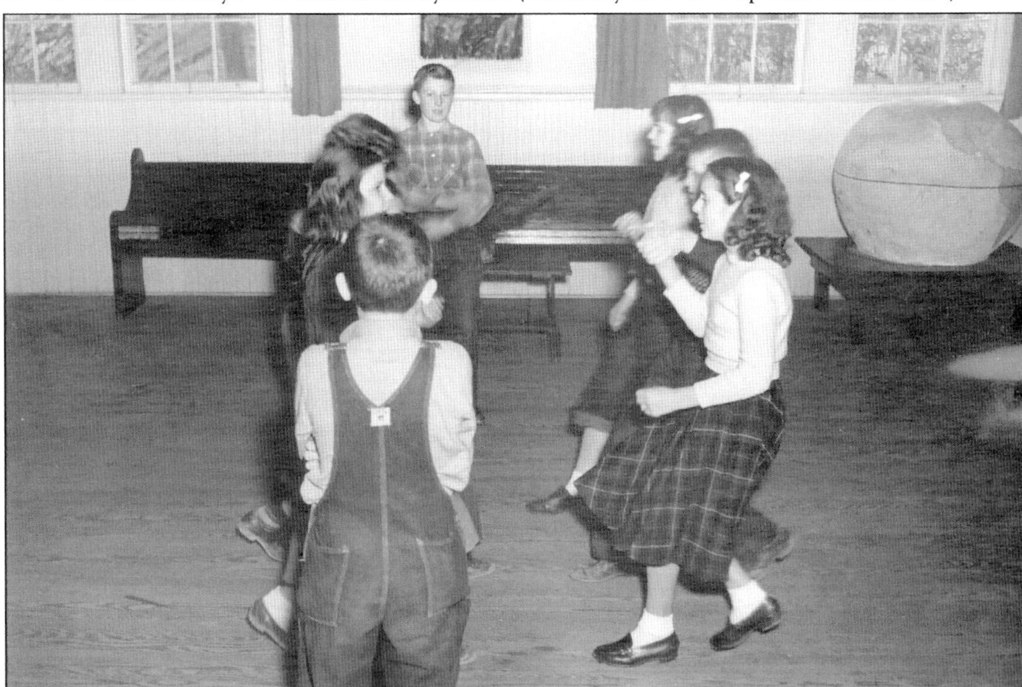

Dance Class for Upper Grades. The Sand Hill practice school continued through the 1950s with seventh graders annually inviting West Georgia College president I.S. Ingram to commencements. With the loss of federal and state education grants in the 1940s and the end of philanthropic funds, other laboratory school programs ended. (Courtesy of UWG Special Collections.)

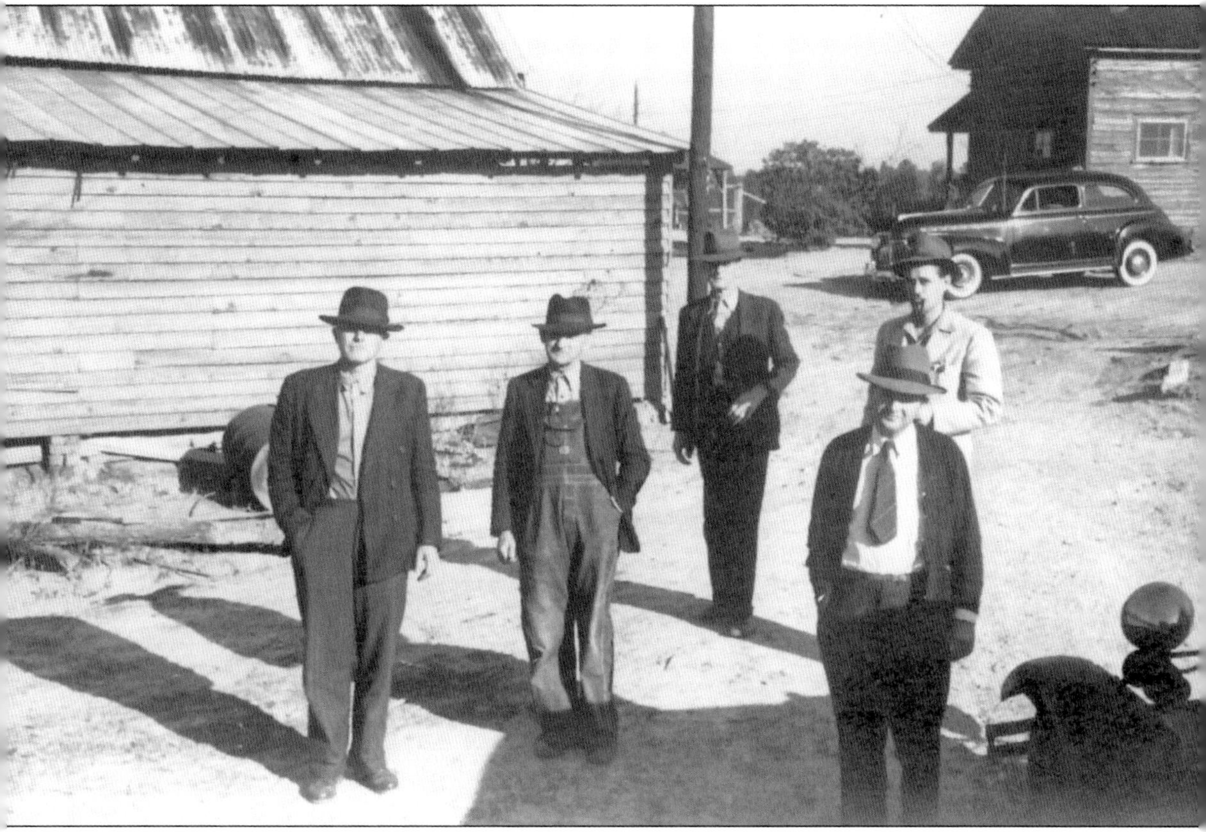

Burwell School Trustees. Educators working with rural communities debated whether they should influence youth to stay on the farm or adapt to an urban society. In the Burwell community four miles west of campus, the trustees confronted the county school superintendent over this issue, complaining that anything beyond book learning was a waste of their children's time. In reality, the schools addressed both educational tracks. Boys from the upper grades at Burwell helped to install running water in the teacherage and to build a kitchen annex at the school, which allowed it to serve hot lunches. They also planted a garden to produce fresh food that was used in preparing school meals. (Courtesy of UWG Special Collections.)

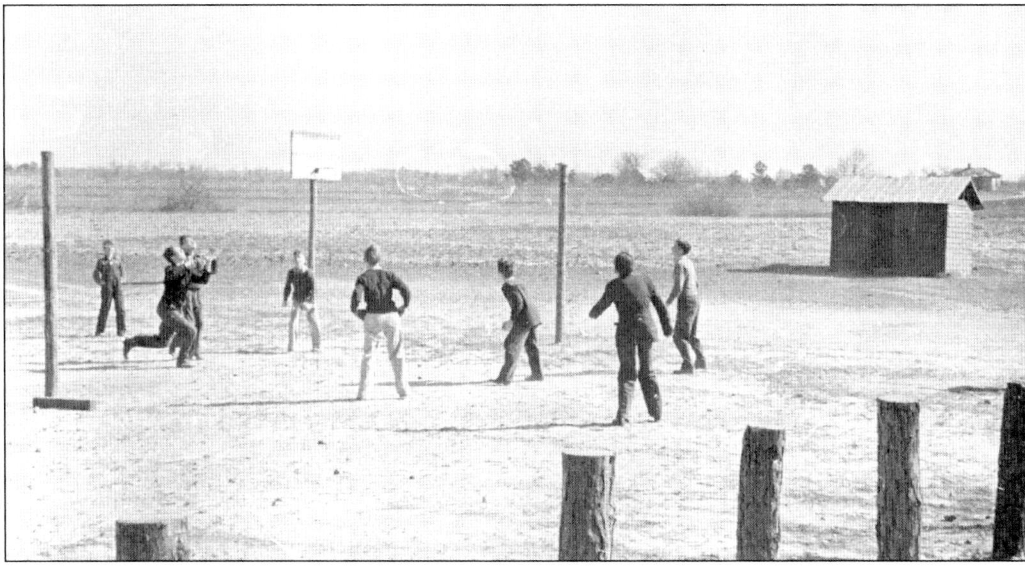

Burwell Basketball Court. School grounds improvements were a large part of the college's effect on community schools. At Burwell, students and teachers planted a tree nursery, painted the pine interior walls of the classrooms, and built seesaws and a basketball court (pictured). The posts shown were installed so farmers with wagons would not cut across the playing field. (Courtesy of UWG Special Collections.)

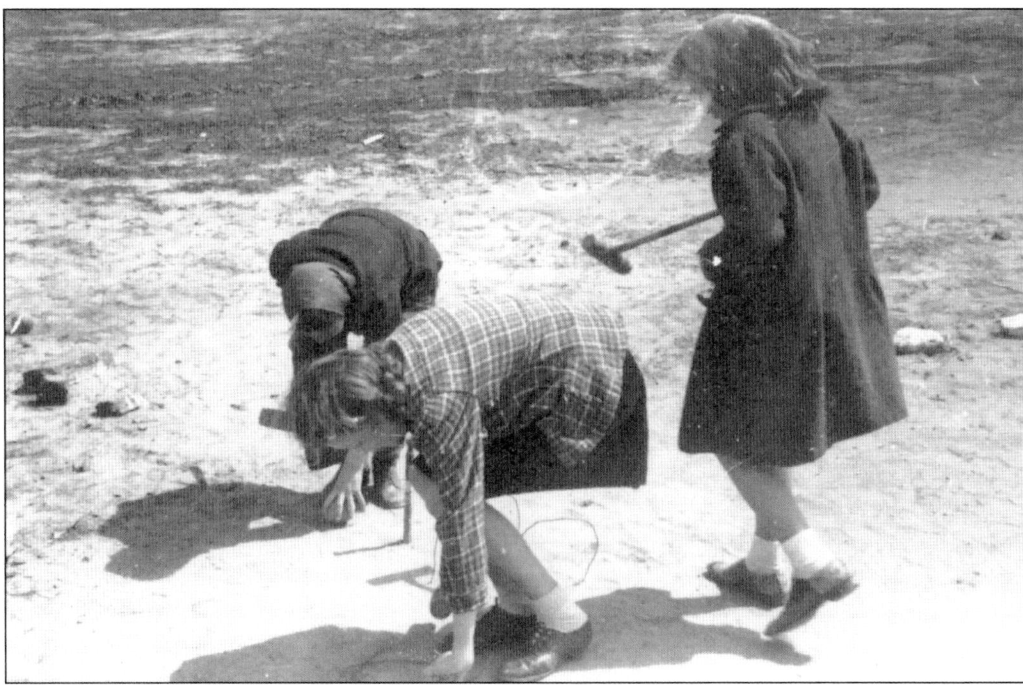

Croquet at Pine Grove School. These students are playing croquet in the dirt at Pine Grove school in northeast Carroll County off Temple Road. Physical education was part of the rural school education. Games included "fox and goose," "drop the handkerchief," and relay games. Children were involved in selecting and making the equipment for their games. (Courtesy of UWG Special Collections.)

Pine Grove School. Two girls are pictured watering their plantings with a coal scuttle at this school north of Carrollton. Beautifying the school grounds was one goal of these activities, but children were encouraged to take their new skills and practice them at home. (Courtesy of UWG Special Collections.)

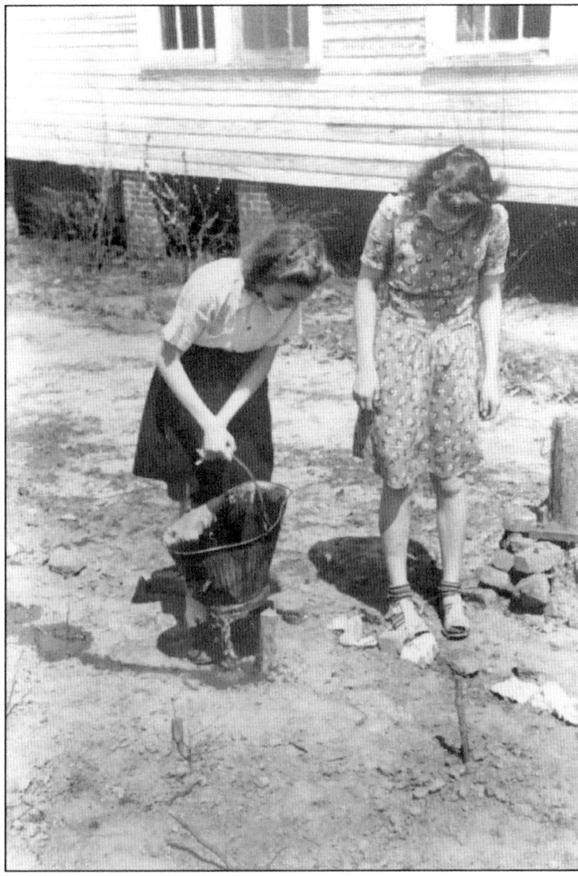

Homemade Whirligig. A pine stump and some rough boards were fashioned into playground equipment at the Pine Grove school. In a 1940 radio interview, President Ingram was asked if farm children did not already have enough practical skills. Ingram diplomatically responded that soil-depleting farm practices and poor nutrition were just two common features of farm life in Carroll County that proved the wisdom of teaching rural youth practical skills. (Courtesy of UWG Special Collections.)

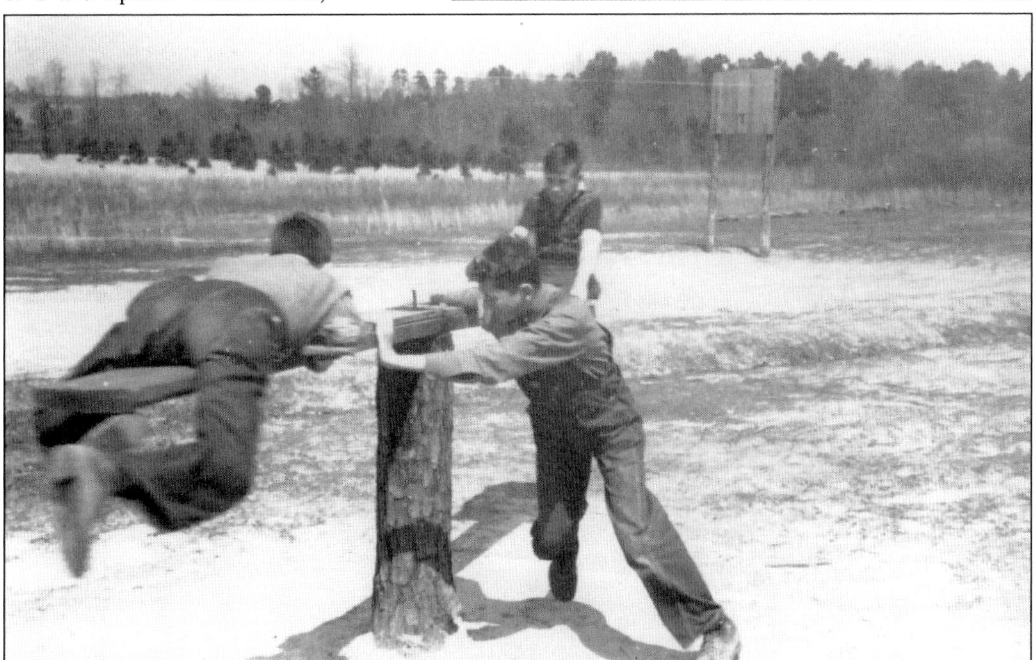

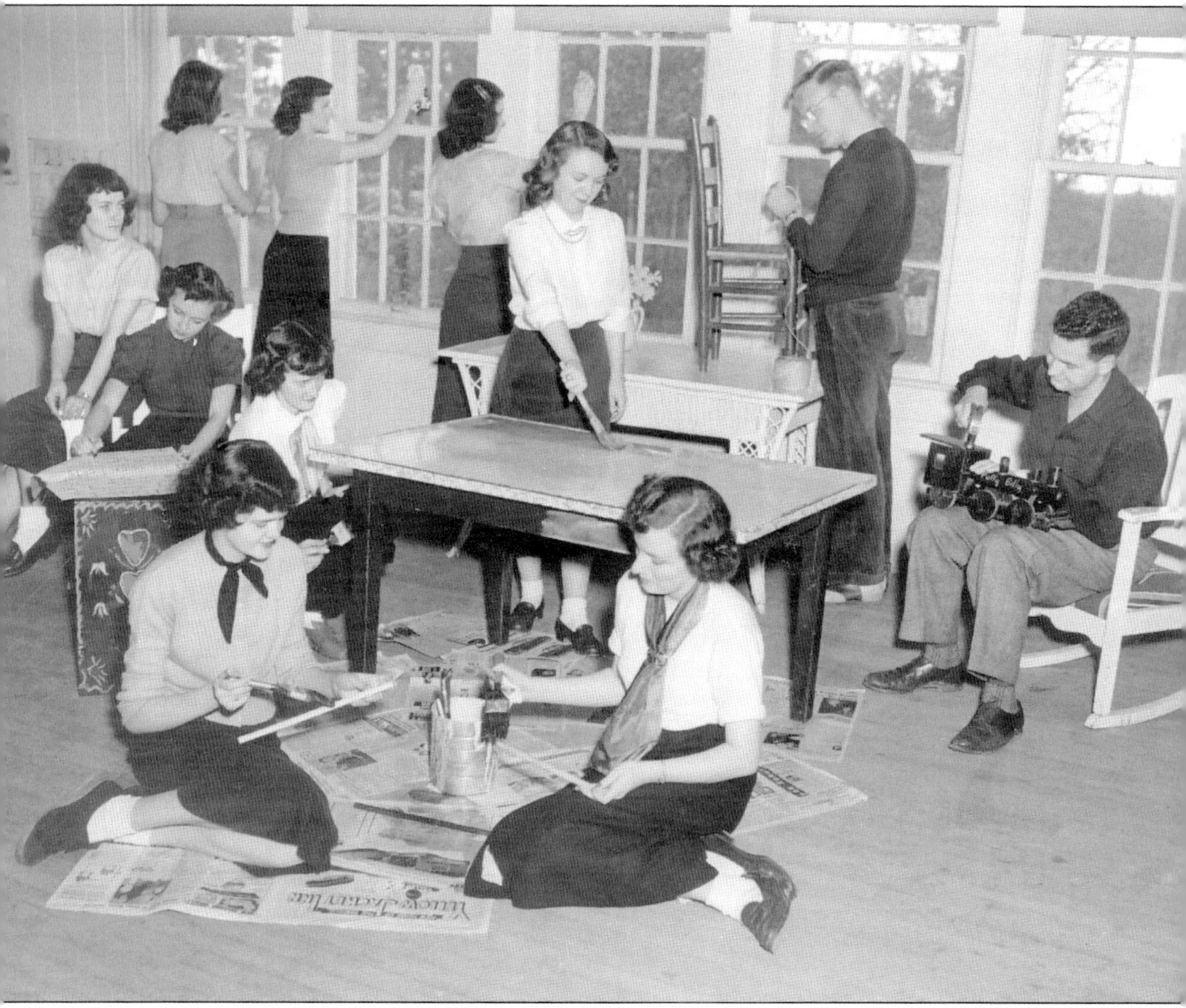

Sand Hill Student Teachers. The Sand Hill School had grown in attendance from 35 children to 180 children within a few years of the college providing student teachers and other assistance in 1939. The rural education program resulted in two new Sand Hill schoolhouses, one a brick building for the upper grades. Community citizens helped dig new wells for the school, and a kitchen was constructed in order to prepare school lunches. In what is obviously a posed photograph, these WGC students are washing windows, making toys, and in general helping to create a pleasant classroom experience for the children in this rural community. In a 1947 teaching document, goals for "social literacy" in children include working for the good of the group, having an ability to enjoy nature, and learning to engage everybody in conversation. (Courtesy of UWG Special Collections.)

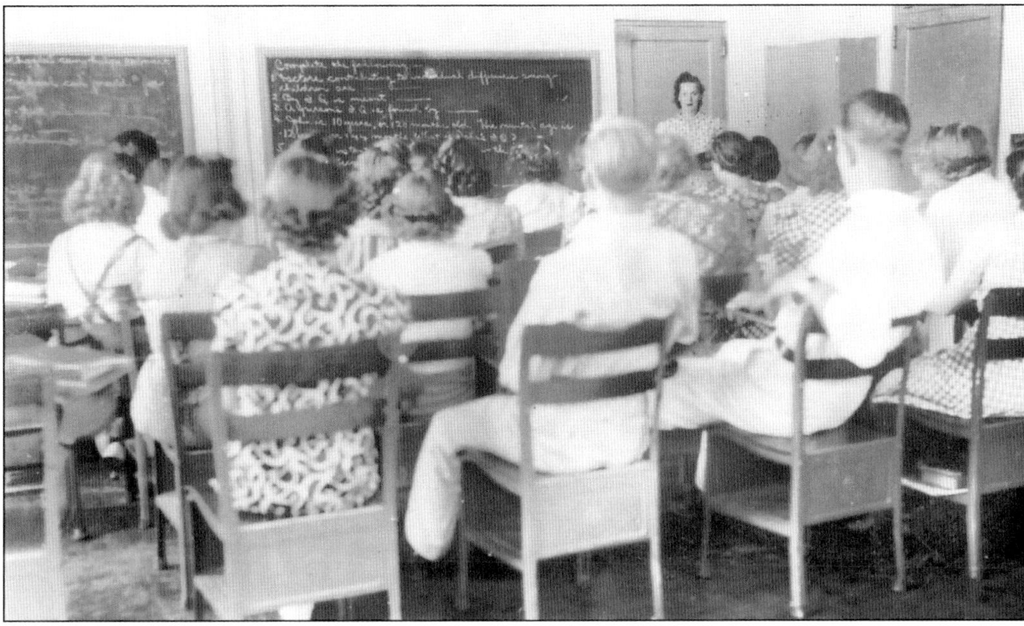

INTRODUCTION TO EDUCATION. These students are pictured in a West Georgia College classroom taking notes. The 1942 *Chieftain* yearbook is dedicated to "those who through teaching dedicate their lives to the making of a better life for our rural people." It also features an image from Depression-era photographer Margaret Bourke-White of a bonneted farm woman holding a plow. (Courtesy of UWG Special Collections.)

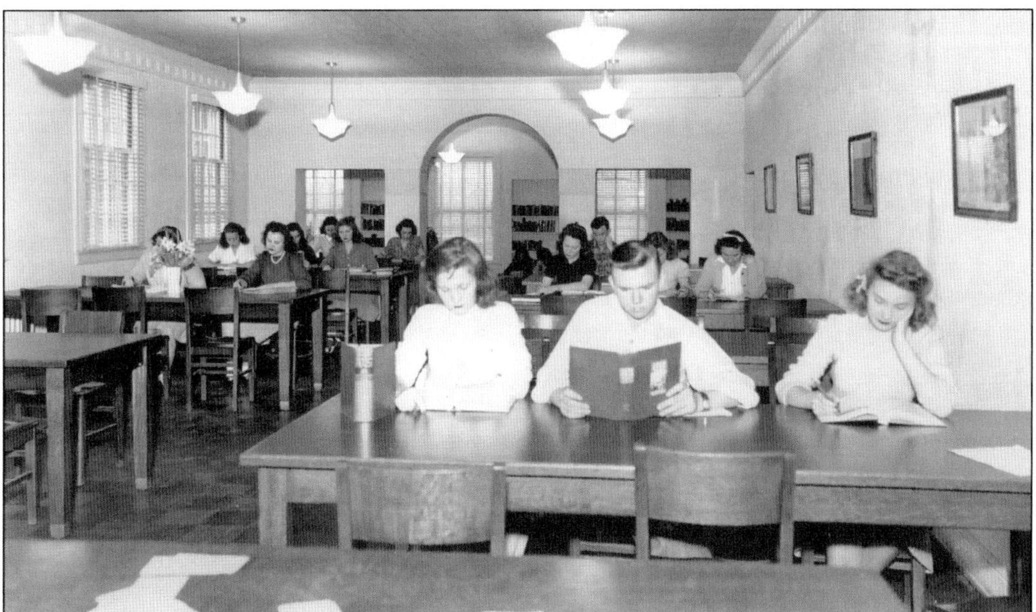

COLLEGE LIBRARY STUDIES. Built in 1936, the Sanford Library on the front campus drive was enlarged in 1941 with the addition of two wings. That was the first year the college offered a third year of teacher training to give new teachers more time to prepare for rural positions that were badly needed. There were 28 students enrolled in the third-year program. (Courtesy of UWG Special Collections.)

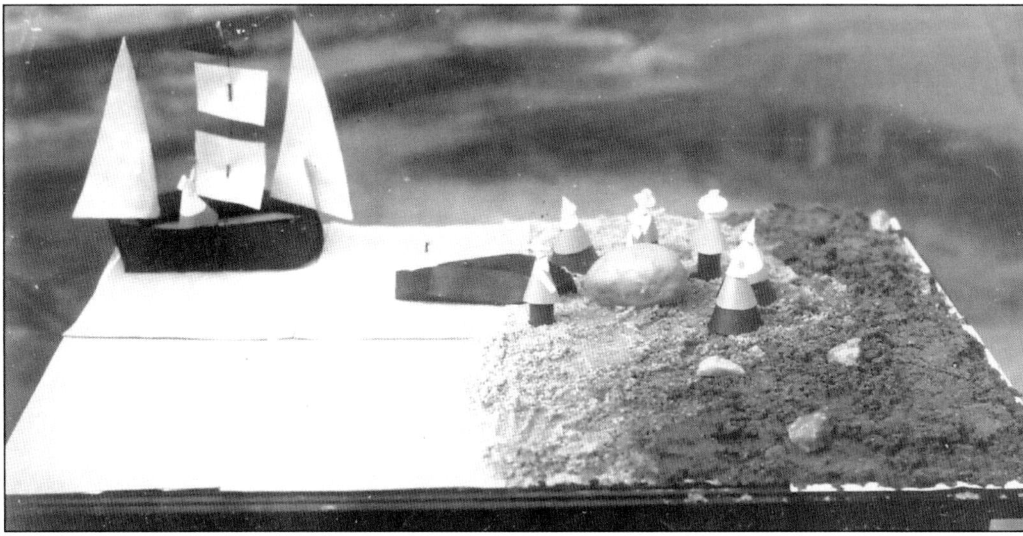

SCHOOL PROJECT. This appears to be a representation of the Pilgrims landing at Plymouth Rock. The "rock" looks like a potato. This photograph is part of the rural teacher education collection, and the assignment was likely part of a history project supervised by the college's student teachers. (Courtesy of UWG Special Collections.)

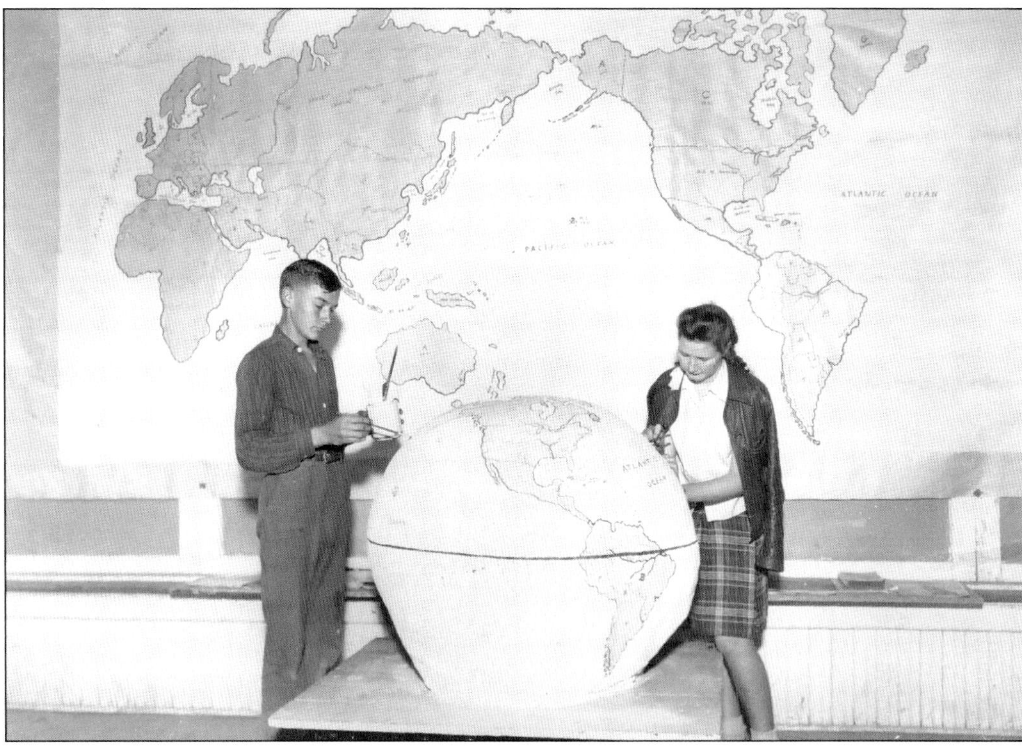

PAPIER-MÂCHÉ GLOBE. With a map of the world in the background, these students are pictured making a globe. Part of the original rural education proposal to the Rosenwald Fund was for stocking a "materials bureau" that teachers could draw from in their classrooms. These would include supplies for students to use in making a map or constructing a globe. (Courtesy of UWG Special Collections.)

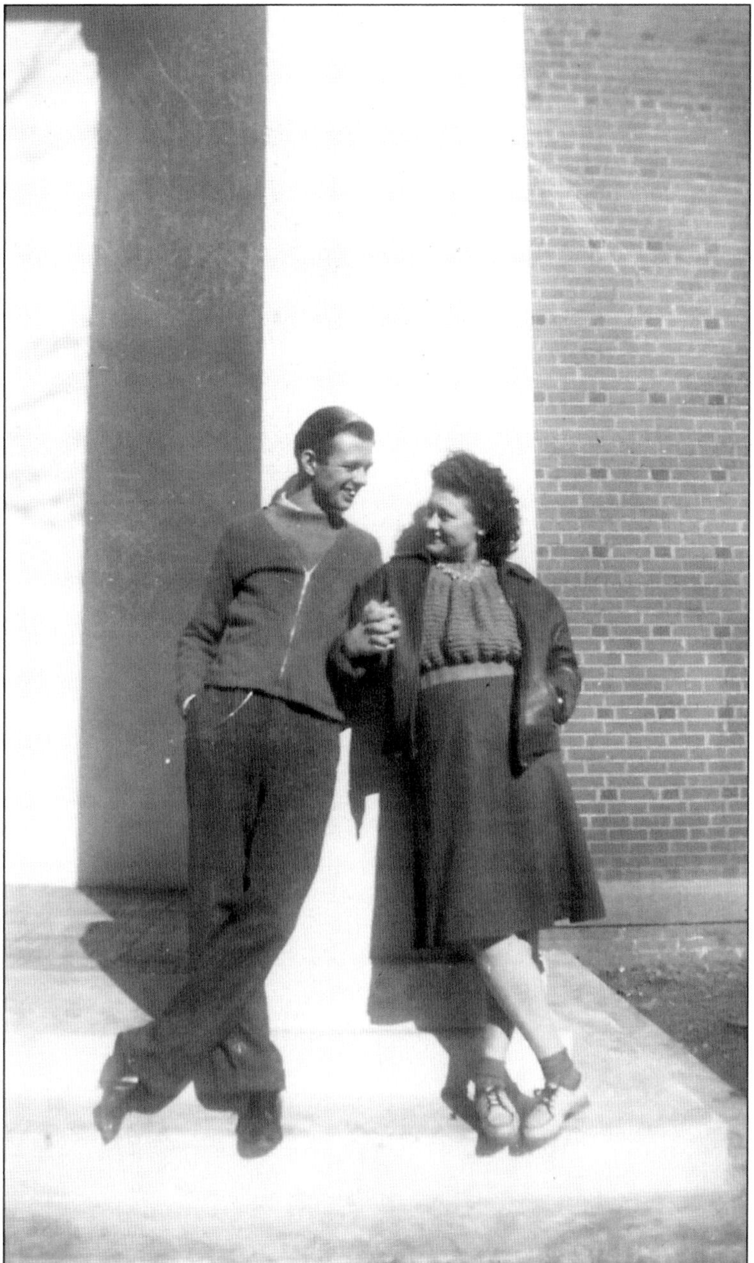

FUTURE TEACHERS. These happy West Georgia College students pose outside the gymnasium, probably around 1942, when the building was only a few years old. Soccer was a new sport at WGC, a band called the Georgia Technicians provided music for the faculty dance for freshmen, and a barn dance was held with pigs and hay wagons and "a well of Coca-Colas." The campus was not within Carrollton city limits, but had its own post office called Genola, with college president Ingram as postmaster. *GenPen* was the campus literary magazine, the forerunner of the current *Eclectic* magazine. The third-year teacher program was in full swing with financing from the Rosenwald Fund and Knights Templar scholarships. These future teachers were hoping to solve uniquely Southern problems through a rural school system. (Courtesy of UWG Special Collections.)